THE
EXEMPLARY
THEATRE

BY

HARLEY GRANVILLE-BARKER

BOOKS FOR LIBRARIES PRESS
FREEPORT, NEW YORK

First Published 1922
Reprinted 1970

STANDARD BOOK NUMBER:
8369-5282-0

LIBRARY OF CONGRESS CATALOG CARD NUMBER:
74-114878

PRINTED IN THE UNITED STATES OF AMERICA

THE history of a book's writing has an interest for its author, when (the worst over) he is able to recall it, that he can hardly expect its readers to share. But in the origin and development of the ideas which I have tried to express in " The Exemplary Theatre " I do seem to find a significance sufficiently impersonal for their recording, perhaps, to be pardonable.

The history begins, then, about twenty years ago at a meeting held in some drawing-room in the further West End of London. My memory is not more precise ; nor does it distinguish who was present. But the meeting's object—the object at least that emerged—was to consider what steps could be taken towards the foundation of a national theatre, and its result the appointment of a committee to draw up a scheme. From this point my memory grows clearer. The committee consisted of Gilbert Murray, A. C. Bradley, Spenser Wilkinson, William Archer, Hamilton Fyfe, and—*longo intervallo*—my humble self. It met several times at Spenser Wilkinson's house and discussed at some length and, as was to be expected, with great learning the principles that should govern the establishment and conduct of national theatres in general. Spenser Wilkinson, I remember, was most apt to turn for a solution of our difficulties to the practice of the ancient Greeks. I trust I sat silent. I was impatient—the scheme seemed likely to be long in coming to birth. I am sure I looked forward to a national theatre in being within the next year or so. I have since thought, as the sequel will show, that our theorizing need not have been wasted.

But one morning William Archer arrived at my rooms in the Adelphi and delivered himself somewhat to this effect :

" We must get something on paper. What you and I have to do is to draw up a practical scheme, and these other fellows may amend it if they know how."

He had only to command me, so we set to work, and the result—to which, I should add, his contribution much outweighed mine—was a considerable mass of detail which we named "A Scheme and Estimates for a National Theatre." My memory becomes vague again. I presume the scheme was submitted in some form to the responsible committee, though I am quite sure that the parent meeting was never reassembled. The committee probably gave up the ghost at being challenged to pronounce upon the subscription prices that should be charged for a second performance of Measure for Measure, whether and when a third scenic artist should come on the pension fund, and the number of charwomen that would be wanted. Archer and I were left proudly alone with our offspring.

We then proceeded to self-suppression : first in favour of seven godfathers—I must name them: Henry Irving, Squire Bancroft, J. M. Barrie, Helen d'Oyly Carte, John Hare, Henry Arthur Jones, and A. W. Pinero—and contingently in favour of any beneficent millionaire to whom their good word might recommend this magnificent opportunity. It should be his scheme for £350,000 or so. There were no offers. The benevolence of the godfathers availed nothing. I fancy some timid approaches were made to the Government. But tariff reform—or the tariff reformer rather—was at that time Mr. Balfour's amply sufficient trouble, and his interest, so he is reported to have said on the broaching of the subject, lay rather in classical concerts with the prices at twopence, fourpence, and sixpence. I fancy, too, that candidates for baronetcies and the like were not quite so numerous then ; besides, £350,000 much overtopped the market-rate.

I recall, amid the barren complaisance with which the scheme was greeted by the few who took the trouble to read it, one piece of harsh and pertinent criticism from Bernard Shaw.

" It's no good," he said, " for no one with the youth and energy to get such a theatre started would do a hand's turn for the sake of such a musty list of plays as you put down. The old drama or the new drama may serve you, but old-fashioned drama's the devil."

We had apologetically ruled out of the specimen repertory Ibsen and Hauptmann and Shaw himself, and a few others (Brieux had slipped in, though), on the ground that it was no advanced theatre we were designing. So that, with a little heat, Archer replied that as quite notorious Ibsenites, Hauptmannites, Shavians, etc., we had made this great sacrifice as a pledge of good faith. To which Shaw only answered that if we hadn't the courage of our opinions we deserved to be ignored.

We were. But that was to have contented us if only the millionaire would have fathered the already well godfathered scheme. And Shaw's criticism, if pertinent, was partial. But it raises one interesting issue. Does not a little self-seeking do more to promote public confidence than a disinterestedness which will either be suspected as hypocritical or condemned as half-hearted ?

Some years later, however, when Archer and I had travelled together to America and were discussing in New York a not dissimilar project, there blazed up in London—public meetings, press paragraphs, and all—a movement to establish a national theatre as a tercentenary monument to Shakespeare. And we returned to find the committee, to which we were added, disposed to adopt our scheme as at least a preliminary text-book. It had, I think, by this time been published, was no longer anonymous, but remained as disinterested as ever.

Into the next ten years' history of the Shakespeare National Theatre Committee I do not propose to go. Enough to say that when the tercentenary came England—and Europe—memorialized it in another fashion. I forbear the usual ironic comment upon the German patronage of our national poet. But I will record the bitterness of my realization—sharpened by the occasion—of the theatre's utter and ignominious failure during the war to lift its head into any region of fine feeling and eloquence. It was sharpened still more by the thought that had our Shakespeare National Theatre been earlier brought to a safe existence that would surely have stood in significant honour above the disgrace.

Well, it is 1921, and the memorial committee is still whistling, and may whistle, for their money —and they need more than £350,000 now. This is not yet a country for the heroic dramatist to live in. And it is no use crying over the spilt years. So, personally, I have turned for comfort upon the subject during these last three or four, to a reconsideration of the theatre's whole position. And this book is evidence of such comfort as I have found.

If we had established our national theatre according to the idea of it commonly current ten to twenty years ago (and the scheme and estimates represents this not unfairly) we might well have

set up something that did not truly or fully represent
our national dramatic genius. We were stirred, for
one thing, to an emulation of the Théâtre Français,
we were inclined to borrow useful items from the
plans of the many good German and Scandinavian
theatres. No harm in that, once we have achieved
an individuality of our own. But have we—in
dramatic matters more important far than organization and machinery ? We talk of the renaissance
of our theatre; dating it, according to taste, from
1870, 1890, 1900 or whenever. And so, no doubt,
we most allowedly may. But, for one thing, this is
a renaissance of the written drama only. Acting—
which is the theatre's original art—has by no means,
if this book is in the right, yet adjusted itself to its
new opportunity. And certainly the theatre, as a
whole, has only begun to absorb the interesting and
often typically English developments of the art of
scenic decoration. Moreover, we are all still under
the dominance of the well-made play. In our playwriting renaissance, if we broke from Scribe, we
fell into the arms of Ibsen and have hardly yet
escaped from them. Not that these embraces
necessarily did us harm.

But to survey his heritage and to prosper its working a man must stand upright and feel his feet.

Now, it is obvious that the drama is, of all others,
an intensely racial art ; whatever the playwright
may do, the actor cannot—and advisedly will not try
to—translate or adapt himself. The genius of
French acting is fitted to the well-made play—
naturally, as the two things have developed together.
Together, moreover, they may almost be said to represent with perfect fitness the genius of the French
nation itself—reasonable, precise, rounded neatly
and completely from cause to effect.

ix

But does it follow that this form and method will be equally expressive of the characteristics of other races? It is noticeable, on the other hand, that the typical French actor turns from the foreign play if he cannot turn it to himself. Consider the work of three such dramatists as Shakespeare, d'Annunzio, Tchekov. Apart from all excellence of content, is not its salient quality—that thrust out for its interpreters to seize—racial expressiveness, and does not this necessarily dictate method and, finally, form? And now consider one or two points in the history of, say, the English and German theatres. In the eighteenth century the Germans borrowed largely from us— they swallowed Shakespeare whole. In the nineteenth they borrowed from the French. They assimilated Ibsen, they gave much original attention to organization and decoration. They have, indeed, a voracious dramatic appetite, and are little inclined to wait patiently for the slow growth of native product. But when this does, if with difficulty, appear, it is remarkable for rebellion, both in minor methods and larger form, against the borrowed models. In England, from 1660 onwards, foreign influence upon our theatre is apparent. Throughout the nineteenth century we borrow, indeed we often steal quite shamelessly, from the French: so shamelessly that our sense of " mine and thine " is gone, and we find ourselves, in our own despite, violently trying to convert the very work of Shakespeare and of Sheridan into the likeness of the well-made play. Our modern actors, bred to the borrowed drama, acquiesce. To the Elizabethan actor, though, Shakespeare's work, as Shakespeare wrote it, came naturally enough; he was one of them himself for that matter. And though we need not trouble to argue why Racine would have puzzled Burbage, and how—

x

more to the point—Pinero and Galsworthy would have upset the Globe Theatre stage-manager completely, is it not true that while other English arts can show—for all incidental breakings—characteristic descent, the art of the theatre to-day is most characteristically un-English? The content of our plays may be native, but the form, as a rule, will be arbitrary and foreign, and will show little regard, or none, for the character of the interpretation the play is to receive. What form does the English genius for self-expression most readily take? What dramatist starts by asking himself such a question? In lyric and epic poetry, in fiction, do we not tend, unhindered still, to run the Shakespearean gaɪ ut of rhetoric and metaphysic, to be allusive, to be passionate, seldom ironic, logical hardly ever? How should we expect to find English actors at their best, burdened with a method, crippled in a form, which, however excellent, is no development of their natural way of expression, is as foreign to that and to them as the words of a foreign language would be? The trouble is, it would seem, that the integrity of the English theatre has been destroyed. The dramatist can serve strange gods and can profit by it ; the actor cannot. But harmony between the two there must be : because, for all the dramatist's importance, acting is not only the original art of the theatre, it remains its peculiar foundation. And it may be that the time lost in setting up our standard of a Shakespeare memorial will not have been time wasted if in it we can profit by this lesson which Shakespeare's own art so particularly teaches us.

But further—and this is the encouragement of thought by which my share of the Scheme and Estimates has developed into this book—it may well be that just as Shakespeare made of drama

something which outspanned all its then acknow-
ledged powers, so we, gathering up tradition with
understanding and measuring our power by our
need, might make in our turn of the theatre something that would not only better, but quite transcend,
its present service to us. Even in its complexity
it is so simple an art, and the pleasure and the profit
of it are so common a heritage. We have been setting, it may be, inappropriate limits to its destiny.

September 1921   H. G.-B.

CONTENTS

Chapter I : The Author's Prejudices, and Others

The uses of dialogue—Dramatists all ; and actors all—
" The " profession—The theatre's appeal to the
mob—Should drama be accounted one of the fine
arts ?—The difficulty of ranking the theatre as a
social service—The difficulty of using the drama in
education—Art's overrated influence—The theatre
as catspaw—The economics of the modern English
theatre—Authority's obligation to the theatre—The
drama's industrial difficulty is that an art shall not be
an industry—Art as a gift to society—Society's responsibility in accepting the gift—There is no such
thing as a theatre in England—The larger idea of
drama

Chapter II : The Educational Basis

Book learning and the educational claims of acting—
The professional theatre's contribution—Public manners—The tradition of our speech—The American
language—The influences of climate and of recent immigration—The drama as a microcosm of society—
The self-realization of a child—The teaching of psychology—Democracy, the newspapers, and the whole
art of fiction—Qualifications and temptations of the
journalist—The public's self-defence—The artistic
synthesis—The popular attitude towards interpretative
art—Theatre *v.* novel—The good audience—The
educational use of drama—The Exemplary Theatre
—The break in the acting tradition—Robertson-Ban-
croft-Pinero—The Ibsen challenge—The discredited
art of acting—The need for a new virtuosity—The
critics—The wrong sort of school—The army of
women—The unprofessional student

Chapter III : The Plan of the Theatre as School

The school's scope—No children admitted—The
broad base of the work—No teaching of acting allowed—The by-paths of the social " settlement " and
the " community " theatre—The picked recruits—
Playwriting classes—Stage decoration—The co-opera-

Chapter IV : The Theatre as Playhouse

THE EXEMPLARY THEATRE

CHAPTER I: THE AUTHOR'S PREJUDICES AND OTHERS

ONE follows a calling for thirty years and forgets its comparative unimportance ; how could it hold one otherwise ? But, pleading its cause to the world, this is the first thing one must make a show of remembering. For a man of the theatre to write of the theatre as if nothing else mattered is only to invite from the man of the world that polite acquiescence which is deadlier than disagreement.

This book is a plea for the recognition of the theatre as an educational force. It is addressed mainly to people whose present interest in the theatre is at best perfunctory. And its first chapter takes the appropriate form of a dialogue between a man of the theatre and a minister of education, and is an attempt to reconcile the general and particular points of view.

To begin such a book with a chapter of dialogue *The uses of* is more than superficially appropriate, for its whole *dialogue* purpose, as will be seen, is implicit in the virtue of this form of expression. We are to argue the educational uses of the dramatic method. Let both parties, then, put their present accomplishment in it to a preliminary test.

The Man of the Theatre—as is only fair— frankly exposes his bias. Why pretend in a book of polemic to be disinterested? It is bad enough that the technical questions involved will prevent the lay reader, half the time, from estimating the honesty of the statements. The Minister of Education replies coolly, judicially. But now consider. Was the admission of bias a disguised appeal for sympathy? Is the reply only let seem more judicial that it may the safelier be made less so? Is the writer's whole show of accommodation only another form of special pleading? How far, in fact, does his art elucidate the truth of the matter, or is he deliberately using it to obscure the truth? If the reader can discover him at his tricks, so much the worse for him—and for his art! If he cannot, so much the worse for the reader and the more need for a little education in this dramatic method! The more need, then, of this book. In one sense its writer is trying, of course, to get round his readers. Why ever else go to the unnatural trouble of writing a book at all? And he shows but a necessary confidence in his case by opening with this demonstration. Yet the gist of the case is that the dramatic form, if honestly used—which is to say in terms of an art, artistically used—is the vehicle for a very vital sort of truth. And this is its honest use. First, to have the courage, not only of the strength, but of the weakness of one's opinion. Not merely to be self-critical: there is little in that, it may lead only to diffidence. But to project the whole body of one's belief into an individual shape, armed and sustained to the full. Then to attack it. Can such an attack be genuine; can one hit oneself in the face? Well, we must not look for a detachment, or an artistry, or an honesty that is superhumanly perfect. But the fact of projection makes all the difference. We shall be tender of a guarded faith : but if it has had its fling, if we have set it free, so to speak, from reservation and control, we shall then be well content to fling back at it and to fling our best. For the harder we fling the greater its credit in sustaining our attack. We may take pride even in showing alien adversaries that we know its weak spots, naturally, better than ever they can. If it sustains

2

our attacks it will certainly be invulnerable to theirs. And if, as it happens, we do demolish it; why, to do so, we must have formed a better opinion and a stronger belief.

The drama's methods are the commonest in the world : they are the methods of everyday conversation. But they are worth study: the more that, becoming suddenly aware we have used them unknowingly for years, we may think ourselves natural masters of the art—which is first to deceive ourselves, and later probably to be deceived in turn, and so to come to the belief that the art lies in its deceiving. *Dramatists all; and actors all*

Now, art is a social danger if it is a continuing untruth. Surely that does not attach an unreasoning importance to the matter if the practice of this art of the drama is as common as eating. And it is. We dramatize our lives; by no other means can we decide upon the parts we mean to play in them. We are actors all; but so many of us, setting out with the best intentions, neither know when nor why the performance begins to go wrong, and tricks to take the place of the fine interpretation we meant to give. Nobody hisses perhaps. But that's the worst of it.

This book's plea for the theatre's salvation is a wider and simpler one than it would seem to be. Technical argument apart, it is a plea for truth-telling (a matter of great artistry) and for the cultivation of a faculty by which the common man may hope, as a rule, to know whether he is being told the truth about things or not. Strange if dramatic art can successfully concern itself with such matters! But if it can . . . .

The Minister of Education . . . . . . But, my dear sir, don't apologize. Every man worth his salt naturally makes high claims for his own profession. *"The" profession* The Man of the Theatre. I don't apologize . . . though I'm readier for the moment with accusations than claims. I recognize, to begin with, that the theatre is not a profession. That was rubbed into me by a kindly editor when I'd written my first public words on its troubles . . . a letter to a newspaper. " Do you mind being accurate ? " he said. " There's a medical profession, a legal profession. The theatre is . . . you may choose half a dozen words for it." I went away sorrowful and snubbed. The distinction had never occurred to me, nor had the subtle contempt come home of the journalists' joke (briefless barristers most of them!) about "the" profession.

I imagine that I fixed upon "calling." One avoids the word "art" . . . though not to escape the Royal Academy's frowns. But how many a programme have I corrected with the actors described not even as artists, but as " artistes " . . . the printer's unconscious fling ; and who invented *that* gibe, I wonder ? Actors, I agree, are absurdly sensitive. I suppose that even this generation of them is not quite free from the struggle to be considered gentlemen. It is mostly their relations, though, country clergymen and the like, that distressfully take up the cudgels. And that silliest of plays " David Garrick "—even sillier in its motive than the silly prejudices it mocks and appeals to—is but just out of date. Better to call the theatre a trade, except for the implication that people make money by it.

M. of E. But don't they ?

M. of T. Out of it, yes. But by following the calling and practising the art of the theatre there isn't, for the great majority, much money to be

4

made. In that it is as honourable as a profession, codeless though it be. No parson or doctor or civil servant could be, in practice, more disinterested than the average actor who has settled down to the life. But they are trade victims, if you like.

M. of E. And is that your first complaint?

M. of T. I shan't press it on their behalf. The bored and barren sympathy which the victim inspires is not at all what I'm after. I want to interest you in the theatre.

M. of E. As . . . what?

M. of T. As social service.

M. of E. Interest on my part is to be official and to imply action, is it?

M. of T. Admission of the need for action.

M. of E. Then I must analyse your phrases carefully. You mean that it should be regulated as a social service . . . as a civil service, do you?

M. of T. Not strictly . . . not altogether.

M. of E. No, since civil service became bureaucracy you're not so eager to entrust your darling schemes to its care.

M. of T. Well, I'll own that I'm thinking of my average Englishman, who'd sooner have a bad bureaucracy than a good one . . . it is a step nearer having none at all.

M. of E. But you were going to begin with complaints. Let us clear the ground of those first. What offends you most in the present state of things?

M. of T. Fundamentally, I believe, that the theatre exists by appealing to the mob.

M. of E. To the public.

M. of T. No, no . . . if you mean to analyse my phrases I must pick my words. The public connotes something, if not organized, at least a little

The Theatre's Appeal to Mob

5

stable, doesn't it? My first complaint is of the mob appeal, the mob standard of success, and the ever-growing confusion of purpose that results. In London, and very notably in New York, it isn't even a constant . . . it's a shifting, hotel-haunting mob. Oh, a demagogic art, the theatre of to-day, if ever there was one.

M. of E. That's the fault of a quality, surely, for democratic, as a normal description of it, wouldn't offend you, would it?

M. of T. On the contrary.

M. of E. Well, then, as to its proper method of carrying on. . . . I sound old-fashioned, but I'm a weary bureaucrat myself and not over in love, it may surprise you to hear, with indefinite increase of bureaucracy. It takes many generations to train competent officials, you know. Heaven knows that so far we haven't enough to go round. What's wrong with the dear old discredited law of supply and demand to regulate the theatre by? Can't even you put up with it for a bit?

M. of T. Well, I admit that it must depend upon current appreciation more than does any other art, more even than music need, because of the greater expense and complexity of the machinery. Therefore degradation is easier . . .

M. of E. I protest now . . . that word is yours. You're horribly self-conscious. I should never have dreamed of using it.

M. of T. You protest, may I say, too readily. You wouldn't use it because you'd never dream of admitting a claim from the theatre to rank with the other arts; music, literature, painting . . . though these, in some respects each one of them, sink as low as the drama can. But you don't cease to honour them for that.

6

M. of E. I don't think the theatre does rank with *Should* the fine arts * . . . no. The drama . . . *drama be ac-*

M. of T. Oh, please don't make that—forgive *counted one of* me—that silly distinction. Drama has no claim *the Fine Arts?* to existence apart from the theatre that it should be framed for. As well praise a yacht for being built to stay safely in harbour as exalt a play because it is more fitted for the study than the stage.

M. of E. But there's a finer distinction. Has any theatre you can name ever lived up to the best opportunities its greatest dramatists have given it? How many first prizes did Euripides win? Do you suppose King Lear was popular with actors, or audiences either? Is it a libel to suggest that the actor of to-day cares very little for the quality of the play he appears in?

M. of T. Yes, I think it is.

M. of E. But the better actor he is the less it affects him, and the poorer the play the greater his

---

* Since writing this it has been decided upon technical grounds, by the Chief Registrar of Friendly Societies, that acting, at least does not rank as one of the Fine Arts. His judgment, upon which immediately depended the liability of the Academy of Dramatic Art for certain rates, is a practical inconvenience to the progress of the theatre as a social service, and had therefore better be upset as soon as possible. The arguments upon which he founded it, though interesting, are vitiated, it seems to me, by his consideration of the constituents of the art as the art itself. And here the drafting of the Academy's charter is also to blame. Had it advanced as the main object of the institution the study of the Art of the Theatre, and left acting, elocution, diction, and the rest in a qualifying clause there would have been a better chance of a favourable decision. For, I humbly suggest to the Registrar, if he will analyse and isolate the constituents of, say, the art of architecture, the exercises in which its students must be trained, he will easily be able to prove that architecture is not a fine art either. The Act of 1843, however, expressly stating that it is so, he was exempt, unfortunately, from the necessity of making the comparison.

personal success. My point is—let me put it quite
brutally—that the chief circumstance of the drama,
its exploiting of the human personality, and the
consequent belittling, instead of exalting, of its every
theme, must always forbid it to be thought of as a
great art.

M. of T. Well, I won't question . . . for the
moment, at any rate . . . its absolute value. But
can you deny the colossal influence the theatre must
have . . . merely by the mass of its output . . .
upon the public imagination?

M. of E. Certainly I deny it. That sort of
energy is expended, as a rule, without direction,
and I incline to believe that in the theatre's instance,
as far as any moral effect is concerned, one-half of it
about cancels out the other.

M. of T. And you're content with such waste?

M. of E. That's part of a bigger question. I don't
want to answer it by saying that a licence to waste
is all man has gained in this latest prosperous phase
of his efforts at civilization. But we do, every one
of us, throw away and wear away in the course of
our lifetime far more than our individual energies
could ever replace. And nowadays we're so many
of us mere *entrepreneurs*. Our lives depend on
machinery, actual and social, and on the willingness
of . . . let us advisedly remember . . . not so
very many people to keep the master-machinery
going for our benefit. Certainly, therefore, emotional
or intellectual extravagance, undirected and meaningless, is undesirable. For one may justly say
that it prompts recklessness of all kinds.

M. of T. You yield me my point.

M. of E. So far.

M. of T. You agree that an emotionally degraded
theatre is a dangerous thing.

8

M. of E. It's anarchical, perhaps. But, I'm not afraid of a little anarchy, of leaving a little of the primitive social mud for men to relax themselves in.

M. of T. Out of which they may make their mud-pies of drama ?

M. of E. Though by all means I'm for clarifying the confusion of mind that leads to the degradation of things of value . . . by all simple means. I see my educational way as far as children are concerned. I'd encourage their dancing, singing, playing games that have rhyme and reason . . . not too much reason . . . in them. I see my way for the adult over architecture, painting, sculpture, even over music. These are, compared with the theatre, impersonal, abstract arts. One can consecrate them at their best, and set them apart. But the theatre you'll admit to be very difficult to handle for such a purpose. And can you convince me that even at its best it would reward the handling as the arts which have permanency of form do undoubtedly reward our care of them ? Theoretically we should take more trouble over all such things, no doubt, and over many others. But shall we be practically wise to direct our spare energy . . . for there's not much to spare . . . towards the theatre ? Should we be even if it were, in its working out, the simplest of the arts ? That's one question. But another, more difficult if not more serious, arises not from its artistic shortcomings . . . I leave you ensuing them . . . but from the complexity of its organization as an industry. You are proud of the theatre as a living art, reflecting the spirit, even in the commonplace life of the time. Why can't you be content with that ? What would you gain by trying to change its nature . . . for that's what you're after, I fear. Now it's a pleasant super-

9

fluity of life. Society makes certain careless and incoherent demands of it. If the theatre's responses excel them we're grateful, and we store up the remembrance to its credit. If its response should become very poisonous we should have to put the police on it. But suppose we do give it rank with life's necessities, put it to the utilitarian tests, strangle it with regulation, hand it into the care of people with highly developed social consciences . . . what then? Convince me, if you can, to begin with, that I should educationally gain anything. I'm fairly convinced that you would artistically lose. Reform your theatre from within as much as you will . . .

M. of T. That's not easy. Of whatever calibre you mark it, the drama is still an art. But the theatre as an industry is a successful one. Please tell me upon what basis of reasonableness you set out to reform a successful industry. It is under the control of business men who are not concerned . . . why should they be? . . . with its social functions. They are only indirectly interested in its artistic development. But they are very particularly concerned that what I have called its mob appeal should remain. All's fish that comes to their net with a piece of silver slipped in the gills, and the bigger the catch the better. What other standard of success, then, should we expect them to recognize than the power to attract the greatest possible crowd in the shortest possible time?

The difficulty of ranking the Theatre as a social service

M. of E. But listen now. What you are after is the exalting of dramatic art. Good. How will its mere recognition (blessed political Mesopotamia of a word) by public authority effect that?

M. of T. Be careful. Once you admit the prin-

10

ciple of recognition I may push you pretty far in its application.

M. of E. Believe me, I see you at it. Subsidized theatres, colleges of acting . . .

M. of T. Well, isn't our standard of musical achievement higher to-day because of the recognition of the art and the endowment of musical training during the last fifty years ?

M. of E. I might question that. *Post hoc* isn't *propter hoc.* That the standard of public taste is . . . higher, shall we say ? . . . well, wider ; that it is more . . . shall we call it educated or sophisticated ? . . . I won't deny. But we must not be taken in by the snobbery which leads people to the opera or to classical concerts . . . intellectual snobbery, the most aggravating variety.

M. of T. Come now, people can only learn to like music by listening to it. I must say that for an educationist you're distressingly impatient. Movements of this sort don't show a real result in much under a hundred years.

M. of E. But remember, once we give authority to professors to spread abroad a respect for some complicated lingo, for their own greater credit they'll go on complicating it indefinitely. Does it follow that the fine phrases mean anything : that Abracadabra casts any spell except upon the credulity of its hearers ? That sort of mystery-mongering is not education. You don't expect me to encourage you to go round muddling up my teachers' minds . . . and encouraging them to make a worse muddle in their pupils' . . . with talk about the civic importance of the theatre and the psychological necessity for the development of the histrionic instinct in children. I enjoy a good play, well acted ; so do they. Don't spoil it for us. I

admit a certain absolute educative value in music.
I haven't yet admitted it in the drama, have I?
And I can't retract, I fear, my disparaging remarks
about the theatre. But shall I put it this way?
Any of the constituents of dramatic art that I'd be
ready to teach in an ordinary school you probably
wouldn't be content to call drama at all.

M. of T. Come, come. We're getting on. I'll
hold you to the admission that you might be ready
to take the poor, pretentious, and accursed thing in
some guise or other within the sacred portals.
I'll spare you the reminder that if you didn't teach
some form of drama in schools you couldn't teach
anything at all . . . or rather, I'll return, by your
leave, to that later. But I'll promise not to be at all
exigent about what you do teach as long as you'll
give it its rightful name, and not disguise it as gymnastics, or as some Cinderella branch of literature.

M. of E. But from the moment I do touch the
accursed thing, and own to touching it, I know I
shall be trapped by one difficulty after another.
You know that, too. I see you dissembling a
malicious grin, and heightening its effect thereby,
like the incorrigible man of the theatre that you
are. That's the worst of art. It gets round you
under false pretences. Give me solid science and
I know where I stand. There's a precise value in
the subject, and I can test the quality of the teaching.
But I'm to put on the list of the school's work something called dramatic study, am I . . . or the art of
self-expression? My dear sir, forgive me . . . that
simply opens the door to charlatanism.

M. of T. Oh, I agree.

M. of E. Well . . . ?

M. of T. You must go further. This is *my*
point. Half measures are what the charlatan

thrives on. If you want to escape him you must go the whole way.

M. of E. To the study of drama in ordinary schools, in ordinary classes ?

M. of T. Yes.

M. of E. And not as literature ? In action ?

M. of T. Yes. In whatever amount of action . . . in whatever *sort* of action the study demands.

M. of E. Well, now, admitting, for the moment, some value in the thing, incalculable but sufficient, my difficulties at once begin. It's a co-operative art, and very unequally co-operative in its practice ; very hard, therefore, to make use of for individual culture. You'll admit that. *The difficulty of using the drama in education*

M. of T. Yes, certainly a young lady can't sit down to a piano and play over a piece of Shakespeare as she can an Etude of Chopin. But hasn't that facility for individual showing-off come near being the damnation of musical education ?

M. of E. Maybe. In my own opinion, yes.

M. of T. Yet how can we properly study any art but by practising it ? For the musician there's nothing, I suppose, like a little hard gruelling in an orchestra. Working together at a play does knock the individual nonsense out of young people so oppressively delighted with their newly-found egotisms. . . .

M. of E. Oh, I'd not mind a class in the drama as an infrequent spree, for no serious attention gets given to it then. Children prefer, though, to be either at work or at play ; and I sympathize with them. But constant class-work in drama, ranking with geography and arithmetic ! To begin with, how would you prevent the distraction of it from wrecking both the class before and the class after ?

M. of T. Oh, that's the trouble, is it ?

13

M. of E. I've not contended so far, remember, that the drama is positively demoralizing. It has its place, and a very worthy one, as recreation. But if you ask me in its name to substitute emotion for thought and pleasure for hard work, and as a part of education . . . education, mark you ! . . . to let loose that spirit in the child which would then find itself very loose indeed in the man, I must find something severe to say. Don't call me old-fashioned. There are no fashions in this. The world has never got on by cultivating its emotions, and it never will.

M. of T. It may ill become a mere expert in emotionalism to tell you that he detects a confusion of thought, but I think I do. In the same breath . . . at least, if you'd had a proper dramatic training you could have managed it all with one breath ; as it was you took two or three . . . you spoke of letting loose emotions and cultivating them, as if you equally condemned both proceedings. But surely it's only dangerous to let loose an emotion when you haven't cultivated it ?

M. of E. By no means. Cultivation, for instance, may hall-mark it with an entirely fictitious value, and it may circulate to the ultimate depreciation of the whole moral currency.

M. of T. Well, I realize that objection. The drama is not free from domestic trouble, so to speak, on the score ; and I must do my best to meet you. But you must let me, for the purposes of argument, idealize my theatre just a little. For we are talking of an imagined future, after all . . . near as I want to bring it.

M. of E. By all means.

M. of T. Then I can face your sternest contentions. You tell me that the theatre does not . . .

you imply that it cannot . . . rank with the other fine arts. Do you mean that within its three hours' limit no possible drama can deal adequately with great subjects unless, perhaps, as with the Greeks, they are formalized almost into ritual.

M. of E. I won't dogmatise. Possibly, though, one reaches in three hours, or in rather less, the limit of man's capacity to absorb such a potent mixture of emotion and thought.

M. of T. But come back, for a moment, to the actual present, to the theatre as it now is, and to what does seem to me this perfectly damnable business by which people . . . young people too, mostly . . . have their uncultured emotions played upon night after night by an intellectually seductive, emotionally cloying, sexually provocative and altogether irresponsible entertainment. Do you approve of that ? Is that a socially sound business ? I can imagine your crying : Down with the theatre altogether. I *cannot* think how you are content to leave it as it is.

M. of E. Once again, I believe you overrate the effect of such emotional indulgence upon the average man.

M. of T. Even upon the average young man . . . and woman ?

M. of E. Oh, for them all emotions get trans- *Art's over-* muted into the one that Nature most requires them, *rated* at their time of life, to cultivate. And I should say *influence* their imagination's digestion is of iron . . . especially the young female's. So you move me very little by " sexually provocative " and " emotionally cloying." Certainly I prefer that they should be stirred to very outbursts of laughter and tears, and for the sake of those sanitarily emotional effects I am quite ready to overlook the simplicity and stupidity of

15

the cause. But when you say " intellectually seductive " you do touch me nearly, for it is these young
people's brains that get green sickness. Un-
intelligence I can forgive. But false intelligence
is the devil.

M. of T. Can't they digest that too, and throw
off the effects ?

M. of E. No, my friend ; you may eat too much
pudding, and a good game of football will free
you from your trouble. But don't try a diet of
drugs. Young people are greedy of emotion, or
shy of it. To the average adult it is a passing distraction, nothing more. . . .

M. of T. And you prefer it should remain so ?

M. of E. Frankly, yes. We must be utilitarian.
You know we're still in the stage of striving . . . for
all our fine talk of " higher " things . . . to maintain
our poor foothold upon even physical civilization.
If a man doesn't respond to the finer stimuli, it is
because he has found that they would hinder rather
than help him in his everyday round. And I don't
want him to be constantly distracted by a sharpened
imagination from his dull but necessary daily work.
He has learnt that it's necessary ; frankly, I don't
want him to find out that it's dull . . . for his own
sake.

M. of T. But wouldn't that be a path to enliven-
ing it and so enriching it ?

M. of E. No, there I'm at odds with you. Art,
with its exaltation of emotional and spiritual
standards, may follow in the wake of social progress,
it doesn't prompt it. You'd admit that of all the
other fine arts, I think. But because in the theatre
you have one so simple, so democratic, so capable,
in current phrase, of " direct action " upon the
sensibilities of the crowd, you want to forge it

16

into a weapon (Forgive my clichés ; I am not, you see, an artist!) of social betterment. You can't. If you could it might turn double-edged, and become, I do think, a most dangerous one. Yes, art is in its nature anarchic. Let it remain so then, happily and harmlessly, and keep it from any share in the control of society.

M. of T. I'll disagree with you to the end of time. You like to say that because art declines measurement by your footrule. Art is constructive, but it constructs from the elements, as life itself does. Refuse it right functioning, and in its neglect and degradation it does become a disintegrating and . . . as I hold the theatre of to-day to be, negatively, at least . . . an anti-social force.

M. of E. Then you must reform it from within, autonomously. After all, your industrial problem is not an insoluble one, and in the last instance you can do without the loathed, and I think somewhat libelled, business man better than he can do without you. Qualified artists in combination could assert something like a monopoly value. But now I want to attack you on your own ground. You theatre reformers . . . I suppose you like the title . . . are not single-minded. You confuse the issue you present. You ask me for one thing when you really want another. Come, get on your guard. Whatever else an art may or may not be, it must, to be healthy, be single-minded . . .

M. of T. Agreed.

M. of E. And I, personally, should add, simple-minded. Therefore, when you make this art, and try to make me, the half-conscious victim of your schemes, I tell you you'll do more harm to the drama than good to the theatre containing it, and

The Theatre as catspaw

consequently no good at all, in the end, to the society you pretend to set out to serve.

M. of T. This is a sounding blow. " Schemes " awakens sinister echoes. Please particularize the crime that I contemplate.

M. of E. Without being personal ?

M. of T. Oh, be personal if you want to be.

M. of E. Well, as a simple instance, will you admit that your anxiety to reorganize the theatre hinges in great part on your wish to get a certain sort of play performed which doesn't enjoy much public favour now ?

M. of T. Naturally. Wait, though, I see where you are driving me . . .

M. of E. And any specimen is nearly always a " reforming " sort of play, isn't it ?

M. of T. I make no more admissions.

M. of E. And is it only a coincidence that many of you theatre reformers are out after reforming the rest of the universe, too ?

M. of T. What's the concrete accusation ?

M. of E. Simply that at heart you care little about the theatre in comparsion with the use you can make of it to forward your social and political ideas.

M. of T. But why, in heaven's name, should a man write three sentences but to express and forward an idea ? And since he's a social and political animal, what other ideas should you generally expect from him ? However, don't let's come down to scoring these barren points. If you'll assure me that you don't want to turn us into performing poodles I'll own up that the theatre, with its seemingly simple art and its direct appeal . . . the mob appeal, though, mind you, it is I who condemn . . . is a tempting platform for the mere lay preacher.

18

M. of E. Whose sermons, being out of place, are dull . . . which art never has a right to be.

M. of T. Not duller than most of the plays meant merely to amuse, as no sort of art surely should ever be. You don't admit that ? I'll argue it later if you like. But as to the disingenuous reformer, take this to your comfort. The theatre is very old, and has some of the wise simplicity of age. Given time . . . and art itself never lacks time, though its exemplars may . . . it can endure and absorb a dozen merely intellectual " movements " and still go its way. We organize and combine all sorts of forces to make a mark, but the only thing that leaves one is genius. And you're ready to welcome any species of that, I suppose.

M. of E. With open arms. Please show me how to organize it into existence.

M. of T. Patience, patience . . . not with me and my arguments so much as with the poor theatre itself. Do you mind my parenthetically remarking on the unreasonable way in which you public men are apt to demand genius in the arts as the only justification for their existence ? If lawyers and doctors and parsons, civil servants, and soldiers could claim no recognition, no protection for their callings, except on such a ground . . . !

M. of E. Good ! One to you ! I grant you that point.

M. of T. Very well. Arising out of that . . . as they say in a place where a good deal of co-operative dramatic effect is expended, and might, with better training, be more profitably expended . . . you admit, I gather, that, of all the arts, the most dependent, under modern conditions, upon sheer organization is the theatre ?

M. of E. Yes, if you like.

The economics of the modern English Theatre

M. of T. Now I must trouble you for a moment with some economic history. Twenty-five years or so back the English theatre began to face . . . belatedly, as is its nature . . . reorganization in the terms of modern industry. Organically the theatre was an industry ; and so that had to come, whether one liked it or not. Most of the important individuals concerned did not like it, and would not face it, until quite recently they found themselves at last overwhelmed, protesting and bewailing, by the accomplished fact. It was left to others not so intimately concerned, but able therefore, perhaps, to take a wider view, to foresee the coming change, and to begin to struggle for the theatre's soul. For that, too, was finally . . . was and is, as we are arguing now . . . involved. They were the " reformers," as you call them : on their behalf I won't resent the name. They saw the theatre as a social service, not first . . . for if first generally last we find . . . as a money-making concern. And so they urged that, by one scheme or another, the community must be made responsible for its welfare. The money-makers did not hurry to the struggle. They saw that the industrial development must come, and waited for an easy market . . . a good vantage. But straightway the individuals most nearly concerned . . . individualists, indeed, who saw " their " theatre as a private estate " situate " very exclusively in the West End of London and to be parcelled out conveniently among them : actor-managers their generic name! . . . took on a fight with the reformers in the name (God bless us !) of fine art and freedom. I fear you'd have been on their side. For you still take your stand under their showy banner, unaware, apparently, that this particular battle is over. It is over. And what was the course of the fight ? And who, does it turn out, was the real enemy ? Why, the money-maker, of course, who . . . in his own good time . . . took them, the fools, in the rear. Yes, I repeat without apology . . . the fools ! They should have known that the reformers' cause must finally be theirs. But no, they would go cockily on until the giant Financial Interest, once under way, now swallows them one by one, each at a bite. Some of them personally and professionally survive, partnered as a rule with business men. But ask them the difference between their old situation and the new one if, for a minute, box office success gives them the go-by.

M. of E. I'll wager that they still prefer the business yoke of the man who makes money out of them, and lets them get as much of it as they can bargain for, to the artistic yoke which would make of them lay figures to illustrate this new " sociological " fashion and that.

M. of T. Well, whether or no, I fear their tastes and troubles are no longer important. They have counted themselves out of the main fight. They must do now what their capitalists tell them. " Backers," these gentlemen used to be called : they are well to the front now ! But to come again to the artistic sins of the reformers. Wasn't it almost inevitable that men bringing fresh blood to an art which had come to exist, you'll admit, much in appearance and little in content, should believe that, for redressing the balance, only ideas mattered at all ?

M. of E. But why not artistic ideas ?

M. of T. But when are ideas *not* artistic ideas ? I utterly resent the implication that art . . . any art, but most especially the simple, democratic art of the theatre . . . is to be divorced from the things of

21

everyday life. It only thrives upon fellowship with them. Moreover, I'll assert that if it has drifted hopelessly out of touch with the current of men's minds, it must begin its association again as a servant, not as an equal. Precious lucky the theatre might think itself that men and women with a lively sense of what was important to the world at the moment should take the trouble to make some artistic use of it. And it was the business of the interpretative artists already in possession . . . it was their duty . . . to help these interlopers, to exploit them, moreover, if they could, to the theatre's profit. The newcomers were not out after conquest and exclusion. There need have been no quarrel except with certain self-satisfied people, who were not only too lazy or indifferent to use the theatre for the expression of any ideas themselves, but objected to their own easy livelihood being discredited by those who could and would. The " reformers " made every effort to work even with them, only to be snubbed and sneered at, or, at best, to be patronized. Men of spirit don't stand that. And how you, as a public man, dare to complain that we occupied ourselves with the socialization of the theatre to the prejudice of its artistry, when it was *your* work we were doing at the expense of our own. . . .

M. of E. Steady ; this is the point we're to discuss. Why is it my work ? That's what you have to prove.

M. of T. I'm out to. That was merely my answer in passing to your gibe at the " reformers," men who were not of the theatre by training or altogether perhaps at heart, but who saw in it something more than an amusement or an easy method of making money, and who therefore, when they

22

came to work in it, turned some of their attention to things that, I grant you, are not strictly of the art of the theatre. I dare say it had from the beginning an ill effect on their artistry. It is, you may argue, just as bad to be thinking while you write or produce a play either of all the social evils you mean to expose, or the rest of the social service your theatre is doing, as it is to be calculating the money it will earn. But if these men remain even now too self-consciously the preachers and politicians of the theatre, unable to lose themselves in the happiness of their work, once again, isn't it largely because the burden of your neglect has been so heavy upon them? So that, even from your point of view, wouldn't you have been wiser to take public responsibility for the organizing side of the job? For, with that done, only quite nice, harmless, " artistic " people would, we're to take it, have been attracted to the theatre at all. And if any of these damnable reformers had happened to slip in they could have slaked their unholy passions upon systems of lighting, or costume designs, or the setting of Elizabethan plays. Still, the mischief mightn't have stopped there. Reform is like jealousy, and makes the meat it feeds on (notice, please, the appropriately theatrical allusion). A passion for reform, according to the non-reformers, springs from jealousy, nothing more or less. So, once they had murdered the artistic conventions they would have sidled for bigger game, and instead of the present paltry misuse of energy you complain of, you might have had to trace a whole social revolution back to—say—a production of King Lear. It is really a terrible problem, this of getting people to keep their noses to the grindstone and mind their own business. And the theatre really is not a good place in which to attempt a pattern solution. For if it is to be alive at all it must be concerned with the life all around it, and that only makes its merry men livelier still, more inquisitive, more impertinent. Come, why don't you suppress the poisonous thing altogether ?

M. of E. Well . . . taking public charge of it might be one way of dishing the reformers and of doing that.

Authority's obligation to the Theatre

M. of T. I'm ready to run the risk. Give me for the theatre the conscience of a public service . . . I return you compliment for snub . . . and I'll trust its own innate life to defeat any bureaucratic stranglings more easily than it manages to escape from the tangle of money-making. Art for art's sake may be a good or a bad cry. Personally, I think it's a bad one on all counts. But there is certainly no art less fitted to respond to it than the dramatic art. And again, while poetry, painting, sculpture can exist for a little in the cloister or the desert, as a reflection from the past or a promise for the future, the drama . . . simple, democratic, crude if you will . . . must be of its age. Therefore, even if I cared for nothing else in the theatre but the quintessential art of the theatre . . . ah, that stamps me as the most pestilent of reformers, doesn't it ? . . . I should welcome its present attachment to some larger idea, to drag it abreast of the times.

M. of E. As an artist, how you ought to hate that phrase !

M. of T. . . . abreast of the *need* of the times. Here is the theatre in the dumps. . . .

M. of E. I don't maintain that. I don't admit it. And, yet again, why am I to be called on for the helping hand ?

24

M. of T. Confound your condescension ! I'll be offering to help you in a minute. It is dignified, and it is historically right, that an art, bankrupt of consequence, should go into service so as to establish itself again. Did not the Greek drama spring from religious ritual ? It at least had the form, it carried the weight of accepted ceremony.

M. of E. Am I to take the appeal to history seriously ?

M. of T. Well, like better men, for bigger ends, I twist the picture to my purpose. But one's view of a winding street must depend—mustn't it ?— upon the point at which one turns to look back on it.

M. of E. Hark to the advocate of the drama as the saviour of society ! And you ask me to magnify such methods by my approval . . . and, what's more, to multiply your chances of using them !

M. of T. Well, as a public man, impressing on us your view of the present, I hope you've nothing worse on your conscience. If we can't find you out, though, that's our fault. However, you may neglect my history when the practical present-day questions come to be answered . . . as I fear you would indeed, however much you respected it. And you needn't grant me the Greeks . . . and I'll skip the Romans.

M. of E. Thank you.

M. of T. But how did the drama struggle to coherent life again out of the Dark Ages ? By clinging to the skirts of the Church or the Guilds. Elizabethan players, remember, were the servants of this lord or that. The best of them were the Queen's servants. That wasn't mere snobbishness, you know : they were formally a part of her household.

M. of E. But they played to the groundlings.

M. of T. So did she ! * The tie loosened later
into the quite formal relationship with the patent
theatres, and has even outlasted their dissolution.
Witness the institution of the censorship in the
Lord Chamberlain's office. The best excuse for
that foolish business would be a royal theatre sup-
ported by the Privy Purse.

M. of E. But that would hardly suit your reformer. I remark to you that these player-folk
were pretty severely kept in their place in those
halcyon days.

M. of T. That mattered little beside the fact that
they had their place. How long would they have
survived interference without it ? Of course, I
don't want them thrust back in it now. What
suited that time doesn't suit this. But notice,
please, that the theatre is but one among many
crafts that have waked up lately to the further implications of their freedom to make all the money
they can, or starve.

M. of E. Economically speaking, of course, why
not to make all the money there is to make and still
to starve ?

M. of T. Why not, indeed . . . as the Russian
proletarian discovers? And while that reduction to
absurdity is being reached, still to be starved . . .
they themselves and all the rest of us, their customers
. . . of all the things due to them and from them

* Did contemporary critics complain of it ? England has had
great political performers since to whom she has given more
dubious reception. But one finds an instance of the histrionic
temperament coming to its own again in a note of Sir John
Skelton's upon meeting Disraeli in 1867: "They say, and say
truly enough, 'What an actor the man is'; and yet the ultimate
impression is of absolute sincerity and unreserve."—Vol. IV of
the Monypeny-Buckle "Life."

that don't get quoted at a market-rate. But men are not born doctrinaires, thank God! They do not come into this world either as little individualists or little socialists, but as something more satisfyingly human than either. And where this impending fool's tragedy has been sensed, watch their efforts . . . scattered and contradictory, no doubt, since, born to this particular inheritance of anarchy that troubles you so little, they can't quite forswear such capital as they have all for the sake of future interest . . . watch these puzzled adventurers in the cause of the greatest unhappiness of the greatest number trying to struggle back into some sort of mutually helpful state of dignity and safety.

M. of E. And, pray . . . letting the rest of the wide world slide for the moment, as you conscientiously can, I assure you . . . what stands in the theatre's way ?

M. of T. I grant you, mainly our own confusion of thought and purpose. We still have to discover . . . and come to a sufficient measure of agreement upon what we want. There are efforts in plenty and experiments enough, but they are particularist still, and they show little perception of any idea of the theatre that could enmesh and might reconcile them all. Playwrights collogue together; the training of actors is in hand; there's an actors' strike in America; in England the Actors' Association, after years of uncomfortable and unprofitable sitting on the fence, dubs itself a trade union. There are village theatres, community theatres, repertory theatres, clubs and leagues and committees of one sort and another; on paper, in embryo, promising well, doing nicely now, or gasping for breath. It's all very interesting, very hopeful, rather exasperating.

27

M. of E. Well, then, go ahead on those lines, and when you and your fellow enthusiasts have gathered enough strength, drop your differences, fight the commercialism you protest against, and then . . .

M. of T. But no mere discrediting of commercialism will content me. I don't even trouble to attack it, for I see it beaten in its very victory.

M. of E. A familiar paradox !

M. of T. And in this case a very obvious one. The commercialists have won everything that I'm not fighting for, and they are quite content with their spoils. I've nothing against them, then. They'll go their prosperous way and I'll follow my star. We can be quite good friends. And I'm only thankful that the general result of their victory, and nothing else at all, should now so nakedly appear. Does it content *you* . . . this is the question I'm framing in every form I can . . . to see the whole power of the theatre absorbed unashamedly in the greatest entertainment of the greatest number upon the best cash terms, to see it making nothing but a mob appeal ? For is a mob only a danger when it gathers in ill-dressed crowds ? What of the well-dressed mob that makes up a dinner-party of ten; the ten thousand mobs of a hundred or so, each calling itself the best set in its own dowdy, respectable suburb; the provincial mobs . . . you'll find a dozen different ones in every cathedral town; the mob innumerable of hard-headed, practical people; the clerical mob, the educational mob, the artistic mob, the medical mob, the sporting mob ? The theatre's business to-day is to talk flattering nonsense to these good people. It may be complimentary or abusive nonsense almost indifferently if only it will familiarly echo them, so that they in

28

turn can effortlessly echo it, till voice and echo, indistinguishable from each other, deteriorate into a meaningless vacuity.

M. of E. Excellent vituperation, no doubt. You combine all the usual targets for abuse into one. But at the worst this makes up, I repeat, a very negative danger.

M. of T. The worst dangers are negative, and the longest breeding. An artist must loathe the mob mind.

M. of E. No doubt. But we're back where we started. This was your original trouble, more or less. I could agree that a self-respecting way out would be for the real workers in the theatre to recover control over their own industry. But you won't take that.

M. of T. It would be no way out. For I won't admit that the theatre is only, or chiefly, an industry, or that the people who make a living by it are the only people concerned. I want to fasten responsibility upon *you*.

The drama's industrial difficulty is that an Art shall not be an industry

M. of E. Well, I'm still waiting to undergo the operation.

M. of T. It now begins. Where any sort of art is concerned we are apt to talk, aren't we, without knowing perhaps quite what we mean, of men and women having a " gift " for the thing ? An absolute gift is it, or one to be held in trust and passed on ?

M. of E. Well, if you bury that talent you certainly get no good of it, you can't even dig it up unimpaired. Still, there's a market price for the use of it.

M. of T. Certainly, we must most of us earn our living from day to day. But isn't it a rather startling fact . . . at least it should surely startle

29

the commercialists if they would stop to consider it . . . that by law one cannot perpetuate property in imaginative work?* Think of the copyright laws, of the hard fight there was even for a term of lifetime and fifty years. What's the other side to that question, if not some conviction that the power to write plays, books, and poems comes as a gift to the writer, and so must in honour be given again?

M. of E. Well?

Art as a gift to Society *M. of T.* What I first want to fix upon you is a due responsibility in accepting the gift. Admit the principle.

M. of E. I am thinking, with some amusement, of the practical consequence of all pictures and sculpture, for instance, coming as gifts to the nation fifty years after their authors were dead and either forgotten or just beginning to be thought of again. Would they then have to be solemnly consigned by some Ministry of Fine Arts either to a public museum or a public bonfire?

M. of T. Ah, these were the things that the nineteenth century really liked to call works of art, conveniently concrete things, " portable property." And please note that this was what gave the artist . . . pre-eminently when dead, but the living exemplars could not then be denied it . . . the dignity of his capital A; these comfortable fortunes that could be made by manœuvring his work.

M. of E. Yes, I've been trying lately to buy a good Cotman for our local picture gallery.

M. of T. I think that a modern Dante might rank picture-dealers with Simonists.

---

* Actors and singers, it may be said, who naturally cannot perpetuate property which resides in themselves beyond their own lifetime, "create" nothing in any case. One could dispute upon this point too. But the main argument would not be affected.

M. of E. On the other hand, if you buy from taste and not for names or schools there are good enough pictures going cheap still.   However, we digress.

M. of T. But take book copyrights.   They fall in due time into public domain : printing is (comparatively) cheap, our benefits in literature due to survive will distribute themselves somehow.   That interpreted the public attitude, didn't it . . . when printing *was* cheap?

M. of E. Yes, I admit this difficulty.   There was always the question though over books that called for any care in production, whether, when everyone might print them, it was worth anyone's while to. And now that printing's not cheap any longer and is not apparently ever going to be . . . ! The other day a publisher complained to me that he could live upon new novels, but that for this year he'd have to leave unprinted a hundred thousand copies of books of learning.

M. of T. Yes, and think of the work done for literature and the wages paid for it . . . and the no-wages.   I won't complain of that, since the scholars don't, though I think they are hardly devoted to poverty in itself.   But could the work itself be done at all but for some endowment ?

M. of E. No, I'll admit that practically it couldn't be.

M. of T. And when we come to the problem of the theatre, which has never been helped out, as literature has, by the blessing (and curse !) of cheap printing, which can find no old endowments to capture and direct to its needs . . . well, I admit it's a tough problem; I don't blame you for shirking it. But won't you also admit the principle that you, as trustee for the public, cannot in decency come into the inheritance of these dramatic gifts and acquire no responsibility for their right use ?

M. of E. I'll admit . . . you'll smile at the banality . . . that something ought to be done for Shakespeare.

M. of T. A Shakespeare theatre ?

M. of E. Yes.

M. of T. I don't smile. I am too angrily weary with the years of balked advocacy of such a simple . . . surely there could not be a simpler, a more obvious duty towards such a name and such a fact in English culture than to make a home in which his plays may live.

M. of E. But they do live.

M. of T. How many have you seen in the last ten years ?

M. of E. I read them. Yes, I assure you, from time to time I really do read them.

Society's re-sponsibility in accepting the gift

M. of T. About as many people can get at Shakespeare's plays by reading them as can appreciate Beethoven's Symphonies by fingering them out on the piano. However, your admission, banal though it be, is enough. For once admit you should care for Shakespeare's plays and you're landed with some responsibility towards the actors of them, and towards the actor's art in general, and so towards other plays . . . the inheritance of the future. How you discharge the responsibility is a minor matter. There are a hundred right ways of doing it to be found ; and then there'll be the interest of finding the hundred-and-first. Provide me my artists somehow with the machinery for giving . . . that is all I ask. They are, the most of them, so anxious to give if only the machinery were there. And the average man, I believe, is innately enough of an artist to believe that. My own belief, indeed, is that the average man himself is in a like generous case ; but that is beside the point. Com-

32

pel us artists to make, or to sell ourselves to those who can make of our art, a commercial machine; or to compete for capital and profit among ourselves and with all the other profit-making industries, and, of course, it's a machine for getting we produce, and the gospel of getting will dominate us. Besides that (you're right) the edge of art is blunted in men who are too much occupied with the machine. For every art and for most industries to-day the common problem is to devise machinery for their conversion to public use that will not impoverish the product. This is notably and tragically true of the art of the theatre. All the better for the theatre, perhaps, if it can march with its fellows towards a general solution. And I want to admit all its special difficulties. So please overlook it if I seem here to speak a little unkindly of a calling I love, and of fellow-workers in it whom I have watched with sympathy and admiration fighting their hard, blind battles.

The chief difficulty, I repeat, of doing anything for the theatre of to-day is that it is so confoundedly prosperous, if we judge it . . . as it is popular to do, as it asks us to judge . . . only by its successes. It is much spoiled, though more than a little despised. The weakness of personal vanity and the hunger for passing praise . . . all about the theatre passes so quickly . . . are played upon and themselves made to pay. Its duty to be of the age and of the hour is debauched to a mere appetite for the favour of the moment. It sustains itself amid such golden clouds of illusion that one finds it hard, to begin with, to turn the thoughts of the theatre itself to a soberer standard; and even harder to persuade men like yourself, for instance, that something must really be done to save it from this damnation of so-called success, and a something which . . . much as it can be asked to do for itself . . . the theatre cannot be expected to do. Especially so when that something will not come easily to anyone's hand, will not be cheap, will need planning and re-planning, experiment here and there, will ask for the patient work of years to make up for the wasted time and the efforts run to seed before one can even hope to build the theatre of one's faith, to endow it with a success so real and constant as to be quite unnoticed.

M. of E. Yes, that is the only sort.

M. of T. But if the men you stand for will do for the theatre the one thing they can do for it, the one thing it can't do for itself, if they will somehow as-sure it a rightful place in the settled economy of society, then . . . yes, I promise you, or if not you, your grandsons . . . that there shall be established among them, as one of the means to their earthly salvation, what I will be bold to describe as a church of art. A body of men and women who will bring their humour, their fancy, passion, and thought to be clarified and formulated in the terms of this art of the drama. Painting, architecture, and music . . . that you are so ready to glorify . . . will take their share in the work ; for the theatre is the meeting-place of many arts. If you'll not have my simile of the church, I'll fall back on chapel, and ask you to remember, too, what chapels called meeting-houses have meant in their time to England and to New England. And this new meeting-house . . . with its doctrines worked out in a human medium, its range from past to future, its analysis in method and synthesis in effect . . . will be, by virtue of the unity in diversity for which it must strive, a microcosm, not only of the social world as it moves,

34

laughs, weeps before our eyes, but as it has a sublimer being in the souls of men.

M. of E. And you ask me to help turn a harmless amusement into something so portentous as that?

M. of T. Don't be alarmed. You won't be " saved " in a hurry. There's the advantage of the theatre as a moral force. It can't go very far ahead unless you keep pace with it.

M. of E. And I am unregenerately just abreast of it now, you think?

M. of T. I'll answer your irony seriously. I don't know. There isn't a theatre to measure you by. There's a mass of material to make one of : plays, mostly on bookshelves, actors with a nightly habit of going through the motions of acting. There are even the makings of an audience, if one may judge by the occasional grumbling . . . *There is no such thing as a Theatre in England*

M. of E. But we should have defined our terms to start with. What, then, do you mean by a theatre?

M. of T. Not one of these houses of entertainment that you now walk tolerantly into and contemptuously out of.

M. of E. Not if the entertainment's so bettered that tolerance turns into enthusiasm?

M. of T. No.

M. of E. Well, positively then, what do you mean by a theatre?

M. of T. That we can't take much further, I'm afraid, by the method of question and answer.

M. of E. Then, to follow up the jargon of the House of Commons, hadn't you better proceed to draft your bill? But is that, by the way, the larger idea you want to tack your renascent art to?

M. of T. What larger idea?

35

M. of E. The drama of the popular assembly.

M. of T. Don't you think that the present performances in that particular . . . and rather un-
popular . . . assembly are often pretty poor ?

M. of E. There I counter you yet once more.
Heaven forbid that with politics national, social, and
industrial developing into a game for everyone to
play we should come to rely on easy effects of oratory. Let's have the substance of what's to be
said as artlessly put as possible; the better can
the worth of it be tested. If you want to turn us
into a melodramatic nation , , , thank you, I'd sooner
you didn't.

M. of T. But you don't counter me. You only
show me what miles apart our minds upon this
matter are still. You think about the performers.
My trouble, to begin with, is the audience. I
grant you they're gullible, and by coarse phrases
moreover, not even by fine ones. But you show
me that you—even you—are equally ready to be
taken in by artlessness. You don't really think
that the more incompetent a man is at expressing
himself the more able and honest he is likely to be.
Suppose we set ourselves to prevent people being
imposed on by absence of oratory, also. For the
larger idea I hitch on to is simply to make
the drama, its appreciation and its practice . . . and
its application through its practice . . . a common
factor in the community's education.

*The larger
idea of
drama*

M. of E. You want, do you, to make me a present
of the theatre . . . of the whole blessed thing ?

M. of T. You've called me a reformer and I
haven't protested. But I have one key-belief by
which I condition my adherence to any stated reform. Does it tend to produce a greater number
of more fully and freely developed human beings,

36

and . , , to push the test further, by the present most urgent demands of our civilization . . , of more co-operative human beings ? Can the theatre, by any contrivance, have its strength brought to bear directly on that job ?

M. of E. I'm to go to my evening's entertainment to be more fully and freely developed, am I ?

M. of T. The evening's entertainment will be but a small part of the business. But do you mind ?

M. of E. Will the process be decently concealed from me ?

M. of T. I will tell you what best can conceal it. A thorough education in dramatic art. By the aid of that you would make the remarkable discovery that good plays are better than bad, and that there are many more sorts of good plays than you imagine. You would find, also, that acting is a very subtle and sensitive art which demands trained appreciation. Plays may not always get the acting they deserve, but audiences mostly do. And, finally, you would find that in learning how to enjoy the theatre you had learned . . . But I'll keep you talking no longer. I'll try, as you say, to draft my bill. If you've the patience to read it . . .

M. of E. I assure you I'm only anxious to be convinced.

M. of T. Don't say that. We none of us are . . .

The Man of the Theatre and the Minister of Education now part . . . but only for the time being, it is hoped.

37

THE schools of to-day are still dominated by cheap printing. As an exact medium was needed for the study of the exact sciences it was inevitable that book-learning should, as our modern civilization advanced, largely conquer the older methods. But the victory extending beyond the justice of the cause, there have lately been notable attempts at readjustment. And if one must write " still dominated " it is because the rescue of the expressional side of education from its obliteration by the absorptional is halted by other difficulties than any lack of conviction in the individual teachers giving thought to the matter that such a salvation is urgent.

The convenient notion that an abundance of books will take the place of talent in the teacher, the strangling of even the finest teaching talent in the grip of enormous classes, the unavoidable drawback that the supply of good teachers will never equal the demand, are major difficulties enough. But what chiefly vitiates the employment of this dancing, singing, acting, now called, still rather half-heartedly, from the play hour to the school hour, is the lack of understanding of the full and proper use to be made of them. This is so, at any rate, as far as the acting is concerned; let me confine myself to that.

The educationalist asks just how seriously he is to take it. And he has a right to an answer before he can be expected to confirm it in the place it is, he will sometimes impatiently say, usurping in a crowded curriculum. Drawing and music and dancing—good reasons enough can be given for their study. If the art of the theatre, of which acting is the naturally first grasped branch, is still viewed askance, if its claim to consideration can only be

38

admitted on the ground that some snatchings at it may be a useful part of the good fun by which the strain of learning must be relieved or by virtue of the extraneous opportunity they will give for practising speech and movement and acquiring self-confidence, its advocates can hardly complain. For, in England at least, the art, as a whole, is neither studied, practised, nor appreciated even by its professional devotees with any sustained intelligence.

As a calling the art is hampered by the conditions of a trade, and a very badly organized trade at that. Gallant attempts have certainly been made, of late years, to improve the quality of the product. With great public spirit Sir Herbert Tree founded a dramatic academy, which pretends, certainly, to no more than the study of acting, but now, under the guidance of representative people, does, no doubt, all it can do for that. There are other institutions and many independent teachers; competent, some of them, and most of them enthusiastic. But, apart from all other drawbacks, they work of necessity with their eyes upon the standards and demands of the professional stage. Now the modern professional stage does not even ask for recruits deeply studied in the art of acting—it has neither the time nor resource to indulge itself in anything so delicately complex. And as for the cognate arts, which the theatre blends with its own, of literature, music, or design, the recruit is not expected to be more than conversationally aware of their existence. The professional theatre demands just so much of the external craft of the actor as will measure up to the critical discernment of its present public, which is, in its turn—and therefore remains—rather low.

The professional theatre's contribution

So it is not to the professional theatre that the educationalist can be expected to turn for advice.

39

" If there's no more in the business than this,"
he might say, " what use can it be to boys and girls,
except as a medium for lung exercise and a means
of uncramping themselves after a long spell at their
desks ? "

And if his use of the drama is to extend at all
beyond the kindergarten and the primary school,
or if he is to give it any other place among the
studies of older pupils than that of a semi-recreational
subject, he must be brought to consider it in terms
for which acting and the theatre, as England now
knows them, provide no interpretation.

Let us first consider the educational claims that
are already made on the drama's behalf and place
them as high as possible. They are even then
by no means to be admitted; and it is ambition
with its fine phrases that is fatal to them.
They will still be urged, nevertheless, with all the
insistent force of narrow enthusiasm. Self-expression, for instance, has become a catchword ; development of the individuality—where parents afford
the money and teachers the time—a craze ; and
into this service drama is dragged by the heels.
Well, it is very fit for children of ten years old to be
learning how to move and to speak, if that is what
self-expression and the rest of the jargon means.
But it is as ridiculous to find adolescents and grown-
up people bothering themselves with such simple
things as it would be to see them conning the
alphabet.

Public
manners
The study of manners is admittedly a very
necessary one. Manners are the lubricant of the
democratic machinery, whether they be the ordinary
good manners of strangers and neighbours to each
other when no law compels them to show respect,
or whether the more complex problem is involved

of expressing—and, as an exasperated minority, sometimes suppressing—our political opinions. As far as personal good manners are concerned one can be done with the mechanism of the business very early. A child soon masters the essential rules ; teachers, by ranking manners as expressive at all, admit the existence of something more than formality, and we commonly find it in the individual recognition of the " right thing " to do and say at any particular moment. To learn to express that in terms of mutual understanding should be easy enough. But if personal good manners—it's a truism—are not based on consideration their foundation is brittle indeed.

Just so with public manners. Self-expression provides but one of their rudiments, and its physical side is so comparatively unimportant, such a mere matter of mechanism, that it is as well to be through with one's study of it before reaching an age when such things have ceased to be wholly assimilable. There is nothing a man need know of the general physical rules of public behaviour, standing, moving, speaking, which can't be mastered by the age of sixteen or seventeen, and which can't better thereafter begin, as rule, to be forgotten. Beyond that there is certainly the expression of his own mental individuality to be thought of. But it is better, on the other hand, that this side of the training should not be too prominently developed just at the age when the ego begins to grow powerful. Concentration upon externals at this time may result in polite affectations, but attention to sheer *self*-expression will cultivate a brutality of egotism, emotional and spiritual. And that this may be only the more effectively masked by a nervous, fragile exterior any mistress of a girls' school can tell us.

41

The tradition
of our speech   Not that one need deny either the absolute value of the externals, or that as an offset to five or six generations of mental cramming any sort of expressional fling which can be granted to young people is better than none. When, for instance, our language is the commonest verbal currency in the world, what shame to us that it should not be expressively used ! Since it has unsurpassed traditions of beauty and eloquence, what a scandal if here, in its home, we are unworthy of them ! Not but that we have unavoidably much to contend with on this head in England. Of necessity seventeenth century English, the last great mould into which our language was poured,* has been broken into by newly-made phrase and word. The Church has a weekly chance to keep the magnificence of the liturgy and the authorized version of the Bible singing in our heads. The theatre, no doubt, could and should do us a like service with Shakespeare. But language must respond to every change of habit. The most, perhaps, that the past masters of our tongue can do for us is to strengthen the bones and the sinews of our speech ; the flesh we must ourselves keep live and healthy by the cleansing process of renewal. Moreover, it

---

* Unless some would evidence Johnsonese. But that never, one hopes, became colloquial. Sheridan's dialogue is delightful, the musical cadence of Miss Austen's perfect of its kind, just as Parliamentary eloquence of the great period was no doubt very fine. But whether—certainly when faith or passion were in question—they did more than refine upon, formalise, and weaken the seventeenth century tradition . . . ? However, I am a seventeenth century man, and, with the best will, unfair to the eighteenth. But compare Walpole's letters with Sir Henry Wotton's, or Lady Mary Wortley Montagu's with—for a simple lady's—Lady Grace Grenville's. Read the Verney correspondence. In a hundred years how much colour and warmth has vanished !

42

is possible that in the last three hundred years some absolutely physiological change has taken place in our speaking of English.* How otherwise account for the extended rhetoric of the Elizabethan drama, its feasibility for the actors, its popularity with the audience ? Can one see a packed crowd of ground-lings *standing*—be it remembered—through an un-cut Henry V or Measure for Measure, unless the long speeches were taken with a Latin glibness for which we have lost, it would seem, both the mouth and the ear ? Elizabethan speech, among people pretending to any culture at all, was normally quick : a swifter, fiercer, more full-blooded business than anything we have the custom of now. It is disconcerting, to-day, to find French actors speaking Shakespeare more appropriately and effectively—for all the loss in translation—than most English actors do. But they can. There is a nation that takes an unaffected pleasure in beautiful words, beautifully spoken. How far we could recapture all this delight it is hard to say, for, no doubt, there were other and psychological causes contributary to its loss. But pleasure in the colour and music of the verse we could certainly have if actors would trouble to give it us. Some trouble on our part, as well as on theirs, is involved, though. If they must learn how to speak Shakespeare's verse we must learn how to listen, the effort being but comparable to the one we must make to appreciate a method of music three centuries old.

Buti for a model of contemporary speech where

* Some hint of this is to be found in the rapid alteration of Cock-ney. Compare Sam Weller and Albert Chevalier; the difference is almost a physiological one. Tongue, breath, teeth, and lips, that is to say, must conspire quite differently together to produce two such dialects.

are we to look ? We ought not to have to look in vain to the theatre, even though the material —be it well understood—is not to be found in modern imitations of Elizabethan drama. Nor yet shall we find it in elaborately built-up prose, taking the form of drama but belying its spirit. But what better model can there be of perfected everyday speech than the dialogue of a modern play if, under such conditions as a good theatre should impose, it can carry to the audience the fullness of its meaning and emotion ? Nor need we rule out for this use the artistic incidents of such streaks of dialect— the Mayfair or Whitechapel variety—as a play may contain. An awful warning is sometimes as useful as an example.

One can admit that the theatre, even as it now stands, does serve this purpose a little. So does the Church. Some part of the population gets every Sunday a lesson in English. The quality of the model presented leaves in each case no doubt much to be desired. The parson's speech may be flat and dead. The actor's will be lively enough, though that may be its first and last virtue. But neither calling is so relieved from other cares and charged with this one as to have leisure to acquire such a thing as style. And it is of no use whatever placing the responsibility for our ineptitude and vulgarity of speech upon school teachers. In the first place because the teachers themselves must be taught, in the second because, though the grounding of a child in the habit of good speech is a great thing, the labour will be largely wasted if he is to emerge into an adult world where he will find no public pride in the accomplishment nor any importance attached to it.

But if difficulties surround us in England, what

about America's mountainous task ? Think of the *The American language* problem of preserving a language in its integrity when thirty per cent. or so of the children in the schools come to it as to a foreign tongue, when to whole sections of the adult population it remains no more a medium of expression than are the hundred words or so of French, German, Spanish, or Italian, with which the average English or American traveller will pick his way through the hotels and restaurants of Europe. Whether and when the process of the melting-pot will extend to language, and what the final residuum will be, is a question that, quite apart from its difficulty, would range far beyond this present subject. That English will remain the language of America we may regard as fairly certain, and it is sufficient for our purpose to point out that its possible remoulding rests upon other considerations than those of literature, and of the present struggle for its soul between the writer of classical traditions, whom nobody (comparatively) reads, and the journalist whom everybody (absolutely) reads. This struggle though is in itself instructive. We note the classicist out-flanking the position by getting at the will-be journalist as he passes—as almost all of them now do—through college. But then, with his guns trained, often enough the classicist won't stick to them. Lest he be thought dry-as-dust he goes back on Milton to encourage the solemn study of O. Henry and George Ade. Or—worse, it is true !—he makes of his Milton and Addison and Pope a mumpsimus jargon, reflected, how horribly, in ceremonial documents and speeches launched from time to time at the public's head.

45

The influences of climate and of recent immigration

But the immigrant, though he brings as a rule little literary culture of his own,* only partly abides by the issue of this battle. For he has brought, let us remember, much else that goes to the making of a spoken language : physical differences to begin with, differences in the emphasis of emotion, long inherited constructional habits of thought. And mixed with all this will be the yet uncalculated influence of climate. Even the approaches, then, to the problem of the standardization of speech in America are complex, and the problem itself is doubtless not within a century or so of anything like a solution. One merely notes meanwhile, as compensations for the present inter-racial disturbance, that when Americans do take the trouble to speak well—and feeling this as but one among many threats to the precious "Anglo-Saxon" dominance, the old stock among them often do take a great deal of trouble—they achieve a purer, firmer English than can commonly he heard anywhere else; except possibly in Ireland, where a sweetness in place of firmness is added to the carefully acquired purity.† And a second compensation may be the bringing to the language, by some, at least, of the foreign element, of a fire and colour of expression and a musical tone of which native speakers seem almost deliberately to deprive it. Did the Yankee twang develop, by chance, from Puritan "psalm-singing"? Our own 17th century Puritans were reproached with making just such sounds. But for fear of treading too debatable ground we

---

* He sometimes brings more than might be supposed. I once caught an Italian workman, solitary under a hedge on Long Island, reading poetry aloud to himself. But he probably went back to Italy later, back to where the poetry came from.

† I have found this among Donegal peasants.

46

might rather say—enlarging our supposition as to the present difficulties of tackling Shakespearian English—bring *back* to America some of the quality lost to England from the time that our own growing political insularity separated us from the cultural influence of the Latin tongues. England gained an integrity for its language thereby, no doubt. But by mid-seventeenth century had not the full benefit of that inured, and since then does not the history of its speaking possibly show, by the drag-back of peasant influences on it, a reversion to slower, slacker, slovenlier ways ?

Not only in this particular may America, without taking thought, be more fortunate than we, who refuse to. The foreign elements, blended into the American nation of the future, may inform it with a much livelier general expressiveness than our closer origins develop. Certainly one would say, even now, that the American is more ebullient than the Englishman. That may be, again, the influence of climate : it may spring from the difference in social—more properly in economic—conditions, under which self-assertion is the first step to success, while personal success must, of course, be the good citizen's gospel in any country pledged to extreme individualism. Political democracy and commercialism are beginning to flavour our English national life to something of the same taste. But the self thus expressed, or rather asserted, is merely an armour, offensive enough—sometimes in every sense—but chiefly designed so that upon it the blows of a battling world may rattle: it is hollow, and the real self within often a timid and essentially undeveloped thing. One appreciates that competitive conditions have called for this weapon, and how, with our educationalists caught unprepared,

47

any sort of expressional fling to counteract the constrictive influence of the hard grinding of facts, and yet more facts, into a few generations of youthful skulls—far more deadening work than the gerund-grinding of old—is indulged and encouraged in preference to none.

But as self-expression—even if that alone be what we are after—does this stoking of the emotional ego and its blowing of steam suffice? And are we after that alone?

Those of us who are æsthetically inclined admit, and should even in opposition insist upon, the importance of these externals. This would be a much more attractive country to live in if all its inhabitants spoke perfectly and moved beautifully, and on public occasions could express themselves with force and distinction. And possibly our countrymen would cut a better figure abroad if they cut a more beautifully expressive one. Not the picked ambassadors of statecraft or learning, who doubtless do express most suitably what they— if not, alas, what all of us—are; but the ordinary traveller in commerce or pleasure, for he is also, be it remembered, his country's ambassador.

The drama as a microcosm of society But we must finally recognize that Handsome does only as Handsome is. And we have serious cause of quarrel with those for whom self-expression is only self-assertion; with no question of the sort of self. For surely this, even æsthetically, is just what does most matter. And further, as in the Church, so in all other society, we being members one of another, expression of the single self is inadequate. If it were enough there would be nothing for the dramatic or any other art to do in education at all. For does not all art release us from egotism? Let us examine very critically any artistry that can

48

be taken as the text of a denial of this : it will, of a certainty, have lodged in some perversion of its true purpose. The art of the drama, viewed in completeness, is anti-egotist to the last degree. It is so in spite of the study of its simpler constituents being self-developing merely, and of its professional practice seeming too often to induce vanity, affectation, or self-consciousness—though these, it may be forgotten, are egotism's least deadly aspects.

Dramatic art, fully developed in the form of the acted play, is the working out—in terms of make-believe, no doubt, and patchily, biasedly, with much over-emphasis and suppression, but still in the veritable human medium—not of the self-realization of the individual, but of society itself. A play is a pictured struggle and reconciliation of human wills and ideas ; internecine, with destiny or with circumstance. The struggle must be there, and either the reconciliation or the tragedy of its failure. And it is generally in the development of character, by clash and by mutual adjustment, that the determinant to the struggle is found. What livelier microcosm of human society, therefore, can there be than an acted play ? Apologically one could push the likeness further. To bring a play to its acting is to discover the following simple law of its completed well-being. If each character in it, even the smallest, is not developed to its fullest capacity the production will be impoverished beyond any hope of salvation by brilliant individual performances. And yet if every actor—the most or the least important—does not play his part with a primary loyalty to the whole play and a strict consideration for his fellows artistic failure is as inevitable. Interpretation of the parable is needless. To the service of such an art, then, one must bring far more than a crude power of self-expression ; and equally from its study we may claim that much else is to be gained.

The self-reatisation of a child But it may be instructive first to probe for the beginning of the simply self-expressive power. Watch a child seeking it. Before he can express himself he has actually, one may say, to create the conscious self that he would express. Now his way of doing this is the paradoxical one of pretending to be somebody else. Children begin to act as soon as they are free of their cradles ; their kicking and gurgling within them may well have a dramatic intention. Throughout nursery time it is games of make-believe that are the most popular. The child is peopling the world of himself. By imitation, by adaptation, he adds one by one to the list of its characters, appropriating and assimilating them by identifying himself with each. By a long process of trial and error, and later by selection and by refinement, from out of this crude amalgam of his imagination's experience the conscious self is formed. And the games go on till a supervening self-consciousness shames him from their public playing. Even then they go on in secret : he has learned by this time to play them in this subtler way, just as one learns to read without muttering the words. It is doubtful, indeed, whether, with many people, the great game of make-believe ever stops. It is doubtless but a pseudo-self that he brings into being, and later he will slough it off, perhaps. But this is apparently the primary and practical way by which a child establishes connection with the outer, developed world. It stands for him as a medium of interpretation, this bound-up collection of characters simple and

50

fantastic—father and mother and pirate king. It is
a various-noted voice, by listening to which he
himself learns to speak. It is the glass in which,
seeing something he may still call himself, he begins
by comparison to see what other people are. It is
the dictionary that he looks into for the meaning
of the strange things he hears. It is, indeed, his
first effort in education.

But does a genuine self necessarily grow up
within this false skin ? For an answer one might
ask again how genuine a self must be ? Original
it cannot be. There is no fresh creation. And
how great is the difference between borrowing
spiritual qualities from one's ancestors, as one bor-
rows their physical traits, and acquiring them by a
conscious effort of imagination from the general
store of the world ? It is true enough that to
play nothing but the game of make-believe all
one's life is to remain puerilely ineffective. But
that is not to say that the child's method,
become acceptedly self-conscious, the historical
and critical sense brought also into play with
it, is incapable of development to a wider and
more serious use.

What are the obligations that dawn upon the
adolescent ? As we have seen, not merely to
develop himself as an individual, but, concurrently
now, to adapt himself as a member of society.
And into what, by a parallel process through the
ages, have generations of artists turned that make-
believe game of the child but the complex, co-
operative art of the drama, this epitome, as lively
as art can contrive, of society itself ? Self-expression therefore need be by no means the end of its
educational use to us ; for even the beginning—
though we practise it almost as simply as the child

51

plays his game—involves recognition that the self, if it is to be intelligibly expressive at all, must reflect and interpret, as well as express and assert. Study of the drama, indeed, should properly begin for the adolescent not from the self-expressive, but from the exactly opposite standpoint. Let the boy or girl—and the man or woman for that matter—continue by all means their exercises in expressing and asserting themselves. It is as useful to ensure such a suppleness as to keep up our golf or our tennis. But from the study of drama we are to demand much else and much more.

The teaching of psychology   How is psychology taught nowadays ? The subject is admitted, apparently, under one guise or another, and at some remove, into up-to-date curricula. One hears of laboratories—dread word !—containing instruments by which the sense of taste, smell, hearing (including, one trusts, the sense of humour, which should surely occasionally abound among the victims of this spiritual vivisection) can be meticulously measured. In all earnestness they are, no doubt, wonderful places ; but the despised artist must be forgiven if he takes a small chance to poke fun at the deified man of science. If, however, the teaching in schools, and the training of children generally, with its undoubted demand for what one must dare to call the common sense of psychology, are to depend upon the degree of understanding of these frigid complexities that can be gained by the casual student, then the joke has another aspect and becomes, indeed, a poor one. As well regulate one's daily life by a text-book of algebraic formulæ. And small wonder if hard-headed authorities call out " Away with such nonsense " ; though a smaller wonder, alas, if they cling to it just because it all does sound so scientific, and is so very

difficult to understand. But does not the essence of
such psychology as we average human beings need
dwell more accessibly in a good play or novel than
in any amount of parrotted repetition (for that,
half the time, is what it comes to) of scientific
teminology? Would not the scientists therefore be
wise to consider what use can be made of the interpretative arts as the channel for whatever practical
teaching they think can be founded upon their researches? One hesitates, of course, to suggest them
as aid to the researches themselves.

But, the plain man may ask, need psychology be
taught? If we could make a vital study of it—
above all, perhaps, if we could get rid of the name
—the answer, surely, is that there could be few
more important for the making of good citizens.
Democracy will not continue to exist upon the
mere basis of the ballot-box; so both its ill-wishers
and its well-wishers predict. Unless the men and
women of the self-governing nations can learn a
little more of the art of self-government than resides
in the making of a cross now and then (the one-
time symbol of their illiteracy!) against the name
of the demagogue, who, upon the platform or in
the press, will descend to the lowest level of political
indecency to cajole it from them then the system
is righteously doomed, rotten before it is ripe. The
key to self-government, surely—to its very beginning
—is self-understanding, which again must mean, in
terms of a community, mutual understanding. Have
we no use, then, for psychology, or—to find the
simpler sounding term—the knowledge of our souls?

The need for such high-sounding lore in everyday matters may not at first appear. But, however
we limit our understanding of democracy to its
being government merely by the consent of the

Democracy,
the news-
papers, and
the whole art
of fiction

53

governed, we yet do find ourselves making pretty constantly all sorts of would-be knowledgeable decisions, though we lack the concrete knowledge that is needed to make them, and always must. Read through a week's newspapers and note the things that are being done—if one is a British subject, being done all over the world—in one's name. We have necessarily delegated the doing; but wherever a point of principle is involved, or a precedent is created, the responsibility will return upon us. For this we prepare ourselves by currently approving and condemning. When we cease to do either, or when we continue for long to do nothing but approve, we are on the way to a moral abdication of our power. It is idle to protest that we will abide by fixed principles of right or wrong, or by the *isms* of a party creed. We need to interpret these in the terms of each difficulty's solution as much as do the mandatories of our will ; though, truly, we have but to be wise after the events, and that is sometimes just a little easier. The task, however, seems beyond us, and the newspaper comes to our assistance. It not only tells us what, but why and wherefore besides. It will conjugate for us the entire verb of any possible occurence. We have but to define our principles and the paper that owes allegiance to them will do all the rest. Or if we prefer we may first choose our newspaper and then abide by its opinions whatever they turn out to be. This is easier for us, and for the newspaper, too, which can then render current history more pleasing by reversing the former process (all psychological processes are apparently capable of reversal) and bringing principles into accord with our vicarious successes of policy.

But some people see almost a moral danger

54

here. They would prefer that a newspaper should present the uncoloured facts alone. That sounds excellent. It seems to betoken unbending integrity. But how procure an uncoloured version of any fact, and should we be better off even then? That Mrs. Jones died at eleven last night is bare fact, and may need no comment ; the cause of her death—should it matter —may always be a point of opinion. To say that there is a boiler-makers' strike in Northumberland or a rising amongst the Mahsuds sounds informative : but is it? The average man asks for explanation, and into that bias inevitably creeps. A factual education, which would enable one to cope explanatorily and opinionatively with the happenings of the British Empire, would involve something very like learning the Encyclopœdia Britannica by heart, would be about as practicable and about as educative.

If then we are not to believe all we are told and yet have only what we are told to rely on, is there a way out of the dilemma? This same newspaper, perhaps, does, though somewhat confusedly, point us to it. For the modern newspaper interprets its news. Confused and inappropriate the method as now practised undoubtedly is ; for who, reading with an innocent mind an account of any matter " by our special correspondent," is to say where the plain tale of facts ends and their interpretation begins, and how much special pleading does not cover it all ? The involved falsity is neatly given away in the office slang, which calls every recounting of news " a story." But if the medium were properly dissected and honestly used falsity need not invalidate it. There is a

Qualifica-tions and temptations of the journalist

55

science of plain statement; but interpretation and persuasion are arts, and no intrusion of the one method on the other should ever be countenanced. Narrative will necessarily thread and rethread the border line. The skill of it will lie in never travelling over either territory upon false pretences. Now it should be quite feasible, and it is the obvious duty of a newspaper, to differentiate sharply between its use of the three forms. And it should be quite possible for us to discover, by the light of our own critical faculty, when any one of them—if it is being straightforwardly used—is being grossly misused. With the pitching of a too tall story we readily reject its offences to our common sense, even too readily sometimes—but we prefer to err in safety, keeping our most precious possession unsullied. And overdone advocacy will often defeat its own ends with us. But by the fictional form we are too apt to be hypnotized and hopelessly undone.

What is our remedy? Useless to demand that the fictional form shall not be used in such circumstances. The method combines too many attractions for writer and reader both, and apart from attractiveness it is in many cases the only practicable way of conveying news. It exemplifies indeed, in another aspect, the democratic principle of representation. " Our correspondent " at Washington or Tokio, " our special correspondent " sent to report upon a conference, a strike or a prizefight, is required not to speak on our behalf, but to listen, observe, and interpret, and that he may do so in full measure we accord him just that individual freedom that is claimed in a parliament. His task demands honesty of purpose, self-criticism, selective judgment and great executive skill. There are times when bare statement is the only effective thing, times when sheer advocacy based on aeccepted fact is all that is needed, and these paths are at least plain. But the knowledge which sifts truth from untruth, the imagination which can vivify without falsifying a narrative, the tact which can weave happening, impression, and opinion without confusion, the ability, moreover, to evolve with some swiftness from the process a readable piece of copy —such are the qualities currently demanded of the responsible journalist to-day. Equally useless to expect that he will cultivate them without our critical assistance. We cannot apply the spur of it directly, perhaps; though at one remove the editor, keeping a watch on his circulation, will be keen enough to note our distaste for his stunts if it checks the flow of our pennies. But the indirect method, though a slower, is a better one, by which we educate ourselves in an appreciative understanding of this art at its best and towards its worst aspect need only cultivate in ourselves the crass ability not to be taken in by a pack of lies. We are at the mercy of interpreters to-day, be they statesmen or journalists, speaking for us or to us. We must at all costs get a hold over them. By the stretch of our own knowledge we cannot out-compass them, neither can we neglect the service they render us, with honest intentions as a rule, though its quality be poor. But their inevitable choice of an artistic medium of advocacy and communication does provide us, in our turn, with a touchstone by which we can test the worth of what they say and do and are. For art is of universal heritage. It will not be an instrument of super-human perfection that we can fashion, of course, but we can make it quite effective enough to defeat the demagcgue and the yellow journalist, or at the very least to set them such high standards of the cajolery and deception necessary to defeat it as will compel them to be much abler practitioners of their craft than they are at present. Now ability may not connote virtue, but it is the possessor of the one that is most often shamed into a wish to acquire the other : to what else should he devote his surplus energy ? Criticism is stimulus. Most men would rather be good than be found out.

The public's self-defence How is this faculty of discernment to be educated in a man ? We must remember that with each one of us there are for practical purposes two sorts of truth, upon which we set very different values. For each one of us the boundaries differ ; we shift them for ourselves from time to time. But tell the average man that the river Volga falls into the Black Sea. He may, upon general grounds, be slightly annoyed with you later when he finds out that it doesn't ; rather more so if you've led him to make a particular fool of himself on the point. But he doesn't, as we say, take it to heart: if he thinks you misled him for no ill-purpose he counts your sin against accuracy venial. Tell him, however, that his wife no longer loves him, that his child is dying, or his country in danger, and he behaves very differently indeed. You have attacked, probably, a vital interest, and before he takes action, before even he can bring himself to believe or disbelieve you, he will sound all the appropriate emotions of which he is capable, will try to bring all his past experience in such matters to bear, will colour the evidence presented with one coat after another of suspicion or prejudice. He will go behind the actual evidence, moreover, and colour with feelings of like or dislike the personal character of everyone concerned— especially your character. And, finally, if his

58

capacity for genuine emotion and direct thought last out, if he have not taken refuge in the formulæ of either, when he comes to a decision he will make it, not in recognition of the truth as it appears to you or the rest of the world (that will be an empty formula), but in the strength of his own innermost conviction of it. This is the only basis on which, in a matter touching him closely, he will dare proceed to action.* This truth is not accuracy, but something fuller if less precise. Let us remark that to reach this conviction a man goes through all the essential processes of constructing a work of art. And, by such means, in the light of consequences and if he have any power of self-criticism, he educates himself in perception. It does not follow, of course, that men, taking action on such grounds, will do strict justice to themselves or to others, but where their affections are concerned what other course can they pursue and hope to sustain? They may apprehend conduct abstractly finer, but how commit themselves to it? For to take any action of personal consequence unsanctioned by the full exercise of one's own thoughts and feelings is to abrogate one's responsible humanity. At the worst, self-betrayal is the only tolerable sort.

The next step in perception will be the discovery *The artistic* that these processes of thought and feeling, alike in *synthesis.* their genuineness and in their tendency to take refuge in formulæ, differ very little as between man and man. The difference, that is to say, will be of intensity (for men are robust, febrile, or weak

---

* We are always asking "Can you convince me?" "I know nothing of the facts, of course, but the man himself doesn't convince me" is a frequent phrase. "That story doesn't carry conviction" says the magistrate . . . which generally implies that it will.

emotionally as physically) or of scope (self-pre-cipiency has come less easily to some than to others). But if Smith has developed any genuine feelings at all over the death of his only son he may be pretty sure that Brown's, on the like occasion, were much the same ; and it goes without saying that their formulæ of expression will have differed very little. If Smith goes into battle himself the chances are his sensations do not differ essentially from those of the man next him. Young people and continuingly self-centred natures are not over ready to recognize this. It seems to derogate from their perfect in-dividuality. But this illusion is worth losing, they discover, for the gain of a power to apply an inward test of the truth of any tale of battle or bereave-ment that is told them.

But, granted the wish to tell a tale honestly, does genuineness of feeling promote accuracy of observa-tion to begin with ? Not of itself ; but inferentially yes, more often than not. To be trying to tell, if not the whole truth about one's feelings, yet nothing but the truth involves such a ruthless discipline as cannot easily be broken minute by minute for the sake of a conscious manipulation of facts. Here, however, the question of education assumes import-ance. For the third step in perception is the dis-covery that, apart from their subject, the processes of thought and feeling by which men achieve convic-tion are so akin as to be deducible one from another, recognized in strange dress, and, to a degree, imagined without experience. It is quite possible to acquire enough general knowledge of the work-ing of interpretative consciousness to be able to apply test after test of the genuineness—and thus inferentially of the objective truth—of a story every circumstance of which may be unfamiliar.

It will not be a scientific test, of course; questions of science should not be brought within the scope of such a method. But we need not complain of its subjection to human fallibility, as it is to the scientifically incalculable stuff of humanity that the method is applied. We must take it for what *we* are worth. Instruments of an indiscriminating and soulless accuracy we cannot make ourselves; vehicles of a selective truth we can. Truth may here be a misnomer. Philosophers, severely contemplating the absolute, will condemn such a use of the precious word, but we need one that will stand for the utmost attainable.

And where shall we turn for its exemplifying if not to the great artists in life's interpretation and the critics who set them their standard? An artist will in this sense be a truth-teller and a truth-maker: that if he is to picture men anew to themselves he must have a keener observation and a nicer sense of selection than commonly serves. Though he deals with mimic circumstances, they will not be of necessity less actual to us than any others outside our experience. For his characters to carry conviction he must first have convinced himself of the truth of them, which will range between the extent of his vision and the limits of his expressional power. We may hold that under conditions of his sole choosing an able man can bamboozle us sadly, and certainly the power of an artist to impose fiction as fact is great. Defoe specialized in doing so. It was said laughingly of Balzac that his Paris came out of his head, and Parisians had to set to work imitating it. But this does not invalidate its educative work to us. Robinson Crusoe and Père Goriot are true in our present sense of the word. For the artist cannot play us false against our will. The medium

61

he must work in—be it colour, form, music, or words—can be only an extension and refinement of some natural power of our own. We are fellow craftsmen all, and artists willy-nilly, every one of us. And the better practised we are the further can we range with the master-craftsman both appreciatively and questioningly too. It is indeed as much our business to make common cause with the critic, who, approaching receptively what the artist has dealt with expressively, matches him at the game.

Now all this might seem unimportant enough, no doubt, if the fictional form, the fictional method, were not in multifarious use beyond the bounds of make-believe. Of such a method of conducting human affairs we may approve or disapprove, but social history has always been deep-dyed in it, and the elaborate mechanism of intercourse which belongs to modern life has tended to increase its sway. One of the great problems of democratic-imperial government is the bringing "home" to the uninstructed mind of strange fact and distant folk. The lively, simple, immemorial means of personal story telling cannot be neglected. Why, how the even simpler art of picture-making—now that the cinema has given it fresh attraction—is being pressed into the service of such education ; and by quite serious people, too. Things, it is true, are brought within the scope of these easier methods that never should be. Upon questions of pure science we should not have to be warned to allow for picturesque statement and the personal equation. But in general it seems inevitable that the further we move from strictly measureable matters towards the contests of which our still incalculable humanity is itself the field this will be the game to be played. Therefore we may as well learn to play it intelligently.

To the mass of people this power and opportunity is recognizable enough in such a directly interpretative art as story writing, if one may judge by the fascinated credulous respect they show—mingled, no doubt, with a little distrust, as such respect is apt to be—for its accredited practitioners. To simple souls the novelist wears something of the aspect of a tribal magician; and " Jones write a play ! Nonsense, I knew his father," has its roots in the wonder at an almost supernatural achievement. So many of us carry the weight of that uncultured self-consciousness which is affliction rather than gift. This can account, if nothing else will, for the morbid attraction and repulsion which the theatre exercises. The horror with which actors were wont to be regarded had a spice of awe. There is, in fact, general recognition that the artist wields a dangerous power.

The popular attitude towards interpretative art

The staying, if not the satisfaction, of the appetite for fictional art is nowadays mostly sought in the novel; indeed, the very word " fiction " has been appropriated to its use. The form has obvious convenience for leisure moments ;* it makes, as a rule, little demand upon critical attention, calls for little pre-knowledge of a subject, and, most importantly, the reader may enjoy his roused emotion in privacy, a boon indeed, though a false one, to the shy and inexpressive soul. But there is more in it, perhaps, than this ; more even than a positive desire to

---

* Train journeys, morning and evening, and the better lighting of railway carriages, are probably responsible for two-thirds of the circulation of "fiction," whether bound in cloth, in magazine covers, or masquerading in newspapers which could not (or think they could not) get their news read in any less appetising form.

escape for an hour into a world of added values and wider sanctions. There is dormant in nearly every one of us the ambition to share this power that can so transmute the common things of life. Fiction does not so often raise it to the point of emulation, for the habit of writing is new enough to be still a severe strain to most people. But see how the older, directer art of the theatre seizes upon anyone who is not steeled against its influence. It may be only a childish, foolish longing to show off, but who has not " seen themselves " upon the stage, or if one is physically fitter for Falstaff than Romeo, or more positive than reflexive, upon the platform at least? Even so, however, the ambition may still not push people beyond the confines of their secret mind. It is within it they are content to exercise the unforgotten childish faculty of make-believe, strengthened, broadened a little by real, sometimes but by fictional experience. But even then, so timid is mankind, they would rather play with images safely and far removed from likeness to their everyday life ; for they feel too unskilled, too unsure, to venture their personal fortunes, even in thought, within viable distance of the beaten track. But upon everyone at times situations are forced in which they must play an individual part. Then see how at once they turn to art for aid. It is doubtful if any articulate love-making would get done at all had not the poets provided phraseology. And what, further, of the occasions—we name them to our shame—when, called on for emotion and unable to respond, we turn, unconsciously, to our " novel " experience, and say: " Well, this—at any rate—is how I *ought* to feel ? " And, be it noted, we commit ourselves thereby to many a false step. For a life whose emotions are so

far reflected fiction that experience passes without
response or interpretation builds up a character complete in falsity. Not an unworthy falsity, we may protest, for our novel reading may have been pleasantly
innocuous. But if we apply the hard, high standard
of artistry to the matter, an arbitrary reaction to
an artificial stimulus becomes the unworthiest thing
of all, and the resulting emptiness of virtue, hollowly
resounding, the deepest damnation. If art, though,
is the reflex of good life, what other standard
should we apply ? Which of us, after all, can care
to own to a character pieced together from scraps of
even the very best novels ? Not that art, if we rightly
respond to it, makes any such claims of slavery
upon us. As its aim is to interpret, not to create,
illusion, so its end is not to hold us by its own
sufficiency, but, nurturing us, even in its own despite
to set us free. It is nonsense to say that when the
glamour of the fairy tale, the theatre, of our first
emotions when we hear fine music, has gone enjoyment goes too, for appreciation is only then beginning. By education we lose, no doubt, some
chances of unalloyed pleasure. But our keener
discernment not only of the qualities of story, play,
or symphony, but of the intentions of their interpretation, more than compensates for the loss.

From this it would seem to follow that we get
most stimulus from the arts that call upon us for
a constant, lively, critical attention. For educational purposes, then, they are surely the best.
A picture makes but little noise in the world ;
you must keep very actively keen and sensitive
not to pass it by acquiescently. But even after
dinner you cannot sit through a symphony without
knowing whether you like it or not. Take up a
novel in the evening. You may read it, or skip

half of it, or throw it aside ; you feel under no obligations to its inanimation. But play-going is a social act, and makes demands upon you that are direct and incidental, both.

Granted, then—apart from the benefit of studying particular arts—our first need for training in this fundamental artistry of self-realization and expression, the case for music will be strong and the case—that we are now more concerned to argue— for the drama against the novel very strong.

Theatre v. Novel

There would be no need to urge the case as against the novel if it did not, by force of circumstances, so easily hold the field, and if the theatre were not on the whole one vast missed opportunity. Compare the two arts to-day, and, popularity apart, the novel is at its best. The theatre, if not at its worst artistically, has yet its economic foot stuck fast in a slough. But in the first are strains of weakness, more than those we have already pitched on ; in the other, of great strength.

For one thing the novel is under the curse— that sort of curse to which uncalculated blessings turn—of cheap printing. Man, having found out how to make cheap paper and marvellous printing-machines, lets himself be caught in the meshes of the big industries that result. It is in their interests that the paper must now be made and the machine kept going, and art is called into service upon the industry's terms. The public, it seems, can be brought to absorb a vast and varied amount of " fresh-and-fresh " reading. It is to this saturation point, therefore, that the captains of the industry naturally strive. Publishers and editors give, no doubt, what consideration they can to quality of output, but the obligation that predominates with them is to do a certain quantity

66

of trade. Now the quality of the world's literary talent has certainly not increased in the ratio of its mechanical power to print, bind, and sell books, or of the multiplication of people for whom, reading being a comparative novelty, any reading passes muster. Therefore the average quality of the output has—let us not say fallen, but certainly tended to adjust itself to the conditions that make for industrial success. We have a smooth supply of rapidly readable and—that more may be demanded —as rapidly forgettable stuff. The average novel calls for neither assent nor dissent on the part of the reader. It is a harmless, agreeable companion. It is not stimulant : an art which has private reading —almost invariably—as the basis of its appreciation is the least likely to be. Reading and writing, it must be remembered, are, for artistic purposes, nothing but labour-saving devices, and therefore very subject to abuse once an unconscious use of them has been acquired. If art is concerned with the operation of human spirit upon human spirit, through the medium of an amalgam of sense and brain, varyingly constituted, but each a necessary constituent, then purely mechanical intervention must always have an impoverishing effect in so far as it places expression and impression beyond the immediate control of giver and receiver. Poets justly complain that the printing press debases their art ; fortunately the habit of testing poems by the living voice is of long survival. Would it be better if we learned to enjoy music solely by the reading of scores, and for the sake of that mental achievement let our sense of hearing and the effect, direct and indirect, upon our emotions sink into atrophy ?

We must think, too, if we are thinking of the novel educationally, of the moral hypnosis which is

latent in solitary and silent enjoyment of the narrative form. We are conscious of this danger as it
affects our consideration of facts, and at present,
perhaps, are in some reaction against it. It is said
that the Russian peasant believes that whatever he
sees in print must, in virtue of the printing, be true.
His late dose of education, practical and other, may,
however, have roused him from this attractive delusion. We, with our book-learning just a little
staler upon the crowd of us, though with the smell
of the printer's ink still sickly in our nostrils and
strange after the farmyard whiffs of our racial boy-
hood, are more in train to a state of conviction that
whatever we read is, other evidence to the contrary
lacking, a lie. But whether we yield or rebel it is
useless to blame the hypnotist. It may be that the
so common use of printing, and the ephemeral
character of most things printed, do inevitably
breed away in those in control their sense of artistic
responsibility, and that moral responsibility tends
naturally to follow it into desuetude, for the two are
finally one. All the more reason, then, that we
should train our critical perceptions upon other
ground. The advantages of the narrative form
are many and not to be denied. It can play, at the
writer's will, all round a subject, unfettered by
any unity of time and place, allusive, argumentative,
didactic. But in this very freedom lies the temptation to the writer and the danger to us. Our
relations with him do seem so direct and intimate.
We, carried away, have forgotten the mechanical
bond, the human distance. Has he? He has
his conscience to depend on, little else. If
he is writing of matters of a knowledge accepted by him and his readers the double
bulwark may sufficiently brace him. But when
68

he begins to roam over the always disputable tracts of the imagination it is much to expect of a man that he be aware, sentence by sentence, of readers, keen and critical to the exact measure of his own creative power. But this and no less is what he needs. And even the most finely developed literary conscience is no good substitute, for, being but a reflex of his own creative mind, it will fasten upon favourite virtues and vices, so that virtues will grow hypertrophied and vices (we must be tender to our own weaknesses ; no one else will) be cockered up and, by careful cultivation, given the importance of virtue. There are instances enough of writers of individuality who, isolated by neglect or unimpressed by criticism, have by simple over-exercise of conscience so turned in upon themselves, so postured before this glass, as to end in a set self-caricature. Art (which is in itself a reflex) cannot exist alone. It needs the continual reminder of an audience. That it mainly gets and suffers under a stupid audience is a curable evil. The clown tumbling in the circus at least functions more naturally than does the novelist, proof-correcting in solitude.

Art needs also the discipline of form—the only imposition of law to which the artist may submit. Nor is this necessarily a limitation. Form is the equivalent of a code of manners by which performer and audience are at once put on terms with each other.* In rigidity it may equally become a

* Notice Sir Harry Lauder, whose capital asset is his ability to put his audience at their ease. There could be no more simple material than his, and one might suppose that his every effort would be to invest it with variety ... not only of content, but of form also. On the contrary, he carefully stops short at the bare assumption of a fresh character. This he will elaborate. But—and just because perhaps

69

nuisance. But as manners are the framework of a free society, so is a friendly agreement upon form a necessary basis for the social arts. And the directly interpretative arts of music, dancing, story-telling are, in their design and essence, social. That cheap printing, then, has ousted them and has brought the novel, not only to every fireside, but into more solitary corners, has its disadvantages from a cultural standpoint. And just as a religion sustained mainly upon reading of the Bible grows to be uncomfortably concerned with individual salvation, so a social culture fostered by overdoses of fiction tends to an emotional and spiritual obscurantism. Appetite is spoiled by silent indulgence. One grows too timid to put oneself to the test of expression and obstinate in the degree of one's tacit inexperience.

The good audience Wherein, now, can the drama better the novel as an imaginative stimulant ? To begin with, it is, willy-nilly, a social art in a sense that the novel cannot be. The defect of this quality, certainly, is that it lends itself to mob appeal : claptrap is its own word though no longer its peculiar stigma. But mob is only social gathering degenerate, unwieldy, or—more hopefully viewed—uneducated and therefore capable of development into a self-respecting organism. The psychology of audiences is too involved a subject for us to deal with it here at large. But no one would deny that they differ in quality. They differ, an actor will tell us, in their attitude towards the same play and the same company, from city to city

he must reserve for each new audience a measure of spontaneity— he preserves a constant form to work within, of entrance, movement, exit, final glance at the gallery. It is all as rigidly conventional as a Greek tragedy He bounds his audience's expectations, that is to say, into the exact space where he chooses to fulfil them.

70

and night to night. Nor does their quality at all depend on their size, or their class, or the prices they pay. It is not a very calculable matter, for most audiences to-day come together haphazard. But imagine a panel of from ten to twenty thousand people from which the great majority of a theatre's audience for any one performance would be drawn. Is it fantastic to suppose that by constant, though varying, association in bodies of a thousand more or less, to form a part, though but a passive and surrounding part, of such a highly-vitalized, single-purposed organization as is the acting company of a theatre, they would not develop a corporate spirit ? Admit this possibility and the theatre's pre-eminence among the social arts is admitted also. Music might run it hard, but no other. It remains to discover how best to cultivate this aspect of it.

The stimulus that a good audience must be to the art of the theatre will not be denied. As audience, we may not get the plays and the acting we desire, for, having no corporate spirit in the matter, our desires are inarticulate ; they are, perhaps, hardly formed. But we do, in art as in government, get what we passively deserve. Even active negation would be more helpful. There will be great hope for the theatre on the day that a play is soundly hissed for its artistic demerits. And who, being a loyal servant of his art, but would wish, not for a pit of kings—they, of all people in these constitutional days, must take what they are given without grumbling—nor even for a front row of his fellow-dramatists, since the expert talker is mostly a bad listener, but for an audience trained in the art's understanding, with taste sharpened by experience. Who is so sure of his own self-judgment that he may despise this test of his work ? The theatre, as we have said, retains

71

as much as in its developed complexity it may of art's primitive strength in the direct impact of human personalities that is involved. The bard chanting his Homer in a Dorian hall was a degree, though but a degree * directer in his appeal. The loss and divergence which ensues upon introduction of the third factor, the play, finds compensation, surely, and more, in the added interest, the richer complexity of emotion now made possible. The spectator of Hamlet, brought to a mimic intimacy with this little world, a part of it yet not a part as he yields himself to the influence of the performance or criticises the matter of the play, typifies, too, not inaptly, the sentient citizen of a more sympathetic, maybe, but a more detachedly knowledgeable age.

And drama holds the discipline of form. This is thrust upon the dramatist by the necessity of a defined relation with the actors ; upon the actors by their need of an understanding with the audience ; the audience, too, are accepting from the curtain's rise a somewhat strict convention. None of the parties to the completing of a play by performance can travel very far without the agreement of the others. Actors and author must have agreed in great detail upon both content and form. The appearance of this agreement must for each occasion be complete, though its extent will be neither constant nor very definable. The simpler phases of the understanding between actors and audience, as exemplified in language and gesture, are so implicit as commonly to escape notice.† But this relation is capable of a

---

* *See* Murray's " Rise of the Greek Epic."

† But let an Englishman watch a play in Sicily. He may or may not understand the spoken language, but he will at once be conscious how the meaning of gesture is passing him by, plain though it be to his native neighbours.

high degree of development. How do we acquire that unconscious knowledge by which the minds and moods of familiar friends are opened to us ? They use only the words that strangers use, but by reason of a hundred gradations of tone, turns of phrase, by looks and gestures, the meaning is doubled, trebled, intensified out of all likeness. It is not the mere fruit of experience, a reading into the present of an accumulated past. Years of external familiarity with a man will yet leave him a stranger ; and, too truly, one's knowledge of actors and their work may, by experience, come to nothing but extremest boredom. But in the relation between the characters of a play as stated and clarified by the dramatist, as interpreted and vivified by the actors, there is a parallel to the bond of friendship. It is reducible, if not to rule, at least to constancy in terms of art. And the audience, further, by appreciation of the actors' work upon the play, by their own assumption, moreover, of a direct intellectual interest in the play, can establish with the actors a relation of imaginative intimacy which by its very limitation, its de-personalization, its dis-interestedness—actors and audience being related to each other only by their interest in the play— is the more informing. And it is upon the possibilities of this collaboration, little explored as yet, that, as we shall hope to show, the theatre may best base its claim to consideration as an educative art.

It has others. Something is to be said for its ability to combine so many sister arts in its service. Music, painting, dancing, literature find a common occasion, and should find a common purpose, in the theatre. Its educational claims as a vehicle of physical self-expression are admitted ; and there is a case to be made—not a bad one—for the purely

73

educational use of its literature. For some study and practice in the construction of plays and the close-knitting of their dialogue is, perhaps, as useful a discipline in the shaping of thoughts and their putting upon paper as "composition," Latin or Greek verse, or précis writing.

The educa-tional use of drama

But, leaving all this, let us see how the "larger collaboration"—as we may call it—of audience with actors and dramatist may be built up. We can begin with the apparently simple plan by which a body of men and women sit round a table and mutually study a play. Not to discuss theories of play-writing or acting or production. Such things form, no doubt, an excellent mental background ; and in this relation they might have, perhaps, about the value that scenery will have to a play's acting. But what we are after now is a dose of this primary virtue of the dramatic form, the direct impact of one human individuality upon another, clarified and conventionalized, by the assumption and interpretation of character, diversified and en-riched by the side-glancing that even the smallest elaboration of a play involves with its interweaving of other interests; and the final development of some unity of idea, some conviction. There are possibly fifty different ways by which this study can be con-ducted and as many degrees of its elaboration. But the essential thing is to keep it upon these terms of impersonative interpretation, for only while in a state of artistic life will a play yield us any-thing of its peculiar quality. With the breath out of its body, so to speak, it is nothing but a con-stricted if interesting form of literature, worthy, no doubt, of the learned footnotes that cling to line after line of its classic examples. How often, though, are these but the barrenest wrangling upon questions that would answer themselves if the play were raised from its tomb of printed paper ? They are appropriate only to that ghost of the play, haunting thus disembodied the dry mind of the solitary scholar !

Not that the study need aim, with the usual expedition, at a performance of the play. That would at once involve us in the penalty under which the professional actor now lies. He may talk about studying a part or a play, but his concern with it is really very different. His work will rapidly be brought to the test of an effect in which, so to speak, all questions must be begged : it will be for him to assume such a complete identity with his part and the play as must suspend his critical faculties in regard to it altogether. His own fortunes are involved, and his concern will be to exploit the play's virtues, especially the more obvious ones, and to ignore or to cover its weaknesses. He will feel, too, that he must add from his own personal resources whatever it seems to lack, and in the process, like a ruthless restorer of a building, will often cut into and disfigure the fabric. This is why a play may often be heard in fuller integrity shouted through whole-heartedly and unself-consciously by a band of school-children than panoplied in the skilfullest acting. The professional actor's is a good way, perhaps, of performing a bad play—if there is any good way of doing what had better be left undone. But it is very often a bad way to perform a good one. And a method that so abnegates criticism is quite unsuited to educational needs. For that purpose a play must yield us what we want of it in its own despite, to its own damnation, if need be.

But if neither the anatomical methods of the scholar nor the exhibitive standards of the actor will

75

serve our purpose, to what is it that we are turning? We cannot have drama in abstraction, so to speak. Of all the arts, because of its collaborative qualities, it formulates itself most elaborately. Its medium is in one sense the simplest possible. Our recipe for the study or performance of a play might begin: Take the requisite number of ordinary human beings. But for its full development it requires nothing less than the complex organization of a theatre. Indeed, if for no other reason than that as evidence of worth we must have instances of perfection (or as near as the human medium may aspire to), and that precept without example will never convince us, drama must be studied concretely; it is not to be separated from the theatre. Yet again, if it is the art of the theatre itself that we are to regard as educative, not merely its component parts made use of as physical and emotional exercises, it will be only in the development of that art, purely for its own sake, that its wider uses will become completely apparent. Our system of study, then, for all its detachment from the present uses of drama, must yet centre in a theatre—an exemplary theatre, we may call it.

The Exemplary Theatre And in what, more precisely, must this exemplary theatre differ from theatres as we now know them? A theatre to-day is, as a rule, a place of entertainment where plays are produced. A sounder purpose strives to make of it an institution where they are kept alive—a library of drama. Following this narrow path of reform we might still hope to better plays, production, and entertainment, all three, even beyond recognition; to sustain and increase the drama's life very greatly. But if what we have said about the wider uses of dramatic art is sound, then to do this and no more

76

would be to make a one-sided effort to do an artificial thing, which would have no more continuing
life in it than have other arts divorced from utility.
If we can think, though, of the theatre as a place
where dramatic art is to be studied and conserved
for its own sake, from where it is to be dis-
seminated in every demonstrable form, not only
in the single one of the acted play, we shall have
cleared our mental ground. The true theatre, then,
is to be a place for the study and development
of dramatic art, and it must have no more limited
function. The striking of a balance, however,
between the art's intensive cultivation in the production of plays and its *extensive* use as a means
of general education is a task that, with the first
activity so familiar to us and the second so strange,
cannot be attempted dogmatically by a few phrases :
it is a matter yet more for discovery than argument. In any given institution a balance could
only be struck, certainly by experiment, in the end
probably by circumstance. But a contention that
various sorts of theatres would always exist, and
ought always to exist, from those devoted only to the
production of plays to those given almost wholly to
study and teaching, does not affect the validity of our
main conception of one which would completely
and comprehensively exemplify dramatic art. And
if we also imagine it in terms of a stark perfection,
which, if attained, might burst the bonds of its
being altogether (for doubtless dramatic art might
develop beyond the power of any theatre to hold it),
we shall still not look too far if our direction is right.
For all our talk the drama is in no danger of ascend-
ing into an artistic heaven, leaving its profitable
mundane mission unfulfilled.

And though we start, quite legitimately, from a

77

conception of the theatre as school, this by no means rubs out, but should rather enhance the more entertaining use of it. For however broad the basis of its educational work, this will properly be conditioned by what are to be the summits of its achievement. Its directors will naturally and rightly assume that if the courses of study there, pursued to their end, make for the perfect production of a good play, they contain, in virtue of that, all the necessary educational qualities. The theatre, in fact, to be exemplary, must exemplify its teaching; it must produce plays. It does not follow that all students need pursue the courses to this actual end, and specialize as actors, playwrights, producers, and the like; and it will be quite as important to insist that, for those who do, any training too extreme, too acrobatic in its kind to be, roughly speaking, of any non-professional use at all will be harmful to them in particular and generally false to an exemplary theatre's principles. To-day few people would dream of going to a school of drama but to learn to be an actor, and, as a consequence, the study of acting is pitifully narrowed. Our theatre as school must be a thing of much wider comprehension than any existing school of the theatre. Nor could we get what we wanted simply by adding fresh subjects to any accepted dramatic curriculum, nor by turning any existing theatre into a school. Every theatre and school to-day is involved in a vicious circle of narrowness—let it even be brutally said, of incompetence—that must be broken before the wider circle can be begun. Now professional acting will be an important product of the exemplary theatre, it will be in a position of mastership there; but, to begin with, it must itself go to school again.

78

It is perhaps worth while to ask why, with the *The break in* circle of the power of the drama widening for this *the acting* last generation, the circle of technical achievement *tradition* in its interpretation has been not merely failing to widen in response, but actually narrowing. For it can hardly be denied that this is true, making all the allowance we will for the occasional touch of spleen in an older generation displaced by a younger —though, indeed, among actors there is oftener to be found great generosity in acknowledging the new régime—and for the subtler difficulty that our impressions of the performances of plays do undoubtedly improve by keeping, and in our memory of them are probably at their very best just as we are at the point of forgetting them altogether. The actor of a generation ago may have needed fewer accomplishments ; he can probably claim with justice that he kept those he had in far better trim. That he did as a rule need far fewer no one would deny. Consider the repertory of plays in one of the " famous " old stock companies, and their average quality, and compare it with what would be as representative a selection of drama to-day! And the old stock company system, with its " line " of parts for each actor, in which, by much repetition, under varying circumstances, he could train himself to a certain pitch of perfection, could only have made for a very narrow, if for a very definite, achievement of sheer skill. In the actors who never succeeded to much more than secondary parts it was even, perhaps, quite superficial skill. Good stage manners were enough to raise the body of the plays in the seventeenth and eighteenth century drama to a sufficiently respectable level of interpretation. Performances of them must have rather resembled the dancing of quadrilles. While

79

if for most of the plays written between 1800 and
1860 any more than this pleasant gymnastic was
desired, not even so much did they deserve. And
for the full effect of the more important parts an
audience relied, then as now, upon a touch of something uncommon in the actor, or, failing it, fell back
upon the interest of the play itself.

After 1870 (I write of England) the leading
stock companies began to decline. There were a
number of causes for their weakening, but eminent
among these certainly was the coming of a new sort
of play into which the actors of " lines " of parts
could not be fitted. The change is mirrored faithfully and wittily, as every student of modern theatrical history knows, in Pinero's " Trelawney of the
Wells." There it would appear that lack of fitness
was the chief cause of the " old " actor's undoing,
and no doubt the peremptory demands of the
" new " dramatist did deal him the first and the
sharpest blow. But economic influences finally undermined the system, since it seemed worth nobody's
while to adjust it to new conditions.* With the
stock system, then, that prticular sort of training
went, and there were few, thinking twice about the
matter, to weep for it.

Robertson—
Bancroft—
Pinero

It is not so easy to determine all the influences
in the rise of the next school of English acting ;
while, as to its fall, the very fact will still be matter
of dispute, much more the conditions that may have
effected it. The school can be pretty accurately
and very honourably described as the Robertson-
Bancroft-Pinero school. One thing should be

---

* The economic influences are to be summed up in the discovery that the touring of complete productions could be made to
pay. The disappearance of the prejudice against Sunday travelling
had some effect too.

noted about the early training of, at any rate, its earliest leading figures. They found the stock companies surviving as opportunities of some sort of apprenticeship. They would probably deny, and with justice, that they found much inspiration in them, though some of the companies made an effort, no doubt, to inform the new dispensation with the spirit of the old. But if they only learnt by experiment what *not* to do they were so much to the good, and were the freer to bring disencumbered imaginations to bear upon the fresh and hopefuller tasks with which the new dramatists were providing them. Priority among these, in time and in influence combined, belongs to T. W. Robertson; we must envisage the effective part of his playwright's career, and the consequences, perhaps, of its untimely ending. He provided material so simple as to be peculiarly suited for the working out by its means of the beginnings of a new way of acting. And it is especially noteworthy that the protagonists of his success were Marie Wilton, till then a burlesque actress—a dainty and charming burlesque actress no doubt, but regarded probably by the mandarins of the theatre of the eighteen-sixties as something of an outsider—and Squire Bancroft, who was currently referred to, one suspects, by these same mandarins as a damned amateur. Reforms and revolutions both are carried through by minorities. Nor could this Robertson-Bancroft influence, by its very nature, be widespread. It tended only to the development of a gentle comedic talent ; it created nothing but a cup-and-saucer school of drama ; a small thing, no doubt, measured against Aeschylus, Shakespeare, and Molière. But the cups and saucers were of the best china, and they were delicately and deftly

F

handled. The influence, however, was not even long lasting. Robertson died, and it seemed that he would have no successors. Albery, who had shown promise—in his " Two Roses " rather more than promise—dropped out of account. What was Bancroft, as managerial leader of the movement, to do ? He lacked material. He made other quite gallant experiments in native drama, and they failed. So, at last, in desperation he turned back to the potent French theatre for a supply. It was, Heaven knows, a broad and already well-beaten track that thus led him away from the straighter and suddenly steeper path to the revival of a national art. We are not here concerned with the temporary wisdom of this policy, with any question of its inevitability, nor, directly, with its effect upon the rising wave of English play-writing. As a fact the native playwright of later arrival, when his talent was native at all, did go ahead, and kept his eyes fixed on his own course with commendable per-sistence. But the compulsion thus laid afresh at that critical moment upon English actors, cast in adapted French plays, to be modelling their style more than half the time upon French acting was a serious matter. This is often magnificent, hardly ever lacks aptitude and significance, and no doubt a study of its methods would be as great an addition to any actor's education as is some study of the French language to education in general. But it would be no good substitute for an in-and-out familiarity with one's own ; and acting is either an art of intensely racial expression or it is nothing.

By the time that the third great influence upon this period came in to play—by the eighties and nineties, when Bancroft had retired * and Pinero's

* 1884.

82

word was law and the discipline of one of his productions the worthy goal of every young actor's
ambition—the bastard style had struck root. How
far Pinero was wrongly attracted by what was
meretricious in it, or was aware of its insuffi-
ciency for his final purposes, or did try to remould
it to his own taste, it is hard to say. Possibly he
does not know: in art one does what one can
at the time. The playing of his farces, indeed,
fell into the true line of our artistic succession.
They were eminently English. Here he may be said
to have taken the Robertson tradition left derelict,
and handsomely renewed and improved upon it.
But when he turned to social drama the French
influence was waiting to overcome his companies.
Perhaps he himself had not wholly escaped it.
He was trying new ground, and a touch, now and
then, of the hand of Dumas fils may have made it feel
firmer. And in any case there were, in this respect,
many weaker vessels of playwriting than he ; so
the general effect upon the interpretation of plays
was unmistakeable.

The school of acting, then, that shone at its bright-
est towards the end of the last century, for all its
charm and its easy mastery over the material, good
and bad, clean cut or hashed, with which it had to
deal, rested partly upon this false foundation, and
was therefore destined, not perhaps to a decay in
the art of its individual exemplars, but inevitably to
a failure of survival in any second generation. Art
may temporarily flourish, but it will not seed and
grow again except upon a native soil. These actors
were, perhaps, too small and too select an aristocracy
of talent to do more than tint, historically, the age of
their predominance with gold. By no fault of their
own, the art to which they contributed their best was,

but for a few fine pieces, the work of a play-wright or two steadily pursuing his set purpose, a makeshift, pinchbeck affair, responsive to no serious test. They brought their own share in it to perfection, though; and if, because of this, they somewhat over-valued the total result, that was but natural. Play-goers of those years will need no list of names : they have them graven upon the tablets of their gratitude.

The Ibsen challenge But the next challenge of a change brought its cross purposes, too. The challenger was Ibsen, and the movement that tacked itself quite arbitrarily to his name. The movement itself after a while took on major importance and a native hue, so that the apt reply from those of the older fashion, accused of subservience to France, that knuckling under to Norway was no better, dropped idle. The resistance put up against this new in-fluence by the interests it offended—critical, mana-gerial, histrionic—had causes enough. To begin with, the new plays were not popular. Now, if popularity is jam to us all, it is bread and butter to actors. Plain bread may perhaps be earned without it, but that's a hard diet to choose. Contributively, if this sort of play dis-gruntled and puzzled the critics, it led the actor also on to uncertain ground. The old rules for measuring up good parts and bad no longer applied, and in a critical battle over the play's demerits his own reputation was apt (so he feared) to go down. And when later the enthusiasts for the new school of playwriting took to exalting it by the easy process of belittling the old, that made things worse for him still : he could hardly seem a party to the befouling of his once comfortable nest. There was often, no doubt, misguided zeal on the

84

one side, but, really, there was more stupidity, timidity, and sheer lazy indifference of mind on the other. Apart from such extraneous difficulties, though, there must still have been the histrionic difference: it was but increased by circumstances, its springs were deeper. The successful actor of that time thought, wrongly on the whole, that the new plays did not give proper scope for his carefully cultivated technique, but he was right in his usually unavowed fear that their interpretation did, besides, need qualities quite without the scope of any training he had had.

Now whether, if the tradition of acting had remained quite native, its exemplars would have been readier for the new development it is, of course, impossible to say. Hypothetical argument is risky, especially in artistic matters, where no instance even comes true to type. But it is at least possible that actors brought up to the playing of " Caste "; taught to go, if not to English life for their models, at least to English fiction (if Robertson neglected his immediate theatrical forbears he at least had not read Thackeray for nothing), and accustomed next to the excellent native humours of " Dandy Dick," could have been put to the very different fences of Galsworthy's " Silver Box " without fear of refusal. This is to take for an example of the demand made upon the actor a play in which there can be little suspicion of extraneous influence. As a matter of history this play appeared when the Ibsen battle had been fought out, and a younger generation of actors faced it with equanimity. But who would say that a company got together ten years earlier would have known what to do with it ? It was a serious play. But where would they have found in it the stigmata of the serious plays they then knew, the emotional crisis, the *scène à faire*, the ravellings and unravellings of plot ? With such materials they had learnt how to make certain arbitrary effects. In "The Silver Box" they are asked by the author to second his direct observation of the most common-place English life, to " be," as near as may be, a few people picked, with apparent indifference, out of Bayswater, out of the London streets; and never to mind whether they were, as actors, effective or attractive, or could exhibit any one of the superficial theatrical virtues. The principle one attempts to deduce would be something like this, If the actor be trained to deal with the *matter* of observation he need fear no novelty. He may attack it boldly and solve its every difficulty by the light of his own experience. Put an English company to an English play and nothing so far could be simpler. But we may take unlikelier instances. We may try a French company with Ibsen, Italians with Shaw, Americans with Benevente ; and though they may present the plays with a superficial absurdity, with every violence of translation not only into a strange language but into movement and furnishings still further from anything the author saw, yet, because they have searched back to the essential common relations between themselves, the play, and its author's meaning, they will be able to bring it alive upon the stage. But actors trained only in the arbitrary effects of a manner of acting will stand timid and hesitant before any new matter that—once they set it working—may bring mere manner to naught, and leave them helpless and invalidate.

Difference of technique in construction and dialogue between the new plays and the old could have been left out of account beside this difficulty of the different content. It was at this that the actors balked. They were, perhaps, wise in their theatrical generation, and we need discuss that part of the business no further. Nor does it really matter if our view of what might have been is a tenable one. We are only concerned now with the undoubted and undoubtedly unfortunate result of the breaking of the histrionic tradition. It was neither a very old nor a very certain tradition : it had been distorted and weakened already by extraneous influence. But, for all that, it was the receptacle of much necessary accomplishment and many desirable graces ; and first its refusal of service to the new school of drama, and later its rejection by that school, have left the English theatre at present the poorer. It was nonsense to say that any duffer could act Ibsen, and Ibsen has in consequence been rather the prey of the duffers to this day. It was equally rash to assume that sympathy with the aims of the new dramatist and a better understanding of his matter were all that was necessary to the performance of the play. But that was an opinion which now quite fatally tended to establish itself, not, obviously enough, upon the accrediting of a new sort of actor—who could hardly expect to rise to great fame upon such a basis—but upon a certain discrediting of the old, when the success of the new dramatists, or more properly the pervasion of the whole theatre by their influence even in failure, forced him into the service. He, very often, did not individually fail, for it became the amiable critical custom to credit the actors at the expense of the play with making the best of a bad job. But his technique—when it was all he possessed—tending to collapse under him, he had to abandon it and put himself on the level of the newcomers, who had neither any of their own nor any use for his. He had, in fact, to go to school again —and there was no school! It was not then so much the actors who were discredited as—far worse!—the whole art of acting, which has fallen, and remains in these days, most sadly in the dumps.

The discre-dited art of acting

How else, at least, to explain the undoubted impoverishment of English acting in the presence of as undoubted an enrichment of English drama? The admission may generously be made that individual actors of this generation of training do often not only fulfil but embellish particular parts by their personal talent and attractiveness. But the main accusation must be answered—and it is freely made—that, taken by and large, the present lot of English-speaking actors do not know their business. Let us put the matter at its worst. From the actor of small parts little is asked but the sheer technique of expression; how seldom it is at his disposal! A hundred excuses may be found, but the fact remains. And those upon whom the main burden of the play is cast are often in little better case. They may have a more sympathetic understanding of the purpose of the work than their forbears of thirty years back would have shown. But, in spite of this, their expression of it is fatally clogged in the outflowing by a voice they can't manage, a face that appears to need moving by hand, and a body they hardly dare move at all, unless with a violence which will mask its lack of all finer articulation.

It is between these two stools, then—of a technique outworn and discarded, and an attempt to do without any technique at all—that the art of acting has now fallen. It has fallen to dullness; a quite unforgivable sin. The writers and producers of

88

modern comedies may be excused for begging their companies " not to act." It would be uncivil to explain that their appeal in its fullness means " not to act like that." Certain of the later dramatists, it is true, impressed by the vast possibilities of the drama and their own contribution to it, but a little contemptuous of the theatre they so condescendingly make use of, are blind to there being any alternative to the " intelligent reading," which will, they hold, at least give their play its naked, un-hindered chance. But the art of acting was the beginning of drama. Before ever the literary man and his manuscript appeared acting was there, and it remains the foundation of the whole affair. And to ignore its possibilities and to decry its importance is to wander into that blind alley which leads to the play more fitted for the study than the stage—that yacht so perfectly adapted to lying in the harbour.

No ; the instinct of the playgoer is right. He goes to the theatre primarily to see good acting, in the never-defeated hope of being carried clean off his feet by great acting.* Failing this, he can perhaps learn to make more of a good play by reading it comfortably at home. He demands

---

* Et voilà
   Le silence rompu qui vole en mille éclats !
   Le public s'abandonne à l'immense rafale
   Qui gronde et le secoue ! . . .
   Et le rire au galop qui traverse la salle
   Emporte tout . . .
   Les chagrins, les soucis
   Et les peines,
   Tu comprends bien ceci ?
   Comprends que c'est pour ça qu'ils viennent !
   A ceux qui font sourire on ne dit pas merci . . .
      DEBURAU (Act IV of Sacha Guitry's play) praises his art.

even—and quite rightly—a certain virtuosity of performance; and when he misses it, being (tiresome fellow!) just a little less interested in the play itself than the author has been, he is apt to vote the whole affair either portentous and dull, or trivial and empty, as the case may be. It is upon this shoal that the new drama has been and still is in danger of being becalmed.

It is a quite avoidable catastrophe. The better the play, the more full of matter, or the more brilliantly evanescent in style, the less excuse has its performance for being dull. But the more does it need acting; not only a fuller understanding, but a greater virtuosity of interpretation.

The need for a new virtuosity Since the old virtuosity was found not to avail what attempt has been made in the English-speaking theatre to cultivate a new? *Solvitur ambulando* is a good motto, no doubt, and appropriate enough to a theatrical system in which actors start their career and are expected to learn what they can of their art by " walking on." And how expect a serious study of principles from a hard-pressed professional theatre, busily adapting itself to change of condition, artistic and economic, living artistically from hand to mouth, and compelled, above all, to consider appearance, to shark up effects, to make a success of the moment at any cost ?

When the break of tradition came there was no new school to supply—as had to be supplied, from fundamentals up and on—the new need. What have the present dramatic academies been doing ? One should have intimate knowledge of their working to speak with entire authority; but, judging by results, not much. One doubts, indeed, whether the need itself has yet been precisely formulated. These academies, too, are mostly, with their obligation to earn fees, compelled to supply not even such sort of study as the professional theatre might find upon consideration most immediately useful in its recruits, but that which the pupils themselves, impatient for a career, suppose will help them to the swiftest successful assault upon managerial favour. And even the American universities, where the most —and the most serious—co-operative study of drama is to be found, devote themselves less to acting than to plays and playmaking, and are driven to be (they too!) sadly impatient for results.

There is as yet no general recognition that modern drama demands a technique of interpretation or could even accommodate a virtuosity all its own. Taking the first at second-hand, it turns a half-disdainful back upon the very possibility of the second. The student of acting will contentedly approach a performance of, say, Hialmar Ekdal, bringing to bear upon it the same technical equipment that he has cultivated for Romeo. And although the actor playing old Ekdal will know (one hopes he will know; if he doesn't he will soon discover it, much to the play's misfortune) that the virtuosity which makes Sir Peter Teazle charming is so out of place in Ibsen as to be merely ridiculous, this mostly only means, alas, that he timidly shelters himself within the part, diffusing from it a respectable dullness.

Now the difference in the technique of the playwriting is so obvious as almost to escape comment. Shakespeare and Ibsen wrote with pens, wrote dialogue, designed it for living actors, and there, really, all technical likeness ends. Is it enough, then, for actors to make no more difference in their technical approach to the plays' interpretation than is unescapably dictated by the fact that in one case

91

strange garments must be swaggered in and blank verse spouted, while in another one wears coats and trousers and speaks prose; is Sheridan's attitude to the world amply defined if a man only carries a cane and a snuff-box ?

In the last analysis, of course, Romeo and Hialmar Ekdal (to contrast the two only) are sentient human beings both, and we have already admitted that the essential thing is to go back to the common point of contact with real life, that it matters far less what diverse paths may be travelled away from it. And if, for the covering of the long distance between conception of character and elaboration of performance, the actor has only a Shakespearean technique available, he must use it : it is absurd to expect any man to discard knowledge—even inappropriate knowledge—for ignorance Moreover, he *will* use it. For however much we may argue for Ibsen underacted rather than Ibsen wrongly acted, he has the responsibilities of performance to face. He is in honour bound to give the best of himself to the audience, as well as the slice of Ibsen carved for his use. He will not, if he has any proper pride, stand there empty of attraction, be driven back upon that dullness which is to him the deepest artistic damnation.

The worst, perhaps, of the use of Shakespearean technique in this connection, and the reason, besides, why the actor may be so blithely ready to use it, is that it is venerable enough to have acquired an absolute independence of its derivative. But in this both its own purpose is falsified and it remains curiously inappropriate to any other. The first thing needful for the building up of a technique of modern drama is to sort out and restore to their proper use the scraps and ends of method, once, no doubt, living growth, but now detached, dry, and applied haphazard according to the taste and fancy of the actor. Incidentally, what is usually called the Shakespearean tradition is not Shakespearean at all, and with a continuance of the now happily revived study of the obligations of Elizabethan stagecraft it will, it may be hoped, disappear. The Sheridan technique and the Robertson technique it should not be hard to put in their places. Then the ground will be fairly clear and it will be possible to think unencumberedly of the art of acting in terms of a drama which differs profoundly in matter and very eminently in method even from its nearer ascendants. The interpreters must follow the lines the creators have travelled. If Shakespeare wrote rhetorically, wove his effects out of strands of un-repressed individual emotion, if Sheridan cared greatly for the set of his prose, Robertson for sentiment, Pinero in his farces for well-bitten comic figures, if the work of Ibsen is most strongly marked by the involute process of revelation of character, that of Tchekov by the way in which his men and women are made to seem less like independent human beings than reflections in the depths of the circumstance of his plays—these traits of each dramatist mould and pervade his work and should dictate a related method for its interpretation. All acting is interpretation ; it can have no absolute value of its own. How much then of the personal praise and blame that is aimed at actors falls beside the mark when their art has not been looked at in its due relation to the play ! And here even pro-fessional critics fail us as a rule, omissively. To the mere casual public the play may be the actors' own. But the critic is too apt to give it his attention to the exclusion, it would seem, of any serious effort to appreciate at all the actors' share in its completion.

93

The critics   It is ill girding at unfortunate beings who, most of them, most of the time, are faced with the impossible demand for an adjustment in a few paragraphs of cold print of the feverish, factitious, often entirely fictitious enthusiasm of the first-night of a play. Nine times out of ten the play itself cannot stand up to the ordeal of a consecutive description, much less of an analysis. Even if it can, more especially when it can, are these the conditions to which any ordinary critic can creditably respond ? There would be excuses enough, under such circumstances, for almost anything he might say or leave unsaid. But it is a pity that he finds it as a rule easier to deal with the play itself at sufficient length, and so is content to let its acting go with a kindly, vague ineptitude of praise or blame. The play, of course, has at least its story, and by sticking to that he need neither involve himself nor trouble his readers with technical detail. Were he to be either precise or lengthy about the acting he would be straying, he may think, upon very slippery ground. But the flat truth, one fears, is that the average critic knows little or nothing of acting as an art. Not that he is alone in his ignorance. The average audience knows less, and cares hardly at all, demands sensation, the stirring to tears or laughter ; by what means effected is no matter.

But what stimulus, then, is it to an actor to appear before judges, the expertest of whom can hardly tell, so to speak, a bad part from a good performance, when, condemned to the one—as all actors must be from time to time—he may still be giving the other. Whether it is this misprision, or the contrasting gush of easy praise—echoed from the unthinking enthusiasm of an audience, for the carrying off, sometimes by sheer impudence and vitality, of something so obviously effective as to be in the cant phrase actor (it should usually be actress) proof—that has a more deleterious effect upon the art of acting is a question. It has become for actors an unimportant question in view of the conclusion reached by most of them with experience of the rough and smooth of their work, that as they never can count upon discrimination they had better measure the worth of these notices altogether in terms of advertisement, and the parts that they play, therefore, by the standard of an obvious effectiveness. But for us, and for the art's sake, this is an unhappy and a deleterious conclusion. All parts, and some of the best parts, are not—in this headline and poster sense—effective, and any effort by the dramatist or actor to make them so must be wholly misdirected. But the actor will be caught by a conscientious panic that he is not " doing his best to make the thing go," and the effort he then makes has only to be shameless enough to be greeted, as often as not, with applause. Yet again, what encouragement is it to a man to cultivate the niceties of restraint and delicate workmanship if, by the end of his career, no one but himself and a few of his colleagues are to be the wiser of his achievement? Few things can debauch an art so much as the lack of any decent standard of public taste. To every sincere and self-respecting artist each new effort is a new adventure, and it is asking much of an actor to keep his aim and his courage high if his audience indiscriminately applauds better and worse, and often, indeed, prefers the worse to the better. His chance of fame is in the present only, the temptation to " live to please " is doubly hard, for he leaves no score, nor canvas, nor printed book by which posterity may

95

justify his own severer, better judgment of his work.

There have been admirable critics of acting, from Fielding, Lamb, and Hazlitt onwards, and in their discriminating pages the quick mortality of the art has for some few outstanding names been stayed. And if to-day we were concerned only with the actor's allowable ambition to leave some less fading record of his achievements behind him than the hearsay of popularity we might look for and plan, under better conditions than those of current criticism, some recultivation of the sensitive, picturesque writing which does catch for us a little of the passing glamour, helps us to reweave something of the personal spell, which the fine actor once cast upon his audience. But we want not reminiscent value, but an immediate critical stimulus. A conspiracy between critics and actors to play into each other's hands in terms of technical achievement and appreciation to the confounding of the ignorant would be no more than amusing. For the circle of appeal and appreciation in which actors and audience, critical and uncritical alike, revolve is a natural one. It is within its revolution that the art of the theatre is immediately enriched. Granted a good audience, good acting of a sort must result. The actor simply cannot get on at all unless (we now speak of him generically) he can make himself understood and appreciated as he goes. By a process of trial and error, then, he would be bound to approximate his work to the expectations of his audience, if they, for their part, both could and would take the trouble to register and enforce them. If this ideal relation could be brought into existence, it would be within it—within this circle of immediate reactions—that all education in acting, as apart from the accomplishments of the actor, could be let lie. And, once get it going, once the magic circle were formed, the process would not be so impossible of practice as the attractiveness of the theory might lead one to suppose. But intelligent and responsible connection between the three parties—between dramatist, actors, and audience—having been so wantonly broken, there needs some external study, some grinding at principles, and a deal of practising, before they can be set up again. In other words, we all need—not only actors, but dramatist, yes, and audience as well, if a plan comprehending us all can be devised—to go to school again, to take a little trouble over the matter, before we can count upon this art of the drama yielding us in its completeness and complexity, pleasure and profit as well. But it must be to a school ranging wider in the scope of its study and plumbing deeper than does any theatrical academy of to-day.*

Consider yet again the disabilities under which *The wrong* almost every school of the theatre now labours. *sort of school* They are filled with young women and men feverishly occupied, as if training for a race; competitive, keen on accomplishment. The work, too, such as it is, is always disbalanced by the women outnumbering the men. As careers for men go the actor's is not very desirable, and so—but for the few who do feel an irresistible call, or whom circumstances tend to push early in—the supply is kept up by drafts of recruits at various stages of disillusionment in the discovery of their incompetence for other vocations. Not the best field of cultivation to begin with ! Things are better, no doubt, in this respect than they were. By the traditional

* I write of England, but I think that no such school as I have in mind does exist anywhere.

romantic course of running away from home was produced—out of the ensuing rough and tumble— some fine, full-blooded acting in those that had the sturdiness to survive; just as the daring of running off to sea can be proved to have furnished the world by the same process with some notable seamen— and pirates. Things were at their worst, rather, when the theatre, having acquired a sort of gentility, began to be looked on as the home of soft jobs, and, by friends and relations of the attractive wastrel who sought refuge there, as a not too reprehensible foster-mother. They would even manage to add a flavour of humorous pride to their protesting re- mark that " Harry had gone on the stage." The very existence of a school or two, in lieu of the vanished rough and tumble, the implied obligation to take the thing seriously, is a great improvement. But they still specialise far too narrowly. For it is noticeable that when an attraction to drama declares itself and is responded to in the course of a man's general education his particular interest is often less in acting than in the writing or producing of plays, or even—for all that the subject seems a dull one—in the management of the theatre generally. Take a stage-struck young man down from Oxford or Cambridge, and it is odds that he sees himself as Romeo. Find a man who has been getting his teeth into the dramatic courses (it is true they are called courses in dramatic literature) at Yale or Harvard, or working still more at large in some college further west, and for him a career in the theatre will be a thing of much wider comprehen- sion.* To such a man, it is clear, the present sort of

* I once met a man who had been studying drama solely as a preliminary to becoming a dramatic critic. He said he thought it a reasonable thing to do !

theatre school, with its nothing but teaching of actor's accomplishments, can have little or no attraction. And its loss of him—be this noted—is the greater.

The attraction of the theatre as a career for *The army of* women, pre-eminent once, for economic reasons at *women* least, as it was one of the few in which they worked on an equality with men, is now suffering by comparison with the many others opening out to them. It is in any case more of a gamble for women than for men. They may win success earlier, but only to lose it the sooner. If a pretty girl looks upon it as a preliminary canter which she means to abandon for marriage at the first good opportunity, the convenience is sometimes a double one—to her and to the theatre that may be glad to make use of her while her prettiness lasts. But for women who stay in the race there is less demand— if competence is all their attainment—than for men.* Many college women, both in England and America, are studying drama nowadays for the use it may be to them in teaching, or in the organizing of social life in villages and factory communities; the up-to-date development of district visiting. And for this, no doubt, the theatre school, even at present, could be of use if its curriculum were so adjusted. Moreover, such a class of students might well be a strength which would a little counterbalance that other, the obvious weakness of every dramatic academy, the crowd of stage-struck young ladies that

* Developments of the modern drama—and the advent of the woman dramatist—may alter this. But it is curious how the proportion of the sexes in the cast of a modern play tends to abide not by the social realities but by the traditions of the theatre built up for the drama of heroic action. Any play of sheer action, it is true, still calls naturally for more men than women. Tradition has something to do with the male overplus, for all that.

99

beset it, possessed by that shallow enthusiasm which is the bane of all art, and to the assaults of which the poor theatre is peculiarly liable. Nothing keeps them out, not the raising of fees; their parents, to be rid of their restlessness, thankfully accede to any such demand. Entrance examinations do not floor them. They have the abounding, crude vitality which carries them lightly over such obstacles; and, being admitted, they mount the first steps of the student's ladder with facility—oh, fatal facility! The casual looker-on at this phase would really think that something was to come of it all. But then—to change the metaphor, as they, at this point, seem to change—like locusts, they begin to occupy the land only to feed on it. They learn, and keep on learning, and what they do is arguably good enough, if argument made good art. But all the while it is they, more than any, that exhaust the resource of the classes and the vitality of the teachers, till they pass on (crowds of their like still to follow them) and pass out to good luck or bad, a sham career, a hopeless struggle, happily sometimes to marriage and cheerful, chatty reminiscence of the time they studied for the stage, or sadly to some greyer industry and the bitterness of regret.

There is no full escape, of course, from this sort of student in any art or any profession. Professions, indeed, seem quite contentedly to absorb them; for they work well to rule. And it is true that out of any such crowd can be picked a real artist or two. But then the teachers must try to be fair to the others, who work only the harder when their secret heart begins to tell them—for all the approbation they so earnestly seek for and logically almost compel—that it is all in vain. It is hard to

100

withhold approbation. And what arguable reasons can one give for saying in each case : " Here craftsmanship should end. Now artistry must begin ? " We cannot all have genius. Has the theatre no place for the craftsman ? How many tried performers—with not even so much claim on public attention—encumber it successfully. Thus they could argue, in return, these well-meaning ones, even when driven to admit that devoted study has brought them only to the knowledge of what they ought to be able to do and the realization of their failure to achieve it.

Now in a school with a wider intention than *The unprofes-* the training of actors they would be in a very *sional student* different and a very much better case. The drama, in some form or other, is sure to be made a part of any scheme of social welfare (so-called). Here, then, would be a legitimate course of study for any school of the theatre to provide, and a useful by-path along which those in whom industry is the highest artistic virtue might travel to fairly fruitful careers.

But a widening of the school's intention would be for the good of any potential actor, even were he (or she) marked out by genius for the straightest cut to popular recognition and success. One of the curses of the professional theatre is the accident of social isolation forced upon it, not any longer by prejudice, but by the simple fact that its work-time is other men's play-time, and vice versa. The need and the means of an escape from this we are to argue in a closer connection, but the preliminary isolation of studentship is as great an evil. And now we have reached the point where the interests of the actor noticeably coincide with those of the public in the theatre as a whole. The problem of his education is the doubled and divided one both of catching him young enough for the elements of his art to be learned and—one could comprehensibly say, forgotten,* but explanatorily—so absorbed that he can bring a freed mind to its larger aspects; and at the same time to keep him fellowed with those to whom this shadow of life is never to become substance; those, they will be—this is the importance of the matter for him—whose lives, opinions, and feelings he is to understand and interpret. They, on the other hand—and here is the coincidence of interest—can find, we are to argue, an educational use in the drama that will later develop, incidentally, into a deeper pleasure in it. And the drama itself, one would say, cannot fail to be enriched and strengthened by an infusion of new blood and by the demand made of it for wider service.

At this point, then, our grumbling at schools of the theatre had better give place to castle-building for the theatre as school.

* To say to a young actor of an old one "He has forgotten more than you have ever learnt" is illuminating and often salutary.

CHAPTER III : THE PLAN OF THE THEATRE AS SCHOOL

CASTLE-BUILDING it had better be, and from foundations up. One could plan for the development of work already in being, and in practice no doubt, and for purposes of experiment, some such nucleus would be helpful. One could both devise and complete a fine new institution suited to a small community making limited demands. But it will be more to our purpose to imagine in broad outline a theatre as school, fulfilling its widest mission under the most exacting circumstances and to beg the question of how it could be brought into being. Details will give verisimilitude, and they are half the fun of castle-building.

One sees this theatre as school—to attempt first *The school's* a parallel—in its status and outward relations, as *scope* one of those great specialist schools which form part of the already very catholic University of London.* Its internal organization would be, one cannot deny, both complex and costly. And if one says, to begin with, that the building containing it should accommodate two fully equipped and actively working professional playhouses, that might be enough to make most people, most practical educationalists certainly, dismiss the whole project as utopian. But it can, I think, be demonstrated that this particular complexity is more apparent than real, and would be an economy rather than an extravagance. Such a theatre would look to produce plays with large casts and small; plays, moreover, that might appeal either to large or small sections of the public. It is clearly economical to

* Such, for instance, as the London School of Economics, or the L.C.C. School of Architecture in Southampton Row.

fit a small audience into a small auditorium; it is extravagant—when, as may be, plays of small casts are making the larger appeal—to leave the overplus of actors unoccupied. Besides this, the scope of the study and its exemplifying, the call, for instance, for student performances, would easily burst the bounds of one playhouse. The carrying on of school-work and theatre-work under one roof would probably be a physical convenience,* and its amalgamation in one educational plan is a fundamental point of the scheme. The rest of the building equipment would be class-rooms, lecture theatres—much the same, indeed, as that needed for any other sort of specialized education.

No children admitted

Let us at once clear the ground of one just possible misconception, if the remark that potential actors are better caught young should give rise to it. The theatre as school would not be a place for children. All that they need be taught in this kind can be better taught here to their teachers. No sort of study would be provided suitable to any boy or girl under fifteen. Indeed, even for those of university age—as the great majority of students would probably be—the curriculum must deliberately discourage any neglect of more general education. Close specialization should in any case be in the nature of post-graduate work. And two hours a day in the less specialized classes would be an ample enough beginning.† For those already determined

* If it were not, there would be less virtue in the provision of a single containing building. And in London, of course, there are always difficulties in securing large and convenient sites.

† I am aware of the practical difficulties, especially in such a place as London, of combining varying studies in various buildings. But this is a more general problem, in any solution of which the theatre as school would share.

104

upon the theatre as a career it, of course, would not seem so. They would not find it a sufficiently swift test of their powers to excel. And no doubt the school would drift into admitting anyone over seventeen or eighteen to a full course of study at the start. But it should be discouraging to them upon this issue even in their own interests. The swift test—even of such an apparently easily to be discerned natural gift as the dramatic faculty—is misleading. Slow development strengthens it and deepens the strength. Incidentally, those parents and guardians with intractable children bent upon " going on the stage " would find in this slowly widening opening for study a useful compromise with their own dutiful refusal. Such an exiguous beginning might lack continuance and not be a serious waste of time for the pupil, nor—a more important matter—for the school. And this process of discouragement, with its implication of other interests to be reconciled, and the response to it, would help to provide, incidentally, the general educational test that the school should demand from its novices.

Let us reiterate, indeed, that though the school *The broad* must specialize, even to the extent of directing all *base of the* its plans of study towards the culminating point of the *work* fine production of a fine play, yet its claim to recognition is that not only is the base of the pyramid to be broadly educational, but that, at any stage of the building, work of quite general usefulness may be found. The base, indeed, would be broad beyond the functions of the school; for all study would begin upon the supposition that much preliminary work had been done in earlier schooldays, from kindergarten onwards. A supposition of the sort would hold true were the school starting fully found to-

105

morrow. Not a child nowadays but is taught (as we have noted) some form of self-expression— elocution, singing, dancing, or the like. But it will be, of course, more satisfactorily true after the school's own teaching has filtered down through students become teachers and has spread in wide circles to primary teaching of all sorts.

The first steps, then, in specialization would be a repetition, or rather a reinforcement, of work already done in a looser, more general way ; it would be a professional stiffening of the standard. It would be test work, the more physical side of it, and designed (once again) for purposes of *dis*-couragement. We may imagine, for instance, a student who had had some general training in gesture plunged at once into the difficulties of an equivalent of the " Commedia dell' Arte ; " or one that had studied diction put to read a passage of prose or verse in twenty different ways, and asked to pitch upon notes in his voice with the absolute accuracy with which they can be tapped on the piano. We may also suppose that when the effect of the school's work has filtered down into general education the co-operative study of plays will be finding, in a simple form, a place in most classes for boys and girls of fourteen to sixteen. In our theatre as school the students will find themselves faced at the beginning with various elaborations of this, for under one form and another it is this co-operative study which must form the backbone of the school's work ; and its justification, therefore, must be the backbone of the school's whole scheme. To its consideration, then, we will return later at some length.

Then there will be the productions of the two full-fledged playhouses which are conceived to be an integral part of the institution. It may seem paradoxical to rank these as student work; and certainly the general public, paying for its seats and enjoying the performances as it would those of any other theatres, will not trouble to think of them in that way. But the productions will truly be—and be the better for being—the fine flower of the study, or—to return to a former metaphor—the apex of the pyramid of the school's work.

And to sum up the school's general policy: it must make the sweep of its studies as comprehensive as possible, must hold back the young men and women who are making the theatre a career, and compel them, within reason, to obtain some mastery of their art as a whole; it must cater for the student that seeks intensive knowledge in but one or two directions, by keeping its sectional standards high, by providing opportunity, moreover, for actual research; and, finally and most importantly, it must see that the study in all its branches is generally educational, and is as much in immediate relation to the ordinary cultural needs of men and women as the drama should be in relation to their imaginative lives.

One of the school's chief difficulties would no doubt be with young people who, if they could not secure an express passage through its every grade and department, would then want to narrow their studies to the one or other branch of the art on which their hearts were set. It is a perennial trouble with the drama that what for other arts might be but simple devotion becomes in most people caught by its lure sheer mania, nothing less. One could unkindly attribute this to the passion for self-expression, self-glorification, of which, to the

107

novice, the art of acting largely consists, were it not that the would-be playwright, the producer, even the would-be manager, is apt to become almost as unbalanced. Perhaps the drama and all about it is in its very nature an irrational occupation, to be pursued only under the stress of emotion and illusion—a sort of elaborate dervish-dancing. Perhaps all that rationalized study can do is, by dispelling the illusion, to damp the emotion and impoverish the product. One does observe in the careers of some actors a continuing process which might be so explained. First has come a quick physical and emotional adjustment to their work; they " find themselves " as it is called. Then this is duly followed by a hardening into conscious method when they have found themselves—out! Let them be thankful that, if the public is slower to appreciate the first part of the process than they could wish, it is slower still to share in the second. Is the rational study of the dramatic art better then left alone ? Had its development better be confined to some training in gymnastics and to the stimulus of youthful high spirits, or, youth failing, to reliance, when all else fails too, upon those of a more liquid ardency ? The writer of this book naturally does not admit a solution which would invalidate it from beginning to end. He believes rather that it is the unhealthy constriction of the art which produces these symptoms in its neophytes, which wearies and depresses its veterans. Bring the drama as an art and a means of education into touch with the normal life of the community and it will develop rationality as a virtue and a strength.

Young people, of course, will always beset such a school as this fired with the one irrational desire to "learn to act." It is in the young—in the very *No teaching* young, as we have seen—a natural and engaging *of acting* impulse enough. But it must not be allowed to *allowed* colour and disturb by its violence the school's whole scheme of work, if for no other reason than the obvious one that the art of acting in its fuller development is not built upon such an indulgence. But here is a danger that calls for deliberate avoidance. Insist all one will upon the concurrence of other studies, loyally, even as these young fanatics may try to detach their minds to them, their hearts will be fixed upon acting—upon nothing but acting. The desire of it will possess them like a sort of original sin. They will be acting from breakfast to bedtime, in the street, in the solitude of their rooms ; they will act in their dreams. Their enthusiasm must be disciplined or it will evaporate fruitlessly, or else it will degenerate into a disease, rather than develop to an art.

To begin with, they must not be allowed to indulge during school hours in anything that can be called acting at all. The rehearsing of plays by callow students leads, under supervision, to their teaching; and to the teaching, moreover, not of the principles of acting, but of its practice—or rather of its practices and too often only of its tricks. Something of this sort is unavoidable when any teacher begins to show pupils "how to do it" ; and, sooner or later, every teacher will. But even without supervision the student, too soon occupied with effect, neglects cause; and has not the patience, has not the equipment, to work through the slow processes of interpretation, but takes short cuts to what he thinks ought to be the result, becomes imitative and impersonative merely, and begins to develop a machine-like efficiency. The more

109

aptitude he has the more easily will he do this damage to his art. Nor will the harm end there, but spread. For to fellow-students who are either less apt or whose interest in acting is more impersonal, more purely educative, this show of a result, this showiness rather, will obscure the whole process and meaning of their study, will at the least upset the balance of the class work.

For his own sake the student should be kept from premature achievement. Acting seems so easy, and like all other art ought, in its accomplishment, to seem easy. In its inception, moreover, to the unsophisticated, happily unself-conscious, young person dwelling in the false paradise of artistic innocence it *is* so easy, that to plunge into the practice of it without having fully faced, not so much its difficulties as its possibilities (its difficulties, that is, in their finest sense) is inevitably to run this risk of developing one's innocence not into knowledge, but into an experienced and hardened ignorance—death to one's own art, blight to one's surroundings! In the amateur that innocence may remain and preserve its peculiar charm ; in the professional it must suffer this change, and, as ignorance, be inexcusable. Then drive these young people, mad to act,—and drive them hard—against all the more troublesome parts of the business. Let them break their shins, so to speak, and spoil their strength over voice production, elocution, dialectics, eurhythmics ; over the principles of playwriting; upon analytical criticism, theatrical history, the history of costume, costume designing, scene designing and making and painting ; not to mention fencing and dancing and singing and music generally. These make up the whole art of the theatre, nothing less, and now the list is not exhausted.

And if the young actor does not mean to acquire at least some understanding of the lot, make it clear to him that, when he emerges from apprenticeship, and comes to occupy his own particular place in any true theatre, he will still be no better than a hand in a factory, his status no more distinguished. Personal ambitions must, one fears, in these first days be tantalized. The student will be led time and again to the actual brink of acting in a play, led round and round, and not till the last possible moment be allowed to plunge in. For once he is in he must swim unaided. His enthusiasm will survive, there's no fear, while his un-expended powers ripen. And if it fails the theatre will be the better in the loss of him, for, failing under such a test, what could he be trusted to bring to its service but a little vain glory ?

And the effect of such discipline upon the school as a whole will surely be tonic. It must never seem to offer the meretricious attractions of the amateur dramatic club or it will be doomed from the start in the eyes of those who look to make a solider use of it. It is to exist for the exemplary study of drama; it will therefore become its integrity to place in its scheme all the component parts of drama according to their proper proportion and worth. For thus, and thus alone, will it succeed in attract-ing as students a heterogenous body of young men and women, and in encouraging them to seek in active study of the drama something that they look but for the shadow of now, even in their enthusiastic vision of an ideal theatre, something that they would certainly never dream of going to any existing theatrical school to gain. If they find it they will re-bestow it upon dramatic art with interest, some creatively, some appreciatively. From our theatre's

III

own standpoint, then, such a body of students, who will, most of them, have no intention of abiding in her service, is best. And the higher standard of general competence that can thus be set will weed out the weaklings, in talent or intention, those whom no entrance examination detects, those whose pledge to continue their training is valueless and worse—for half-hearted students are the best to be rid of. The half-hearted and half-talented of tardy discovery are the curse of all such schools ; and their gradual accretion like barnacles, once they dare not cast loose, upon the body of the actor's calling is more than a curse ; it is a prolonged disaster.

The bye-paths of the social "settlement" and the "community" theatre　And a student body with aims other than professional acting is an attainable object. We have already noted that the extended and varied use of drama in general schooling, and its probable spreading as a means of recreation among " community-conscious " people (themselves a growing class) can provide useful bye-paths into which students that remain whole-hearted enough, but yet must discover that there are no personal theatrical triumphs ahead for them, can be deflected. " He who can, does; he who cannot, teaches " the aphorism has it. But it is possible in any art, and—this being, at any rate, an imperfectly put together world—in an art which uses the haphazard gifts of physical personality as its medium of expression it is very likely that a talent may be developed, none the less real that it will be somewhat inappropriate to its possessor. It is not so much that the heart of a Romeo may exist in the body of a Falstaff (Nature is usually apter than that. Besides, what a theme, comic or tragic, for the dramatist !) as that a man may be able to cultivate in

112

himself almost all the qualities of a successful actor, and yet for lack of one of them will fall short of his apparently legitimate ambitions. It may only be perhaps that he cannot respond to the test of physical endurance ; great acting is pitifully dependent on the possession of bodily strength; many an actor must be left out of account because he is not a " fourth act " man. And if again such a good man's chances are to be narrowed by the theatre's own narrowness as a channel for the drama generally, the calling seems bound to become a reservoir of disappointed men and women. One will find in it today more such women then men. Anno Domini is, of course, a swifter enemy to them, and they do not find such opportunity of adaptation, such a variety of parts, as a man may suit himself to.

Now to these disinherited heirs of popular success the socialization * of the drama should come as a godsend. As administrators of village and community theatres, superintendents of dramatic work in schools and colleges, a career worthy of the name would be open to them. Nor would they be the theatre's left-handed gift to society. Granted the early discipline of its comprehensive study, they might often become more truly masters of their art than those whose too continued practice of it made them rather its servants. The instinct for acting is such a common one that we can seldom foresee whether cultivation will strengthen or destroy it (early strength is no guarantee of maturity) ; but it must undergo the test. There is no reason whatever, though, that the development of a general understanding of the art in place of a faculty for individual expression in its medium should rank as

* The word is used in its strict sense, not as necessarily connoting any doctrinaire form of Socialism.

failure if only the opportunities for exercise and influence are there. At present it is as if—for a parallel—fiction and poetry were the only forms of literature. But the drama also needs its pure scholarship.

The picked
recruits

Conversely, one might anticipate with a certain mischievous satisfaction that were the study of acting made wide enough in its application (as for the sake of the actors themselves it should be) people bent on more serious careers—in the church, at the bar, in politics, and asking only by the way for what little help in self-development they thought that dramatic art might bring them—would halt at some moment to recognize their more fitting career in the theatre. For certainly there are men now in the church, at the bar, in politics, so-called successes, who seem to have nothing but histrionic capacity to recommend them. Whether the theatre would profit by their acquisition may be disputable, but their present professions do not. And if, now and then, the theatre did seduce a possible good lawyer or priest they ought not to be grudged her. If she is not a calling fitted for the best men it needs but a few of them to help make her so.

Finally; as we began by admitting that, however broad the basis of study, the school's work would rightly be directed towards the perfecting of dramatic art itself, exemplified in the finest achievements of the theatre, so it would aim to find among its students a small surviving band whom deliberate and sustained choice and the discipline of hard technical training had only confirmed in their desire for the promised land of their art. Well, too, if their choice can be kept to the last possible moment a little free by fellowship with men and women working towards other ends ; while the school's

114

usefulness to these, for whom study of the drama is to be a mere means, will be a controlling test of the theatre's own wider fulfilment of its purpose in the community at large.

Into a more specialized category of study would fall playwriting classes.   To those familiar with the work of this sort, originated by Professor Baker at Harvard and now imitated and developed all over America, there is no need to insist upon its pertinence in any school of the theatre.   Its effect upon American drama is already patent.*   *Playwriting classes*

Such classes † are most conveniently made up of from ten to twenty students, of whatever seems the right number for free, informal discussion.   From the nature of their procedure one might better describe them as seminars.   A student—or two, or even three, it may be, that have joined in collaboration—will bring a play for the consideration of the class.   The authorship remains as far as possible anonymous.   The play may be brought in an unfinished, but not an unformed, condition ; it may lack, that is to say, a last act, but its dialogue and

---

* An advisable, an almost necessary, beginning to any practical attempt to realise such a school as this would be a careful critical report of the remarkable and very varied work being done in almost every American university and college.   Some of it is doubtless experimental and may be without permanent value, some of it is inco-ordinate and under the curse of being expected to show immediate and effective results.   Much of the best of it is carried on under every sort of discouragement.   But, as a whole, it is a body of endeavour, which, while it cannot create a great American drama—foolish to expect that it should—is providing every chance for its development.   It is fertilizing the soil.   Later may come a sense of the equal need of organizing the theatre itself, where alone, under as wholesome conditions as give it birth, a drama may flourish.

† What follows is not accurate description of any existing ones, but it indicates, fairly correctly, the lines on which they may be run.

scenes must be consecutive. It is either read aloud by the conductor of the class or distributed in MS. It is then put upon the table for discussion, destructive criticism, constructive suggestion. The author will disguise his identity as best he may, either by partaking (this needs some histrionic de-impersonative ability besides) or abstaining ; the anonymity is only important in helping the class to discuss the play with absolute freedom. The author may take advantage, negative or positive, of the criticism, and bring up the play again in a further stage of development. Its ultimate destiny may well be the waste-paper basket. It is admittedly prentice work, and although the apprentice may prematurely produce a masterpiece he is not to be expected, or even encouraged, to do so. Early achievement in this, as in all else, is inimical to sustained study.

It will be seen that this procedure, with whatever possibilities of variation, is simple enough. The validity of the whole idea of such classes has been questioned, but chiefly from the point of view of literary men, to whom composition is an extremely individual, and generally a solitary, thing. For an answer one may note: first, that the playwright's work is not primarily literary at all—the writing down of a play is mere convenience ; secondly, that he is part artist but part craftsman, most akin, in his methods perhaps, to an architect, essentially, therefore, a collaborator, even though his be the creative beginning of the collaboration ; thirdly, that as he is far more concerned with technique than other literary men his work is the more discussible quite apart from its inspirational side.

That no amount of criticism within class or without will make a man a great playwright need not be questioned. The claim of the class is that he will at least learn there the nature of his materials, and will see their possibilities in the handling. It is to be supposed too that the class critic, by attack and defence, learns as much as the class author.

Nor need a career as a playwright be the student's single goal. How far an application of the excellent rule that to be complete master in any one branch of art some service in every one is desirable would bring into the playwriting classes future actors and producers we need not inquire, for we have held that any broadening of study, and for the actor any suspension of graduation, is desirable. The generally educational value of the work is very demonstrable. If Greek and Latin verse, English composition, precis-writing, and the like are good training in literary expression the discipline of playwriting can certainly hold its place with them. As a lesson in conciseness the well-made play is only to be beaten by the sonnet. Of construction, exposition, clarity, consistency it can be made a perfect example. It is notorious how many accustomed and easy-going essayists and writers of fiction will fall short when they try their hands now and then at the more exacting task. And, for all their protests after failure, it is not ignorance of a few unworthy theatrical tricks that has betrayed them, but often a sheer inability to realize or compass the hard planning and austere practice of the dramatic form.

There are tricks, as in every other trade, to be learnt if you like, and then for their poverty avoided; and a very little more appreciation of good drama would render the worst of them (except for their sleight of hand fun) ineffective and worthless. It is true, of course, that the content of the best-made play may be inferior to that of a rambling novel or a

117

slovenly biography. And these, again, have their constructional virtues, which are not those of the play form. But as a training in any sort of writing the play has its peculiar advantages. It is hard discipline.

One aspect of the playwriting classes needs comment. The work has no relation to the workaday activity of a theatre, and it may seem that as the playwright will exercise his craft detachedly he might better study it so ; that there is a real objection to his being exposed at such an impressionable time to influences which may belittle his work's value, may tend to reduce it to the importance of a sort of verbal scene-painting. With the theatre as it is now, in a school that was only its annex, the objection would be very valid. But if this theatre as school does not, by everything else that is in it, turn this drawback to advantage it will exist in vain. In all reality the playwright is a collaborator, and his work but the part of a whole. Its inception may best be individual and solitary, and no doubt such a man is intellectually better off in the society of those whose minds are not over-occupied with the derivative processes of the theatre. But the remembrance of the coming collaborators should always be with him, and as soon as the completing phase of production begins he should personally assist at it if possible. The best of producers is no good substitute for the playwright himself. But, again, if he is not to be more of a nuisance than a help he should know at least as much of the inner workings of the actor's craft as he may expect the actor to understand of the exigences of his, and he can only learn this in any useful sense by experience or close observation.

It is noticeable that the playwriting study groups

in America are apt to carry on in what are called workshops,* having discovered, one presumes, that their members write more practical plays, at least, if they take the responsibility of acting them, of painting and shifting their scenery too. That is sound, without doubt. One's only criticism would be that the full rounding of this particular circle of experience does not atone for its minuteness. The gain would probably be greater if the prentice-playwright could see the work that is complementary to his own more proficiently done than he himself need ever aspire to do it. What he needs is the chance to sense sharply the comparative value of his own share in the complete process ; and he will do this most profitably by being brought into contact with the rest of the work at its positive best.

In as close, but in a contrasted, relation to the *Stage* school's work would come its study of the decorative *decoration* arts of the theatre. While playwriting may begin intimately and will cut loose, the dress designer and scene-painter must obviously look elsewhere to be taught their particular A.B.C. No more need for a theatre as school to involve itself in that than, on the ground that it calls for music now and then, it should be required to set up a class for trombone players. The basis of study could be made too broad.

There could be classes in the history and the technical planning of scenery, in the history and designing of costume, equally suited for students completing a general education in drama and those that were making a career by studying painting and drawing elsewhere but had an eye to possible work

* Professor George P. Baker's Harvard habitat is known as *The* 47 *Workshop*, and it is the exemplar for many others.

in the theatre later. But practical work would need to be that done to meet the theatre's actual requirements, and could be joined in only upon such conditions as these dictated. We must not forget that this is the theatre as school, and not a school of the theatre operating at large. It would be clearly impossible to set up large studios in which scenery was experimentally built and painted, and costumes were made just for the fun of making them, so to speak. For one thing, the cost would be prohibitive. But, apart from this, we should be at once betrayed into the worst errors of particularism.* A dramatist who works without reference to the acting and staging that his play will need, an actor who takes such an absolute view of his art that he hardly admits obligation to the dramatist, are alike guilty, and pay the penalty of their detachment in the ineffectiveness which will always result in the co-operative drama from individual over-assertion. Not less mistaken is the artist (so he claims to be *par excellence*), to whom the demands of the theatre, are first and last, material to be compassed by his own imagination. Having sated it, he will be good enough to allow dramatist and actor —if he cannot see himself rid of these altogether— to polish off, at his dictation, the few details that remain. This really will not do. It can have no relation to the realities of the theatre. Vision is above all things to be respected and served, but when it can only exist and prosper unfettered the visionary must abide by his isolation and the conditions that attach to it. When the message comes down from the mountain the workers on the plain must make the best use of it they can,

* An imminent danger, apparently, the moment a decorative artist sees the theatre in his grasp.

and, one fears, adapt it, like the poor day-by-day labourers they are, to their current needs. Useless to plan the removing of very complex and mundane machinery to a mountain top, for there are many prophets to serve, and each prophet has, and prefers, his own mountain! The theatre is not the place for the unchecked expression of a dominant individuality, and any attempt to make it so is a step towards its destruction. Much could be learned, no doubt, from seeing a theatre glorified and destroyed by an individual genius. Much would be gained by the theatre as a whole taking example of what to do and—it might possibly be—of what not to do. Such experiments are to be hoped for, and from a surplus of energy should be provided for. But we deal here with general principles; and subversive doctrine must therefore rank as heresy and suffer condemnation, certainly until the true and more catholic faith has been safely established.

It should, though, be possible to provide for some free experimenting within the walls of the exemplary theatre itself. The most fruitful time for it would probably be when students, towards the end of their prentice tasks, were straining upon the leash of them a little, but were as yet uncommitted to a daily round of responsible work. Some natures, of course, retain an impulse for the untried through a long career. It is the final triumph of any institution to be able to give these untameables fair scope and still keep them loyal to its service, and it will be well worth the stretching of many points of discipline to do so. For in them, all appearances to the contrary, will often lie the spirit of its survival. Losing them, no way to it may be left but by the violent process of destruction and rebirth.

121

The capacity of the theatre workshops to entertain apprentices might not equal the demand for practical experience that students would make of them. A certain amount of sheer demonstration for their benefit could be attempted; some benefit accrue from a handling of models. But, generally speaking, the workshops would be the narrow neck of the bottle through which only picked students could hope to pass ; and only a further selection of them could hope for definite and continued employment in the work of the theatre. On the other hand, remembering that the demand for this work must always be limited, the supply of students wanting to devote an apprentice's full time to it might well regulate itself accordingly.

The co-opera-
tive study of
plays
But the main artery of work in the theatre as school is likely to be the co-operative study of plays. It will be, that is to say, if the drama of analysis— and especially of social analysis—with its peculiar interpretative demands, continues the remarkable development of the last thirty years. Classes in finite and attractive accomplishments may be more closely besieged by the tentative crowd. But the student committing himself to the theatre as a career will find that here is the core of the matter for him: he will be drawn to relate every other study to this. When they have receded in his experience to rank as mere training, or remain as a pleasant gymnastic, the practice of this will endure, for his final maturity is to be that of the supple and sensitive interpretative artist. Moreover, it is upon the broad development of this study that the claims of the drama itself to be generally educative can most safely rest. Now, as the playwright has often moved momentarily beyond the reach of his interpreters, so, it is obvious, the student could elaborate

this aspect of the drama beyond the containing power of the theatre. And, working apart from the co-ordinating influence of the theatre itself, he might well do so, and another drama, more fitted for the study than the stage, might be gendered. But working within its circle there is little such danger. The student whose place when study is over will be not upon the stage but among the audience, whose approach to his subject will, as is to be shown, differ considerably in later stages from the actor's, may indeed most aptly fulfil the very useful function of pointing to, and testing, the extreme development of the dramatic form in this direction. Who is to say, for instance, that a Platonic dialogue or the like is not a possible play—given suitable interpretation and suitable audience? The one cannot be developed without the intelligent sympathy of the other. But it is by such disinterested study, which incurs no obligation for immediate effect or even for ultimate success, that art as well as science is given life and continuance.

This co-operative study of plays must, of all others, proceed from the very beginning less upon the lines of a class than of a seminar. It may well be the best plan for the study of any art. One notes its traditional use for painting and sculpture : the pupils at work in a common studio, a professor appearing at intervals as critic, constructive and destructive, of the work under way. The resultant freedom of the novice to feel and find his own path—saved only from too disastrous blunderings, and then more by example than precept—is certainly a necessary basis for any such work as we are to outline here.

We must note as we proceed where the differences *Critical and* of approach as between general and particular *interpretative* student, as between the use of a play for the educa- *bias* tional purpose and its preparation for the stage, are likely to lie. They will tend to develop at different times in differing plays. In some they will be of no practical import till presentation to an audience is in question, and then will be merely practical matters—to put it crudely—of dressing-up and moving about ; in others they would be from the beginning so marked—the approach being obviously, as with a mime play, on the lines of pure performance—as to rule out the usefulness of such plays as a medium of study altogether. But it is most to our present purpose to insist upon the identity of the methods that can be employed for both study and production, and to comment, if but by implication, upon the fact that each process, as now followed, lacks an essential that the other could supply. Production, for instance, lacks concurrent criticism. What the actor thinks of his own part he, as a rule, wisely keeps to himself—wisely, if heroically, for he, at one with the part, is soon to be criticized himself, and a disclaimer of identity will then avail him little. While for co-operative criticism no provision at all is made ; and, indeed, under ordinary conditions of rehearsing it would only result in chaos. The position of the author is god-like—worship and obedience being offered to him according to the credit of his cult. Mutterings of unbelief must be low, for under this banner, after all, everyone concerned is now pledged to march to victory or defeat. Loyalty, then, is a self-regardful virtue. And if the producer told the actors what he really thought of the play it might depress them unendurably. When the actors discuss each others' parts the effect is commonly disturbing, though a kindly provision of nature somehow always makes the part that you haven't got seem the better one.

It is the worst manners to comment to your fellow actor upon his potential performance except in the terms of the most formal (or fulsome) compliment ; reasonably enough, since his artistic life is at stake and you cannot be responsible for saving it. There develops, in fact, as rehearsals proceed, a conspiracy of rather desperate silence as to the merits of the whole affair.

On the other hand, the detached and critical study of drama now lacks the first, the most essential, condition of fruitfulness. For until a play has been brought to life by the assumption and setting in motion of its characters no criticism of it can be valid. It may be said, indeed, that the task of the seminar— our proposed combination of the two methods— will be for the students first to bring the play to life and then destroy it again by criticism if they legiti- mately can. The poorer the play, of course, the more easily could this be accomplished. There are many plays, it goes without saying, that now pursue their way to production, but never could have survived two hours' preliminary destructive criticism. Far better had they thus perished at the righteous hands of their actors before ever the footlights illumined them. It is less obvious, but as true, that drama may make the bravest show on paper, and even—treated by actors with that respectful dislike which they suppose to be due to the classic and superior—maintain a sort of gal- vanized life, when it would collapse quickly enough if charged with any real vitality; or there may be preserved the illusion of a play which has really been dissolved into the atmosphere of its acting.

What amount of technical training in its ex- pressive side will a student need before he can use- fully join in this work ? Not very much. For it will be noted that a class of this sort will have to accommodate more than the number required to cast any particular play. For one reason, any alternate shrinkage and increase of numbers would otherwise be a nuisance. For another, and a better, the elasticity which an overplus of students brings to the discussion will be very valuable. One does not want merely to have the cast of the play discussing the play, for—bearing in mind our preliminary obligation to vitalize the work by impersonation—this procedure would tend very quickly to harden into a sort of rehearsal; good enough in itself perhaps, better than any one may find at present, but unsuited to our present non-productive purpose.

The play would be cast, of course. It would not do to start every meeting by a fresh or a haphazard allotment of the parts. That would give us no continuity of development in its study. But there is nothing against a temporary turning of critic into executant, nor against the exchange of parts—nothing, indeed, against any device which would turn the play's every possible facet into the light of discussion. It will be seen, then, that while no " dead wood " is to be desired, no perforcedly silent listeners, no crowd, these classes would yet accommodate indefinite numbers. Not only that, but there would be an actual advantage in composing them of students in varying stages of training ; by no other means would a man learn quicker how much of his art he didn't know and what was the worth of all that he did. An equal and an obvious advantage lies in forming the classes of students who would approach the plays from various points of view—the playwright's, the actor's, the critic's, as well as from that more broadly, and perhaps destructively, critical stand-point which may be taken by the outsider, concerned only for the value of the whole business in its application to whatever is for him (and for the moment!) ultimate reality.

It may be surmised that the conductor of the seminar will not have an easy task. We are now imagining one twenty or thirty students strong, and its control will call both for authority and experience. But smaller affairs are not to be ruled out, and half a dozen students working upon a play might well be left to elect their own conductor, for it is in this post that the training of a play producer will be found. His powers will be roughly those of the chairman of a committee, and the best conductor, by that parallel, will be he who exercises them least arbitrarily. When he is indeed a producer with responsibility for results his powers will need to be both increased and more strictly defined. For a play's production involves agreement, even if that has finally to be imposed; but for its study an intelligent disagreement may be, to the end, more important. The task of the seminar will, of course, be to come, if possible, to a common understanding of the play : that will be the hall-mark of a quite successful session. But the unity will be of no value unless it has proceeded from diversity ; unless, indeed, it is a genuine reconciliation. And if diversity does not exist to begin with it will even be the conductor's business to produce it. These things are a parable, and they are the gist of the drama's educational claims. To bring a mere show of unity out of diversity is a trite task, which might be achieved by vote-taking in a debating society. Let us be clear that this studying of plays is a very far cry from that, and must never be allowed to

Bringing the play to life

127

degenerate into that. Its mainspring is not to be disputing, however mentally clarifying that may be. Our object is to create a unity *in* diversity—a very different and a far more promising thing. Unity in diversity must be our social ideal, and it is this that drama in its very nature does expound and, through the sympathetic power of impersonation, interpret. This is the drama's secret. Our understanding of things human will be barren unless we have emotionally realized them first. Experience teaches us, it is true, and if we were wholly unimaginative creatures it might remain our only master. But individual experience at the best is not wide, and it is hard to summarize, interpret, relate to the common lot, and re-value in these wider terms. Not more than once or twice in a lifetime, perhaps, do we stand so revealed to ourselves. We are too intimate with our own hearts ; that is the trouble. And nothing ends in them till life ends, nor can we look back with certainty to any beginning ; we know that our causes are really all effects. Therefore we turn to interpretative art for a synthesis, but—so incapable are we of applying a direct test to anything but the demands and satisfaction of our crude appetites—we must even then trust to the vicarious experience it offers to recognise the validity of the very elements that most largely compose it. Now, it is drama, the dramatic power of the assumption of a second identity, that can provide for us best in this kind. Of the directly interpretative arts it is the strictest in form ; in no other can the argument be rounded up, or rounded off, so completely ; in no other, if our criticism be keen, are the fallacies of the artist more nakedly exposed. And from no other art do we gain the essential life-giving virtue, without which the best reasoning is barren, of this personal

128

realization of the human material of a problem, and, for the time that we imaginatively occupy that second self, as genuine a responsibility for its welfare as we take, day by day, for our bodily life and limb. But the unity in diversity that we seek must be achieved as a crown to this responsibility, never by its sacrifice.

It will be remembered that upon acting itself as a part of the school's work we had—paradoxically, did it seem, in a school mainly ordained for its study? —placed a ban not to be lifted till the last possible moment. It is in the work of these seminars of play study that the advantage of the prohibition will be chiefly seen. Imagine a set of young students keen, keyed up, and yet restrained by hard technical training in the gymnastic of their future art, all impatient to be showing what they can do. They are necessary to the seminar; without them the more coldly critical minds would bring the work to sterile debating. On the other hand it will be for these, who are students of the drama only as a subject contributory to their general education, to put every obstacle in the way of a conscienceless ignoring of the weaknesses, or a facile overpassing of the difficulties, of a play. Not, though, that one would attempt to confine them to criticism. When later, as audience, it is their taste and judgment which sets the standard of plays' performances they will exercise it the better for having come as near as may be to acting themselves. In the seminar they must prove their points of criticism, and as much accomplishment as they need for this— it will not be much, as for purposes of study only the play is to be halted far this side of staging— they had better acquire. We have assumed some power of dramatic expression to be a part of every

education ; here will be a test of its quality and
value. If a man disputes the conduct of a scene,
or the reading of a part, let him take over the part
or conduct the scene himself. The whole scheme
and purpose of the work implies that he can and
should. There is no division yet into actors and
audience. We are not concerned with effects, but
with causes and process—above all, with process.
And a third party, the student-dramatist, will find
his use in the work, not only as actor and critic,
but as the observer of both. For here is a performance in embryo ; and he is always to remember that only in its performance will his own
future work be complete.

How the
seminar
works

Let us outline, however roughly, the progress
of one of these seminars.

One supposes, first, a straightforward reading of
the play ; twice or thrice repeated, with the readers
varied. That stamps its meaning upon our minds
as far as the author's own words, barely assisted,
can convey it. The next step is to discover how
far we are all at intellectual agreement upon
the play's meaning, when expressed in other words
than the author's, upon its implications and applica-
tions. There is room now for a general discussion,
a sort of " second reading " debate. The tact
of the conductor will be taxed, no doubt, to keep
this within reasonable limits. He must remember
in particular that the discussion is only of value
as a preparation for the next stage, in which the
seminar's characteristic work begins. However,
in six plays out of ten the issue is apt to be so closely
defined that agreement upon it may seem almost too
easy to come by. And the next step is to demonstrate how the importing of emotional values may
completely upset conclusions arrived at without their

consideration. This is the moment when the play must be brought to life by a selected body of interpreters. They will need to band themselves together for its integral expression and, so to speak, for its defence. For their interpretation—the importing of their personalities—will certainly give offence to the intellectual agreement upon the play. This is bound to be so, all intention apart. The interpreters may protest that they remain in perfect agreement, that this is merely how they express the preliminary opinion arrived at in common. Now the measure of the difference between the two things, as it will appear to the critical listener, is the measure of the importance of the human factor in any problem. If the critic had not exercised his brains on the matter first, and in conjunction with the interpreter, he would probably take the protested identity of opinion and expression for granted. But now it will seem to him almost fantastic that men can so deceive themselves as to imagine this thing they so apparently *are* to be of a piece with their mental pretensions. Well, let him analyse and prove the discrepancy if he can. We are now at a point where mere argument no longer avails ; it would only lead to a re-stating of agreement. So the objector must illustrate, must interpret in his turn. And then he in his turn will provide the exhibition of inconsistency.

But at this stage something else may happen. *The absorp-* The process of interpreting may work a genuine *tion of the* change of opinion ; first, and perhaps but half-*interpreter by* consciously, perhaps quite unconsciously, in the *the play* interpreters themselves ; then, by the light of the interpretation, in their critics. We are trenching now upon discovery of the extent to which an actor is a dramatist's collaborator, of the extent to

131

which an idea is in such a case only completed by its expression. This is slippery ground; but upon it, for whatever reason, the biggest playwrights and the poorest stand closest together. The emptier a play, of course, the more easily can an interpreter of creative instincts fill it with his own personality ; though this habit, it may be said, will as a rule seriously disable him from the tackling of more commanding stuff. On the other hand, the greater the play the more easily it will accommodate the height and breadth of an interpreter's legitimate endeavour. One turns for instances to the recognized classics, the Greeks, the Elizabethans, with their manifold and divergent interpreting by scholars and actors, both. We must remember, though, that distance lends these things the enchantment of an obscurity of their surface meaning, even while time may deepen and widen the bearings of their philosophy. The Elizabethans were not drawn to dispute, as we are, over "Hamlet," because the indications of the character had a contemporary, perhaps a very topical, clearness to them. Language alone is an uncertain register of all but the simplest and most material things. It loses veracity with time, as a colour fades and turns. We must in any case translate a poem or a play from the past even as we translate it from one language to another; and where the meaning of the original, made misty by time, can be questioned the translator has freer play. He may even make a mistranslation his own, and so bind us to it that we reject its correction—witness our preference for the mistakes in the English Bible. And it appears therefore that the great playwright is not he who can define his meaning most rigidly, but he who has planted in his play ideas vital enough to bear development, to demand

132

development, yet to defy both belittling and falsification. This may seem an easy truism to enunciate. But when we come to its application, under such conditions as our seminar will provide, its import is apparent and will become the high test of every play's value, and our response to it a measure of the drama's educational use.

The kernel of the seminar's work will be the discovery and development with regard to each play of the possibilities of this collaboration between playwright and interpreter. Note that the discovery must always be a fresh and a genuine discovery. It always can be; for each new body of interpreters is new material to be worked in, even though the play itself be well quarried; and so the development, if genuine, will differ naturally with each change of interpretation. Nor will it matter if the would-be collaborators range for a time widely and perversely beyond the limits of the dramatist's intention. They will thus best discover their own limitations. The retreat within its obvious boundaries, the reaction to a sober consolidation of expression, may then exhibit the play's own. It can be seen—given a play well charged with vitality of idea, a well-balanced fluid gathering of interpreters and critics, and a conductor apt both to provoke differences and to reconcile them, with a keen sense, too, of the direction and goal of the work—what scope there is for a struggle of minds and temperaments. From which obscurity some enlightenment should come.

What sort of a play should be selected for this purpose? It is easier to determine the various sorts one would rule out. A play whose characters were unresponsive to analysis by nature or by fault would be of little use to us. A play making early demands for its realization upon sheer rhetoric or external

133

graces would not be of much more. It is odd to be ruling out *A Midsummer Night's Dream* and, say, *The Doctor's Dilemma* for very much the same reason, but one reasonably could. For a lesson in beauty of diction *A Midsummer Night's Dream* is hardly to be surpassed. The would-be political public speaker who neglects the study of the technique of *The Doctor's Dilemma*, of *Major Barbara*, and *Man and Superman* deserves to remain ineffective. But not the greatest bardolater (as Mr. Shaw has nicknamed the tribe) would contend that the characters of Theseus, Lysander, Hermia, and the rest would repay much analysis (Bottom the weaver might !); while most of the Shavian drama calls for interpretative collaboration of a sort so clearly defined in the text as to be scarcely susceptible to argument at all. That is to say, there is apt to be very little written between the lines.

Now, in choosing a play for our seminar this particular quality of workmanship will obviously be valuable. If it is to be found exemplified in Shaw's work we should look perhaps to *Candida*, *John Bull's Other Island*, *Blanco Posnet*, and in parts of *Getting Married*. But the supreme exemplar of the method is probably Tchekov, of whom it may almost be said that he has put more between the lines than in the text itself. The words of *The Three Sisters*, or *The Cherry Orchard* are indeed but symbols, each sentence merely a prescription by which the actor prepares the intended effect, very much more being left to his perception and discretion than the forceful elocution of his speeches based upon a generally correct realization of the character. When Mr. Shaw, therefore, describes his *Heartbreak House* as a fantasia in the Russian manner, and thus seems to challenge comparison with Tchekòv, he omits (no doubt be-

134

cause it doesn't greatly interest him : his attention is to content) consideration of this question of technique, a most important one for the interpreter. The one method of writing, it may be, can result in as good a play as the other ; though, by the rule that the more you ask of an actor the more you may get from him, Tchekov's work, complete in performance, will acquire certain virtues that Shaw's must lack. One might offer as a proof of this the contrary demonstration that while Tchekov's plays inappropriately acted are quite unintelligible, Shaw's need never, at least, be misunderstood. And though we class his plays mostly as modern comedy they call primarily for heroic treatment.

An instance of the two methods much less violently contrasted can be found in the work of a single author by turning to the volume of Sir James Barrie's plays containing *The Twelve Pound Look* and *The Will*. Apart from the fact that the first is a masterpiece—had one to instance perfection on this scale in its adaptation of means to end one could hardly do better than name it—while the second is, perhaps, worthy of its author but no more, it is most instructive to project both plays towards performance as one reads them ; one should, of course, never read a play otherwise. *The Twelve Pound Look*, for all the necessary sparseness of its dialogue, is essentially a " full " play. You gather that what the characters say is but a small though significant part of all that they think and feel ; you follow them off the stage and back through the years with ease ; half a dozen more plays, it seems, might be written about them. While in *The Will* all is well said and well done ; but then and there it is obviously done with.

Of two such plays, therefore, it is patent which is

the better fitted for the purpose of our seminar. One could continue, of course, to canvass through modern drama for the more and less suitable ; and the individual method of each dramatist and his variation from type will always be worth consideration in the light of any particular seminar's composition.

" Strife "
quoted as an
example

But for a normal illustration of the work let us imagine the collective studying of such a play as John Galsworthy's " Strife." It would probably answer the current demand very well. It is not over-encumbered with dialogue. The characters are within the personal observation of most of us, and in themselves not primarily difficult of assumption. It is a play of no very violent twists and turns ; delicate, occasionally, but not over-subtle in its psychology, homogeneous in idea, its two main divisions are simply contrasted, and its general effect is one of mass. There would be no need to spend much time in arriving at intellectual agreement upon its meaning. This is plain enough. Objective criticism of its characters might detain us longer. It would be pertinent, of course, to discuss their type and their truth to type before impersonation began to individualize them. But without much delay we could begin to bring the play to life.

So the struggle can start at once. In the first act typical difficulties and opportunities alike present themselves. For most of the parts there is little material in the way of dialogue. The interpreter will have a hard task to hold his conception of the character intact and to strike its note surely when his turn comes. He will be caught at underemphasis—an offence against his fellows, since it denies them support; at over-emphasis—a sin against the unity of the scene if by any too highly-coloured effect he shadows his part's surroundings

136

in which effects of greater importance may be more patiently preparing. The discovery that all parts develop in a different ratio according to their nature and their importance to the play, that no parts develop with any constancy of pace (it may be necessary to wait half a scene, half the play, and then, in a few seconds, gather up all the preparation and elucidate its intention in a sentence or so, for that matter by a change of attitude or a gesture)—this discovery may well reduce any novice to a puzzled impotence. The discernment of one's place in the scheme, patent to the looker-on, is lost in the excitement and concentration of partaking. Tact of emphasis is hard enough to come by ; let any pianist bear witness. But when to this accuracy is added the further demand for an observant variety and so apparent a spontaneity that the qualification must be forgotten ; and when this whole performance has to be given upon an instrument so fallible as one's emotional self it will be seen that something more than sheer skill is needed.

Moreover, the sparsely-speaking part encourages *The listening* the interpreter in vagaries. He has spare time to *part* fill in. He must at all costs keep the silent intervals alive by presenting in them a clearly defined figure. And here the dramatist may most easily have played him false. It is simple, if you can draw character in dialogue at all, to draw it in dialogue that is both sustained and consecutive. One differentiates the terms because so many dramatists in practice do not. For fear of letting a character slip from their grasp they will fill up every crack of its development, so to speak, with words ; and thus they rob it of life past any actor's recovering. For words are but a part, at times the minor part, of the true dialogue. Nevertheless, the unspoken things are not the actor's concern merely ; the dramatist must not leave them as a provision of empty spaces and opportunity. He can, and he must, by implication convey to the actors these complementaries of the dialogue. If he cannot dictate them positively—and this is difficult, for words are his weapons of precision—he must at least safeguard his characters against mis-interpretation. There are means enough to this end. The spoken sentences can, of course, be made to do it by the form and the colour of their phrasing quite apart from their surface meaning. But the elaboration of physical " business " will, on the whole, fail one here. There are, naturally, certain things which can be marked to be done without comment, and if their doing is effectively placed they can be eloquent. There are things of which later comment will complete the significance. These are legitimate devices and may be made *The placing* positive indications of character. But to detail, *of a character* for an instance, the gestures, the expression of *in the scheme* face with which a man shall receive the news of *of the play* his son's death is, for the dramatist, as great a mis-conception of his share of the whole task as it is if he describes his heroine as five foot seven in height, with golden hair and blue eyes. If these are *essentials* for the heroine it is a doll he wants, not an actress. In the same way all *method* of expression is a matter for the actor, and to dictate this to him is as bad a crevice-filling as the multiplication of words. No, the dramatist's part is neither so obvious nor so simple. He has certainly to indicate to the actor what to express, but the freer he leaves him as to how to express it the more he demands from the actor and the greater must be the value of the response. Therefore, for him the method of implication is the right one. And apart from the

138

primary uses of dialogue, of things said by a character, there are the things said in reply, the things said of one character by another;* there is, more importantly, the position of a character in the scheme of the play and the relation to its fellows— all these devices are open. The actor should find himself like a piece on a chess-board, with only certain moves and certain attitudes possible for him. This ascertained position must be the foundation of the actor's study, as it was of the dramatist's intention precedent to any writing of dialogue at all. There is, finally, the character's play of movement and his relation, active and passive, physical and emotional, to the particular scenes he is a part of. This it is the actor's chief work to elaborate. The dramatist must have prompted and safeguarded him by the scheming of the scene. Its writing, as we have noted, is only a part of the business. This scheming can be done simply, it can be done subtly. In its simplicity it is probably achieved by most dramatists by instinct ; by what we call, in this connection, the dramatic instinct, the gift without which even the best writers fail to become tolerable playwrights. It is shown in never forgetting that your character is there, in losing no chance, when, by reference no less than by speech, he may be observed and felt. He must pull his weight in the scene. He must be kept consistent, denied no opportunity that he

* Though these again are either less valuable when the play's whole account is made up if they are so positively the dramatist's own point of view, so obvious an indication to actor and audience as to re-dramatise the character that says them, or if they introduce yet another complication in the allowance that must be made for another dramatised point of view. This last plan is legitimate and amusing. If Browning had made *The Ring and the Book* into a play he would, seemingly, have committed himself to this method. But it wants using sparingly, or with great skill.

would not deny himself. He must do nothing misleading; nor useless—for that will be misleading.
He must be used with economy : that is to say, he
must have no empty moments. There must never
be a time during the scene when, however silent the
character, it is not possible to ask " What are you
thinking ? If you did speak, now, what sort of
thing would you say ? " ; and when the actor could
not reply, but must reply according to the dramatist's intention. A character that is not a living
part of the scene is a dead drag on it. But all this is
simple—the commonplace of the dramatic art.

The apparent development of plot from the characters and scenes themselves For subtlety in this scheming of scenes we may
turn for an example to any of the four great plays
of Tchekov. Of them it is possible to say that the
interplay of motive which makes up the action so far
transcends any mechanical rules, is so much the
outcome of the idiosyncrasies of the characters concerned (though one doubts if any play could be so
written, yet it does seem as if the meaning of the
whole were but a quite fortuitous outcome of the
independent action of the parts), that the scenes are
positively unactable, their sound makes no sense,
unless a basic understanding of the characters has
been achieved ; and this achievement is only to be
reached by those who can relate characters and
play itself to the larger drama of Russian life, of
which Tchekov's mind was so perfectly the mirror
that he interpreted it as he would have his characters interpret the purpose of his plays, the broken
lights (never too broken if true) finally giving the
full view. No other plays known to the writer ask,
as Tchekov's do, for the collaboration of the actor.
It is hardly too much to say that they are *libretti*
waiting for music. Yet they are masterpieces of
their kind, and of a very noble kind. It is no de-
140

gradation to a dramatist to confess himself so dependent. They are a technical triumph, to say no more. For, granted they can be misinterpreted, there could be no doubt then where the failure was. And if, as complete works of art, they defy translation, since so much of their beauty and purpose cannot be written down, cannot be packed, so to speak, and freighted; that is true of most fine poetry, too. They can stand, however, to anyone as object lessons. One finds in them an example of the length to which the method of unsustained and inconsecutive dialogue can be carried. It does not follow, of course, that there is not sufficient virtue in a more moderate use of the device. We need not try to define how much material should be left in the rough for the actor to mould, nor what should be the exact proportion of implication to definition in speech. Even if some law were discoverable— like the one which controls the floating of an iceberg, two-thirds to be submerged to one above the water—we should get more fun from our ignorance of it, and from the topplings that must result from the empirical practices of art.

But—and so to end this long parenthesis— it is easy to see how much of a dramatist's skill must go into the implications he provides for the more sparsely dialogued characters, and what skill an interpreter needs to discern them. And in such a play as " Strife," for instance, it matters very much that they should be accurately discerned.

We have said that it is a play of mass effect. *Mass effect* It may seem to go without saying that a dramatist has no right to employ masses without being certain that in themselves they will be effective. But one can conceive of good plays—and find plenty of poor ones—in which minor parts do little more than

141

" feed " (to use the expressive theatre slang) the protagonists. The characters may be deliberately chosen
and placed so that they are negative, inarticulate,
appear for a minute or two on a particular errand,
then disappear for good, are anonymous almost.
In this case their interpreters' discipline, and a
sensitiveness in response or contrast to the tones
or moods of the dominant players, will be the most
important thing. And incidentally a play of this
sort will be the least suited to co-operative study.
But in a play like " Strife " not one of the characters
is negligible. The effect of the whole is quite
genuinely made by the right co-ordination of all
the parts ; the meaning of the whole is only to be
reached by a correct accounting for all the values,
and if the sum is wrong it is little matter where
it is wrong. We speak of an ideal " Strife " and an
idealized interpretation ; but, of course, no play
was ever so perfect that it did not encourage a little
maltreatment, no criticism ever so refined that the
erring interpreter had not his own case against it.
We must know what to aim for, however, and when
our object is simply study we may aim high, and
aim vaguely even. We have not a performance to
think of, with all the imperfections, of dramatist,
actors, and audience countering each other, and an
air of human tolerance—a " will to enjoyment " en-
veloping it all. Performance, as we shall see, stands
finally for accommodation, compromise, and a unity,
forced perhaps and unreal. But students in our
seminar may have their free fling between the best
and the worst possible. They can measure themselves very well in these scenes of mechanical complexity, but, on the whole, of psychological simplicity (of a familiar psychology, anyhow), both by
their own ability to conceive and sustain character

142

and, critically, as against the play's own capacity for expression ; once, by change and change again, by each battling his way to acceptance, the likeliest exponent of every part has been found.

We are now in sight of the branching of the paths of study and production. We should note, incidentally, that a cast for the performance of a play, while approaching their task at the beginning from this same standpoint of study, would, for extrinsic and intrinsic reasons both, not be committed practically to such a mêlée of wits as may profit the students. The actors will be from the beginning each in his allotted place. They will criticize the play and not each other. And, having forgotten, as the saying is, more than the students have learnt, or are, many of them, likely to learn, dispute about technicalities will mainly be passed over. They will come much more smoothly to the point where dispute ceases and identification of play and interpreters begins. *Where student and interpreter part company*

And it is just on the nearer side of this point that the paths must branch. The student will never need so to identify himself except, recoverably, for the purposes of his study. The distinction involved is a fine one, no doubt, and operative more in the collection of a class or a play's cast than over individuals. As we shall see, and as indeed is obvious, a company performing a play has by then abandoned all critical sense. It must be the conductor's business to see that the seminar as a whole never does so. In questions of sheer effect, too, the student will hardly be concerned, in the ebb and flow of feeling—for instance, among the crowd of strikers in " Strife." And a final advantage of this play and its kind, for the purposes of study, is that such questions can be long left aside without the main interest

143

being lessened. There are many where such effects are an integral part of the play's inner workings ; and many, admirable for study, classics like the "Agamemnon," for instance, where the ritual, the swing and the sound of it, is bound very closely with the play's mood and actual meaning; like the Molière farces, whose volubility is most intimate to their character. Then the study of all poetic plays, and of prose plays, too, for that matter, will hinge —for some more, for some less—upon beauty of execution, without which they cannot be brought to life and so made, according to our definition, the subject of true study at all. But they are not to be ruled out as good educational material for this reason. Rather the contrary. It is for the student to realize—and over no sort of play does he need more to realize—that an understanding of a poet's work lives upon sympathy with its passion, and that inarticulate sympathy is sympathy stillborn.

It goes without saying that the choice of a play should depend to some extent on the composition of the class and the disposition and abilities of the students, equally without saying that every sort of play—every play, one might say, ideally—demands a different method of study. It must be faced, too, that just as in every instance the path of study and production branch at some point, so in the choice of plays the interests of the general student and the embryo actor will not, after a while, remain identical. The actor, intent upon the completer processes of production, will look for plays upon which he can most quickly try his skill of expression ; the student will profit more by those which give him the greatest variety of mental and emotional exercise. One does not conceive of " Love's Labour Lost," "A Midsummer Night's Dream," or " The School for

Scandal " being very fruitful themes for dissection and abstract discussion. But the would-be actor, though he were chained to a table and bidden rationalize his work to the last degree possible, would find ample opportunity in them for the development of his sense of lyrical speech, of comedic phrasing. Certainly these are things that he will study to some extent apart as technical exercises. But one must not try to do too much of that sort of work *in vacuo*. The would-be actor is to be kept from acting till the very last moment. But no one would advocate that he should not be given a chance to co-ordinate his faculties before he takes the plunge ; a swimmer—to follow the metaphor through—needs to feel his way in the water before he strikes out.

This brings up, however, a question of quite *The misuse of* another sort with regard to the choice of plays. *the classics* The familiar classics—the finest in most cases, that is to say—are at the present time shamefully misused in the interests of education. Nothing probably has so vitiated our taste for Shakespeare as the commandeering of his great passages for exercises in elocution—unless it be the cold-blooded dissection of his plays in the professorial study.* If the classics are to be kept alive their expounders must first of all be kept alive to them. They must preserve for them, as far as ever they can, a freshness of eye, ear, and mind. It would be well, then, for an actor never to have looked at " Hamlet " in his student days at all. He had far better break

* This latter process applied to the great Greek tragedies robbed them of the very semblance of plays, even, apparently, in the minds of the professors themselves. Professor Gilbert Murray's restoration of Euripides to his place as a *playwright* was a far-reaching service.

his shins over "Troilus and Cressida." And for "A Midsummer Night's Dream " and " The School for Scandal," as we called them into service a while back it would be better to read " The Sad Shepherd " and Farquhar's " Recruiting Officer." The risk that a nascent judgment might thus be permanently perverted would be very small. If neglected masterpieces were rediscovered by this plan, all the better : the student adventurers, just out of their apprenticeship, would be their best possible sponsors. There would rather be a certain danger, perhaps, that, flung upon examples of second-rate classic work, the student might fall back bored and defeated ; but that would not greatly matter. And, quite apart from the question of the degradation of fine work involved in their educational misuse, the importance of the classics as factors in this sort of training is over-estimated. They are more delectable meat for maturer years—for more catholic minds—and the great thing is not to blunt a man's love for them.

The would-be actor admitted to the playhouse at last

It would be well, too, that with their near approach to graduation the would-be actors should be kept from the use of the plays, classic or modern, which were a part of the repertory of the theatre itself, and from the influence, therefore, of the performances of them. For their last year's work, and for that only, these particular students, and these only, should be brought into the closest touch with the theatre as playhouse—of which side of the institution we have yet to speak. But we must presume the existence there of favourite, perhaps famous, actors, who will possess methods and mannerisms of their own. Now it is a truism that one *copies* nothing from an artist but his faults. The tendency of the student to copy will always be great,

146

increasingly great if in this last year he becomes an understudy ; nor much diminished, even though, his training done, he goes to another theatre to play those parts which the favourite actor has made his own, unless he has been deliberately kept from studying them during his pupilage. One needs, indeed, some very definite countervailing influence if study of any sort in dramatic schools is not to result in the transmission of the very individual methods of half a dozen popular actors in an ever-widening circle of impoverishment. And the more the popularity is buttressed by real ability the harder it will be to get from under its shadow.

By this time, of course, the students who are to graduate as actors will be practically cut off in their work from those that are to pass out else-whither. Their study-seminars for this final year might well be quite self-contained affairs. They should now be set to the task of bringing plays to production. Groups should be formed for this purpose, and split up, and differently formed as often as possible, by the teaching authorities. But the group might well elect its own conductor-producer, and the work should be seen no more till it was at some near stage to completion. The plays, as aforesaid, should preferably not be familiar ones. But, further, the groups might flesh their steel upon completely untried plays, and upon untried sorts of plays ; though, as prentices themselves, they had better not be confronted too exclusively with the mere prentice work of dramatists. There is some-thing to be said, of course, for an occasional student production, home-made from beginning to end ; student playwright, actors, costume designers, and scene-painters, too. But let us sharply beware of too much indulgence in that sort of thing. It has a

147

specious value. At its best it brings all concerned into too narrow a circle, and by lowering their standard of achievement may, at its worst, cocker them up into a lamentable state of self-sufficiency and conceit. The plan works well enough with amateurs. It is, perhaps, the plan of all others for them. They should be master of the processes they employ from A to Z ; it is in this grasping of the whole that their enjoyment of the art will lie. Not for them, it stands to reason, the closer concentration and more hardly earned triumph of the expert. They must cultivate an art as primitive man cultivated his ; then their simple pleasure in their own success will be attractive and allowable. But those who mean to take a worker's place in the organized republic of the theatre, and to be inheritors and sharers of the achievement of their forbears and fellows must, from the beginning, measure their own weakness against the finest strength they can find.

Experimental work for students in their last year For students in their final year plays to experiment with could without difficulty be found. We shall see later how this requirement will fit in with one particular need of the theatre as a whole. And of plays experimental in themselves one may make yet another use. We must remember always the conservatism that any institution breeds ; and the better it is organized, the more comprehensively, the stronger will be the growth. Conservatism, if an eye be kept to its drawbacks, is not a bad thing for the drama. So much, at least, this book in its very theme supposes. The English-spoken drama certainly at this moment suffers from a lack of it— calls loudly for any sort of organization at all. But let us see, by all means, to a provision of the means of freedom, of legitimate revolt. For no one will

148

deny that students, graduating from this school to its playhouse side, or leaving for any other playhouse of the sort, will tend to accept, with little question, the routine they find there. Routine of action certainly they must accept. But the machinery of a theatre is so elaborate that no artistic activity need feel cramped by it. It is routine of mind that would be the danger. Some natures can always contrive to keep a freshness and rebelliousness of mind, and any institution will be lucky if it can attract and hold them, active and unspoiled. But for those readier to accept convention—likely, too, to prosper best by following it—it may be said that their fruitfullest time of individual development will be when they have finished their formal training, are pre-eminent on that scale, and have not yet had to sing small in competition with their elders. Now we have done our best, by every device, to keep the student actor free from the teaching which will force him, at the teacher's convenience, into a rut, into the deepest ploughed, directest way to some sort of accomplishment. We can do him a complementary service by setting him in this last spurt of his training at a few quite impracticable and impossible fences, in the shape of plays that are (as the saying goes) not plays at all, and at some whose title to practicability has been lost, or has yet to be proved. It is a pity even—so much is the routine mind to be dreaded in training—that he cannot come at these fences in company with the general student, with his (presumably) still less particularized point of view. And it would always be worth while to consider, instance by instance, whether the two interests could not be combined.

It does little harm, of course, to the general student to be working at a play in common theatrical use. Indeed, if he is slow of dramatic instinct, and unready at bringing the thing to life by impersonation, it may be a necessary help to him to have seen the play in full being and at its best. There need be little fear but that the method of work we have outlined for our seminars will effectively prevent their degenerating over such a play—as far, at least, as the slow student is concerned—into facile and flashy imitation of acting. But with the right, and a rightly assorted, collection of students it should be possible to find work of an unconventionally dramatic form which the student actor could approach, to his continuing advantage, in fellowship with minds more detached from the theatre, in its now narrowing sense, than his own. We can hardly over-estimate the benefit to everyone concerned of this assortment of minds and purposes. Particularism is the curse of the arts. In the theatre it is largely a needless curse, so direct is the reflection of life in the art's process. From the theatre as school particularism must at all costs be banished. The keenness of the actor student, with all his technical training so ready to his hand, would make of such a play as " Strife " too slick a mouthful altogether were he not to be checked and his cheerfulness disgruntled by minds more intent on the things themselves, which the play at its best does but reflect ; though, again, these minds might remain unperceptive of half the play's meaning were they not stirred by the brightness of its reflection in this keenness to interpret.

The limits of a play's use to the seminar At what point this mixed company will have made the most of " Strife " and its like, experiment must determine ; and, indeed, every such seminar should be in itself an experiment. A play, after all, is only complete in its performance to an audience.

150

It might sometimes be well, after lively discussion had thrown up the best possible cast for the play, to remit it to such a caucus for final shaping in terms of a performance, the whole seminar meeting again to consider it finally in those terms. Where this trespasses against the general forbidding of premature acting one must consider whether one should not make it one of those exceptions that are the life of all rules. Or one might possibly devise some pseudo-performance which this ideally critical audience could have licence to interrupt by their comments at suitable points. And the advantage in this connection of the " impracticable " play, or the play that was not a play at all, would lie just in its natural resistance to the ordinary conditions of performance. Set a seminar to work upon a Platonic dialogue, upon Lowes Dickinson's " A Modern Symposium " ; or, again, upon the " Evidence before a Royal Commission," the verbatim report of a trial, or a Government interview with Labour leaders—set them to extract from that sort of material its last ounce of effective meaning. The verbatim report in particular would have its use. It would furnish for the actor a chance to learn where the substance of drama lies, what it is that he must learn to divine beneath the finely worked surface, prose or poetry, of the plays that are plays. And the more critical mind may come to distinguish, in the light of an artistic test, poverty of matter, flaws in the fabric, pitiful fooleries which passed muster for good sense upon the important occasion itself, which would then have passed muster with him perhaps; but will not now, not in this laboratory where his faculties are fined to their utmost perceptiveness.

These seminars of play study, then, are to be

the centre of the school's work, the hub upon which the whole idea of the theatre as school revolves. It would be absurd at this juncture to try and plan their proceedings in greater detail. If the idea of them is vital they would in time develop in many forms. If it is not, then the centre of the theatre as school would shift, and with the shifting we should probably soon be back at our present conception of the theatre as playhouse alone—and, though it is unimportant, the writing of this book would have been wasted labour.

Subsidiary school work; lectures, etc. The subsidiary work of the school we need now do little more than catalogue. One looks for lectures on all sorts of subjects that come within the compass of the theatre's influence. These are more numerous, perhaps, than might be supposed. The history of the theatre itself is important to those who work for it, and of some interest as a side issue in sociology. The history of costume is akin, and here would be the proper centre of its study— for the making and wearing of clothes is no small part of its understanding. There is, too, more practical knowledge stored in the brains of designers, costumiers, and actors than goes to the compiling of dozens of prettily illustrated books on the subject. We should need, then, a lecture theatre and a library. There would also be studios, where practical work was done in designing and making costumes and scenery. But these would be in effect the workshops of the theatre as playhouse, and it would be a question how much time and opportunity could be given to these students, who would, one fears, be apt to throng them rather overwhelmingly if no barriers were put up. In this connection several things must be considered. Training in the elements of design in drawing or

152

painting is, of course, no part of the theatre's business. Students would arrive so far equipped. How much further they could be usefully taken by working at costume designs on paper or at scenery in models it is hard to say, but probably not very far. Facility in making pretty pictures on paper is just what the theatre does not want to teach them, and a reliance upon the good effect of model scenes is a trap in which it is fatally easy to be caught. On the other hand, it is clear that dresses cannot be made and scenery painted in bulk merely for practice. The likely solution would be a system of " going through the shops " by a selected number of workers, who were giving their entire attention to the work; by an even narrower selection, there might be set up quite advantageously a system of definite apprenticeship. The advantages of this will be better seen when we come to considering the workshops themselves in connection with the theatre as playhouse.

CHAPTER IV: THE THEATRE AS PLAYHOUSE

THE division between the theatre as school and the theatre as playhouse is a convenient one for the purposes of discussion ; otherwise it should have only a very uncertain existence. On the school side of the boundary there should certainly remain the general students (as we have called them) and, needless to say, the more shifting crowd of people who might be working with special objects of study or research. Passing through it at the proper time would be the students for whom, in one way or another, the theatre was to be livelihood ; though not all of them, not many of them probably, could graduate into the playhouse service of this particular theatre. But for the fully qualified members of the theatre staff—actors, producers, designers—no boundary should exist.

No definite boundary between playhouse and school

For this will be the determining feature of the theatre as playhouse, its relation to the larger, the inclusive, entity of the theatre as school. Public performances will be found there, in quantity as in the theatres we now know, in quality improved we may hope. Plans for this particular improvement abound, and later it may be worth while to discuss their mechanism ; one must never underrate the importance in the theatre of the machinery of organization. But we are now to think not of plans but of persons. Let us imagine, to begin with, a playhouse company for whom performances will not be the one and only goal. For our playhouse is still a part of the theatre as school, part of an institution intended for the study of dramatic art and only incidentally for its exhibition—an exemplary theatre. Not, on the other hand, that we are to consider the acting company as teachers, who may (as did the gymnasium instructor of our schooldays) occasionally, as a relief to them-

154

selves and their pupils, indulge in a little display. It has already been made clear that teaching of that sort is to have the smallest part in the school. They rather remain students, fellow-students with their juniors, taking all the part possible in their study, an increasing part always as that study advances, but students also in their own occupation of the theatre as playhouse. It is only that the completion of their study there takes shape in the performance of plays, since (once more to insist on it) it is the audience which must receptively add the final touch to the work. This may seem the finest of distinctions, and, as we may allow, to the casual theatre-goer not an important one. But the difference involved in the admission or non-admission of the audience as an artistic partner is enormous ; a difference of point of view, of aim, of conduct— one after another all three will be involved.

To start, then, from the human foundation of *The sort of* the whole matter. What sort of man and woman *actor and* do we want for such a theatre company, and by *actress this* what inducements can they be caught and kept ? *theatre needs* There's an idea still about—it is not so much a fiction as a simple truth, a century late in expiring, kept alive perhaps by some touch of romance— that an actor's life is an agreeable artistic vagabondage. Young people condemned to a career of dull routine and old people regretting their lost opportunities of adventure are its chief fosterers. And, truly enough, for a few years a young man or woman will get little harm, may, indeed, gain a great deal of good, from the comradely atmosphere of the travelling company, and the chance of seeing, if they keep their eyes open, more of their own country, more of the world, and an aspect of both that office work and their summer holidays

155

would not give them. But a lasting career of casual labour is merely demoralizing, and the life of the touring actor just about as romantic as a commercial traveller's. One may take it for granted that any development of the theatre that is to appeal to actors and actresses must include their rescue from financial insecurity and vagabondage. Who can defend indeed that other part of the present theatrical system which obliges seven actors out of ten to calculate—if they dare do so certain a thing—upon an average, at best, of one week's idleness in three? Is it to be held that these haphazards of existence are what give the mummer that air of careless abandonment which is so popular with young ladies? Even if that were a necessary spice to our enjoyment of the play it would be rather hard that he and his wife and children (young ladies, he often has a wife; the creature even has children) should have to pay the price of it. Why should the art of acting, more than another, more than any other human activity, thrive upon fecklessness?

Success, of course—real success, such as may come for a while to the three out of ten—will carry a man out of this category. Not, though, that a lodgment in it denotes failure; that is the altogether damning and damnable thing. If it did one could honourably throw up the game altogether. But a man may do more than moderately well as far as his acting goes and yet be ill-done by indeed in the grip of this system (so-called!), which, at its best, offers him no permanence even of unsatisfactory employment. He is at the mercy of fashion, of the even more demoralizing speculation in fashion, and of fifty other uncertainties of livelihood—all avoidable. It is *bourgeois*, I suppose, to quarrel with such a condition of things. But it is possible that the theatre may be quite advantageously considered as a rather *bourgeois* sort of an art. One might add the query whether any art would be the worse for a few *bourgeois* virtues?

However that may be, the exemplary theatre—this theatre as school—would certainly need to attract a company of cultured men and women, who incidentally had learned to be good actors and actresses. No set of strange, egotistical creatures, living upon and consumed by what is called the artistic temperament, and caring for no solider sustenance, expert though they might be in curious emotional gymnastics, could, upon any count, find their place in it. One must allow for an occasional eccentric: lovable, fascinating in art as in life. Genius will arise, dominating, compelling, impatient of all regulation, apt, at any difference, to be up and away. But one may usefully question whether, in a calling where right regulation counts for so much, even genius will not welcome the freedom to work more intensely that the good ordering of a community gives. This supposes certainly the upbuilding of a community of sympathy, not a binding together by rule and regulation. But why is this impossible?

The rescue from vagabondage is even more called for in America than in England. The successful English actor establishes himself in London, and for the most part point-blank refuses to leave. It is pleasanter, better for his reputation, and pays better.* In America every actor, whatever his

The rescue from vagabondage

---

* Exceptions to this rule are one or two actor-managers of undoubted reputation whom the provinces pay and London does not. But I don't imagine they prefer constant touring. They choose to hold popularity they have won rather than tempt fortune in London. And any English actor may be tempted by an American engagement.

157

reputation, must tour—and does tour, for, perhaps, two-thirds of his career. For it is this that pays better ; but there is no reason to suppose that he likes it. One must not presume, though, that he equally dislikes playing the same part night after night. If he is a leading actor the presumption is that a part calling for three or four hundred repetitions is a good part; it is in any case hard for him to apply any other measure to it than that of its success. His next play may be a failure. Now, the penalty of failure will not only be loss of prestige and of money, but the worry—far outweighing, as a rule, any pleasure in the work—of deciding on and rehearsing for a third. He cannot be expected to despise the long run. And if the pleasanter life of a settled career in one theatre, even as we now know the theatre, is to appeal to the actor, as we now know him, it must offer, besides, some compensation for the inevitable dimming of his personal lustre by the greater light of the institution itself. And it must also balance in his favour the account by which, as against his being kept from exploiting his success to the popular limit, he is to be freed from the equally extreme penalties of failure. Then we may expect him to consider with a more open mind the purely artistic pros and cons. The money question itself should not be such a crucial one. A star of superb brilliance may, of course, fly off from any constellation either on this account or on that of personal fame ; if the temptation is sufficiently great this must be expected. But the average successful actor does not make so much more money than he spends in the making of it that at a time when his choice had to be taken between the certainty of an honourable competence and the many uncertainties of freedom he would not be very likely to choose the more settled career.

We might then without great difficulty draw the actor into new paths and attract to them, moreover, a more desirable sort of professional pilgrim than will be contented with the old. For though the life of the theatre is doubtless one of vocation, which many a man will follow against his better judgment, still the interaction between the desirable life and the quality of the talent that will recruit to it is close enough. And we shall reap an artistic reward—all of us—if we are right in believing that dramatic art prospers by the intimacy of its relation to social life, and so will be the richer for such a variety of new-comers. Something more, however, is needed than rescue from vagabondage and reorganization of work. It goes without saying that the present system, by which a theatre company is kept damnably iterating the same performance eight or more times a week, is to be utterly condemned. But one of the less obvious corollaries of the system is just as harmful and as stupid from every stand-point except the all-dominating one of finance. The matured actor's best chance of developing his art and observing its progress lies less in the per- *The need of* formances he gives than in his opportunities for *the actor to* study, and especially for the co-operative study *study more* (the only valid kind, as we have seen and must *and perform* further see) involved in the rehearsing of a play. *less* It is true that he may develop his playing of a part before an audience, but he can hardly then alter its main treatment ; apart from the disturbance to his fellow-actors he would no more choose to do so than does a general to change his dispositions under fire. The system, then, by which this precious time of preparation must be meted out to him as parsimoniously as if it cost (as it now does) the eyes out of his manager's head, and the whole valuable process be debased into money saving, time saving, thought saving drill is as much to be condemned as is the ceaseless reiteration of the play once it is successfully produced. No actor should perform a part of any length or importance more than four times a week : he should not appear at all, on an average, more than five times, rehearsals and performances should divide his time as equally as possible, and as much, and more, consideration should be given to his being fit to rehearse as now only can be (though it seldom is) to his not being too over-worked to play.

These are obvious considerations ; and there will always be theatres unable to sound this part of the problem of their relation to their art and the community any deeper than to abide by them: repertory theatres, well organized, with their time fully occupied in giving to the public as great a number and as wide a variety of performances as it will absorb. Nothing here said is meant to depreciate their work. They are to be hoped and prayed for. They are possibly the necessary foundation of the exemplary theatre that we are trying to outline ; for only in them, or something akin to them, will the actors attain that solidarity of purpose and that sense of being an integral part of the community, if but of that particular section of the community, which gives them its constant attention ; and only from the appreciation of such a theatre's work will come the lively interest in drama which will fill with the right sort of student the theatre as school. The repertory theatre is the only sensible theatre ; and it is at least a genuine theatre, not a shop for producing plays. But it may have the fault of all self-contained machinery—inadaptability. There is nothing to prevent and much to encourage such a theatre's becoming academic in the worst sense of that word. Discipline, organization, these are absolute needs. But no art rejoices in mere bonds. And for an art that depends so utterly upon its human factors the danger that in the daily round of routine these may become devitalized and their depression grow into the "sleepy spot" by which the whole fruit will be infected is one that must be pursued to its last hiding-place.

Therefore we look to do even better and to provide for the company and the whole staff of the exemplary theatre not only such an assortment of work and leisure as will let a man lead the ordinary citizen life, but such a constant connection with (one hopes) students of diverse dispositions, working with varying aims, as will keep him—in work even more than in leisure—well in the current of the public ideas, and emotions from which, and only from which, is the stuff for his interpretation of life to be drawn.

And as we are clear of the idea that the student's only use of the theatre as school would be in learning to act, let us also get rid of any that the actor of plays must necessarily be incapable of anything else. He will specialize in acting, no doubt. One would not actually demand of him a talent for making and painting costumes and scenery ; though by all means let him do either or both if he can. And the writing of plays he might equally not take to. But here let two things be remembered: the one, that there is a playmaking as well as a playwriting art. We have of late years been obsessed by the literary drama to the point of forgetting that acting can exist independently of the dictator-

The actor's need of other work than acting

ship of words on paper; and, if acting, plays.
Why should it need anything but the habit of close
co-operation and the conditions of artistic freedom,
which we look for in these theatres of the future,
to encourage our actors in the re-creating upon a
new basis of some form—of various forms—of this
self-contained drama? That there is talent for it the
work of pantomime and revue comedians has always
amply shown. A little too self-contained their work,
as a rule, perhaps; too individualist, even selfish!
But one can recall instances of remarkable co-operation. And that this should not be capable of extension, that the horizon of such work could not be
quite notably enlarged is a matter to be proved, not
by any means taken for granted. We may find any
day a quartet of comedians improvising fine foolery;
they have brought their faculties to a high pitch
to do it. Why should we not expect a company of
actors, as highly trained to a harder task, to produce
improvizations of beauty and of sense? They
would run upon lines of extreme simplicity, no
doubt. Literary association is the beginning of
complexity for the theatre; and, rightly balanced
by histrionics, this indeed lifts the whole art far
above the competition of any minor combinations
of its elements. But, if only that they may the
better take their part in the whole, these should
assert themselves all they can.

The second thing to remember is that the art
of acting could draw many people to it whom now it
keeps or drives away, because the actor's calling
demands such exclusive attention. A first-rate
actor, it is true, may not wish to do much else but
act—nothing but a little contributory teaching,
lecturing, producing, enough to ease the single
strain, to lift him from the rut. How far one can

be a first-rate actor upon any other terms than these is no doubt a question. It may be answered in terms of particular individualities ; it may become a part of the general question of double occupations.* That is too wide a one to trench upon here. But we may premise that, if this be a problem calling for solution, it will be at least more easily solved when, as in a theatre, the occupations could be cognate and complementary than when they would differ so widely as to bear only the present relations between a profession and a hobby.

But there is no good reason that a man should not be a first-rate actor and give equally serious attention to other work ; whether kindred or contrasted would be a matter for his own temperament and depend upon his capacity for boredom and the sort of stimulus he needed. That the art of acting would profit—quite apart from the question of personal relief or private advantage to the actor— by the chances of varying employment there can be no doubt at all. It is but an extension of the student's profit when he works, not cooped among his kind, but as one of a medley of minds and purposes.

And in other directions we must revise our notions of an actor's relation to his work and of our own relation to it. To many playgoers, even to hardened ones, the enjoyment of a play lies in the illusion created. To this the realistic methods of

The destruction of illusion as a step to appreciation

* Mr. Graham Wallas deals most enlighteningly with this problem in the chapter on Professionalism in " Our Social Heritage." He takes for his main text the question of teaching and the impossibility for all but a few devoted natures of giving a lifetime of unchanged yet fruitful devotion to the calling. It is possible that the social psychologist may come to think that exclusive concentration upon the practice of any art exhibits and develops a morbid disposition in a man.

163

production that have now found half a century's favour—a favour still enduring, though undermined —largely contribute. They find a parallel in the facilely emotional fiction for which the great spread of the habit of reading has provided a market. But this surrender to illusion, however allowable, is only the crudest form of enjoyment the theatre provides. And it is the cruder sort of acting that contributes to it ; the impersonative, not the interpretative. When W. T. Stead, at the age of sixty something, went into a theatre for the first time in his life as dramatic critic to the *Review of Reviews* one of his first remarks was that, if plays were to mean anything to him, no actor, having appeared before him in one part, must ever appear before him in another, or the illusion would be gone. This was charmingly childish and most instructive as a reduction to absurdity of that particular demand upon the drama. But it is hardly more sensible to ask the actor (after this one fine and free outburst) to limit his art to impersonative attempts to deceive Mr. Stead and his fellow children. They must really seek some other standard of enjoyment. This is easy enough to find, though for its full attainment a little serious attention to the technique of the art is certainly needed. Over any familiar play, indeed, we admit this standard already ; and far more readily over any opera, familiar or strange to us. Illusion in this last case can hardly be said to exist ; we are thrown entirely upon interpretation for our enjoyment. Now it is not only because of the fuller meal of sensation it provides, its appeal to the eye and its multiplied appeal to the ear, that we go to an opera a dozen times and to a play but once. We have from the first applied a more fruitful method of enjoyment to it. And we take to a performance of " Hamlet " no hunger for illusion. Many of us, no doubt, have sighed after that fatally lost chance of being one among the very first audience that saw it. Not to have known what was coming ! * But we now go to see the interpretation of a play which is so familiar to us that many of us could play prompter if need were; and however much its poor interpretation may fail to stir us it is not for lack of illusion, or because of its familiarity, that we come away disappointed. We are not necessarily bored by the fiftieth hearing of a Beethoven Sonata. Indeed, the closer our familiarity the greater can be our enjoyment if our knowledge of Shakespeare's work is balanced by some appreciation of the technique of acting. For then we ask more of the actor; and, generally speaking, the more one appreciatively asks (in this instance we ask in the negative sense of refusing to do without) the more one gets. The simplest way to some understanding of the actor's art is through knowledge of the plays he performs. Hence, the far more intelligent interest taken in acting in the days when the " classic " repertory was the basis of every actor's reputation. But one may also acquire a technical knowledge which will let us appreciate the interpretation of plays which are neither familiar nor dependent upon virtuosity of treatment—such a simple virtuosity as will raise the enthusiasm of a French audience for any finely

Our interest in inter- pretation the only one worth cultivating

* There is, of course, another side to this, exemplified in the story of the man in the pit who turned to his neighbour at the end of the first act of Irving's performance of " Hamlet," just as the great actor had withdrawn from before the curtain amid applause. " I beg your pardon, sir," he asked, " but have you ever seen this play before ? " " Oh, yes," was the answer. " And will that young man in black appear often ? "—" Fairly often." —" Eh ? " said the questioner, " Then I'm off," and left the theatre.

given screed of verse. This interpretative method
of acting that we desiderate will certainly differ so
much in degree as almost to seem different in kind
from the crude impersonative realism which belongs,
properly enough no doubt, to crudely realistic
plays: and of its elaboration more later. The
point now to make is only that any identification
of the player with the part implies a lowering, not
a heightening, of artistic achievement.

It is undesirably limiting for the actor to be
tied too strictly to acting; for he will lose thereby
catholicity of interest in the theatre. And upon no
account should he be allowed to attach to himself
in any theatre particular parts. True appreciation
of his work in them will only come by comparison
with the work of other actors. The idea that even
a new part should " belong " to the actor who
" creates " it is based upon the childish view of the
theatre. This has been reinforced by false methods
of production, evolved for inferior plays, leading to
paradoxical attempts to combine the weakness of a
part and the weakness of an actor so as to produce
an appearance of artistic strength. It is only an
appearance; and, even so, a deceptive one. For the
identifying of the actor with the part dissolves
rapidly—with an audience in whom sophistication
takes the place of education—into a loss of the part
in the personality of the actor. And so the ill-
gained illusion vanishes. But good plays not only
endure, they profit by variety of treatment. And a
good actor neither wishes the fact that he has been
acting to be ignored, nor looks to suffer by comparison with successors—unless they are to be imita-
tors also, when they may expose his insufficiencies by
thus revealing their own. And once we join our faith
to the interpretative as against the impersonative

method it becomes obvious that, as there is no final
and correct way of playing a part, so there are no
degrees of artistic dignity involved in a second and
third actor following the first. Therefore, once
this is recognized, a reasonable amount of change
in the casts of the plays given in any theatre will be
a stimulus to their attendance and a simple means
to the understanding of the actor's art. Of course,
players will always find their favourite parts and
audiences their favourite players in them. Some
indulgence in such fancies will do no harm ; for
of all places in the world a theatre is the one where
allowance for the human factor should be made.
It is the establishment of the principle that matters.

When we speak, then, of the theatre as playhouse *The relation*
we are to imagine it, not as a body separate from the *of the actors*
theatre as school, but rather as the head of that *to the*
body ; and of the theatre company not as being so *management*
much an assortment of well-trained actors, producers, *of the theatre*
designers as a homogeneous body of men and
women of the theatre, perfected as much in the
broad understanding as in the narrower accomplishment of their work. Specialization there must
always be ; people will do predominantly what
they do best ; it is a question of degree, but the
degree is all-important. Had there been in the
English-speaking theatre an uninterrupted development from the stock to the true repertory
system we should still, in accordance with the exi-
gencies of modern plays, have long left behind the
old divisions of the acting company into leading
men and women, juveniles, light comedians, first
old men, heavies, singing chambermaids, and all
the rest of the menagerie. How much further
upon this path of freedom the enlarged conception of the theatre as school would carry us is a

question that can only be satisfactorily answered by experience.

But from that question springs another. What share in the administration should be given to the company ? The pros and cons of this problem are being argued and fought in half the industries of the world at the moment. The theatre of our planning may look to profit by any general solution effected. It has few particular requirements to be satisfied ; but such as these are it is worth while to note them. It would no doubt be practicable for the theatre as a whole to be actually managed by a committee of the company themselves; practicable, but not, perhaps, very advisable. They would have to delegate most adminstrative powers ; policy would be their only effective province. And whether the devising of policy from such an interior point of view is an advantage to an institution whose very life lies in its reflection of the more actual life without its walls is to be doubted. The company's united influence could probably be most fruitfully exercised through advisory committees, which could appoint small sub-committees to deal with some of the administrative work of the theatre's internal organization. And they should certainly have a full say in matters that personally concerned them.*

* The classical instance of a committee having real power in a theatre is that of the one for the selection of plays at the Théâtre Français. I do not pretend to know how, in practice, this works ; but I seem to remember that of the many inevitable and, no doubt, salutary attacks upon an academic institution a large proportion of those levelled at the Français have been based on its alleged myopic attitude towards the new playwright or the unaccustomed play. Now, for one thing, committees that are large enough to develop parties tend always to a policy of compromise; that is one good reason for condemning them for such a purpose as this. And even if the plays chosen by a committee in which actors pre-

Another step brings us to the consideration of *The theatre* the permanence of the company's connection with *as livelihood* the theatre. Here again we have to consider both absolute conditions (as far as such things can ever exist) and the tendencies of contemporary development, very patent to us. The theatre's every effort at the moment is to establish fixed conditions of employment. Now a certain fixity is dictated by the work of such a theatre as this. Apart from the welcome that might be

dominated—even such sublimated actors as we are forecasting— were not always likely to be more remarkable for the superficial effectiveness of their acting qualities than the dramatic soundness of their content, there would always be the danger of a subtle and very fatal form of compromise in the disposition to give each leading actor (and one presumes a committee of leading actors only) his turn at a good part. " It's a long time since so-and-so had his chance : this will give it him." These words might not be spoken, but the understanding would be there. Nothing is harder to break than a ring of mutual interests, and the people composing it are the most powerless. It is cemented by such admirable qualities, but the cement does harden. Loyalty to comrades—what can be finer ? But one should give it no chance of undermining the higher abstract loyalty, harder to achieve—to the theatre itself. And even if in this supposition one is unjust it is never well to place upon actors themselves the burden of choosing plays. For they it is who must face the audience. When a play fails they are, as a rule, the last to be blamed. To be frank, one has known actors responsible for a failure, who yet, by merely giving that last evidence of their inadequacy for their task, the appearance of good men struggling with adversity, have roused the more sympathy for themselves ; and to the minds of the audience, who knew no more than the presentment before them, have transferred their own shortcomings to the play. Well, it is better this should be so, for playwrights—even managements—may look to the further future for compensation, while the actor cannot. To-morrow he must face his audience again. Better relieve him, then, of these re-sponsibilities. Let the failures always be accounted the manage-ment's bad choice, and let the actor take all the more credit for successes.

169

offered to an occasional distinguished guest to
lecture in the school, or—a much less likely event—
to appear in the playhouse,* and apart from the
probationary engagements of young people graduating from the school—and even these could not
conveniently be for less than a year—every member
of the company should be at least encouraged to
acquire a permanent interest in it. How closely
that interest would need to be sustained is another
matter. For several years, certainly, without inter-
mission. After that an insistence upon a sabbatical
year might be very advisable, and an even looser
system of furloughs might have to be devised to
meet the case of individualities whose work did not
improve, whose spirits were dulled by too strict
home-keeping. The theatre would run the risk
of losing them, valuable talents perhaps. It would
be better to take that chance. The theatre might
be the better for their loss, whatever the value of
these talents, if they could not accommodate themselves at least to self-discipline. Moreover, the
best way to hold such temperaments, and to hold
the best in them, is by the bar of an ever-open door.
    We may note, besides, that the wider scope

* Much less likely, because, however distinguished the actor
and warm the welcome, he could not hope to feel or be made at
home in his surroundings. For the company would have been
cultivating something more important than their own talents, and,
strangely enough, something more individual, but less dispensable,
than an amalgam of their personal talents : the genius of the theatre
itself, which will both exceed and transcend the sum of all the
personal efforts employed. Pitting himself against this—and he
would be compelled to—the most refulgent star would shine less
brilliantly than was his wont. There will be found in the " Scheme
and Estimates for a National Theatre " a very ample discussion
of this point. My mind abides by the plans there detailed ;
though I should trust less to financial than to artistic interests
to keep the actors tied.

of the work of the theatre as school would bring a
practical freedom in this direction that not many
mere repertory theatres could attain. Companies
nowadays that are organized for the production
of particular plays pass from the intensive worry of
rehearsals to the more or less extensive boredom of
the run. The great improvement, by which a
theatre could not only produce, but keep its plays
unexhausted and alive, would give it a more reasonably, but at the same time a very fully occupied
company. The management of such a theatre
would concern itself closely to avoid the waste of its
human material, and—with one peg to each hole,
but no more, being the economical rule—dislocation
of its nice arrangements would be a serious matter.
But, in a theatre of the still wider scope we envisage, if the work of the school and the amount of
pure study bore a proper proportion to the whole
it would absolutely force upon the institution not
only an increase of staff, but an elasticity of the
playhouse organization that would both permit and
encourage the wider distribution of activity we are
seeking.

What the earnings of the company should be we
need not discuss in any detail. Ordinary wisdom
makes one or two things clear. There will in time,
one hopes, be many exemplary theatres, but for all that
the example is admired and followed it will be followed with many a difference. No academy but becomes both a city to leave and a stronghold to storm.
We aim at the virtues of an academy; we shall never
escape being, at the least, accused of its vices.
Besides, the more thoroughly the exemplary theatre
fulfils its purpose the greater number and variety of
dramatic outcrops there will be, each with its appropriate market for its particular wares. And the exem-

plary theatres themselves must, for certain purposes, keep in the main market, if not of it. Nothing is less to be desired than the creation of institutions of a cold and cloistered superiority. Therefore the economic conditions under which the company would work should be better than (by which one does not mean only that the pay should be larger), but not essentially different from, those its individual members could find elsewhere. For instance, while an actor, devoting himself to such a theatre as this, should be assured of the decent competence which is his appropriate compensation for preferring to invest his abilities rather than gamble with them, there is no reason he should not be allowed to register incidental success in money value either within the theatre or without. His furloughs should serve this purpose among others, and he should be free to depart altogether without great sacrifice if he has served the theatre for, say, seven years or so, built up a claim to a pension or what not,* and if he then discovers, or it is discovered for him, that he does no more particular good by remaining. The branches must at any cost be kept living ; dead wood is even the worse in that it does not kill the tree. And what does this theatre finally exist for, but the profit of dramatic art generally ? Even the loss, then, of a member of its company, fully seized with its methods and ideals, would be presumably the general gain. A gospel is often spread by apostates.

One thing only—and that on principle—should perhaps be altogether avoided : profit-sharing, with its further implication of some sort of joint control. It is no stimulus to quality of production, the only

* " The Scheme and Estimates for a National Theatre " deals with this question, too, in some detail, and, I think, quite sensibly.

172

thing for which we are concerned to provide. There can, indeed, be no direct financial profit for anyone concerned in the exemplary theatre, and those who cannot work without the prospect of it had better go elsewhere.

In these days there is bound to be a committee somewhere. Let us then be certain of one thing : the foredoomed failure of the exemplary theatre, or of any institution of the kind, if a committee with administrative powers is at the head of it. *The fallacy of adminis-tration by committee*

Administration by a committee spells compromise, and not even that in its admitted entirety, but rather as a divided purpose which is the rightful damnation of all art. There would, no doubt, be much that committees might do in such a theatre, given consultative, legislative functions merely. They could usefully co-ordinate the various branches of the theatre's work. And a supreme body of this sort, a council, a board of trustees, would be the pattern link between the theatre itself and the community it serves, and as such valuable beyond question. Much of the theatre's mechanism must be devised, as we have seen, to keep this bond alive, automatically, unconsciously. And the key function of this supreme committee would be to do this actively and deliberately, and to see that all the time it was being done.

Conceive the theatre as part of a university and its governing body could be provided for more or less according to custom. This would be well enough as far as the theatre as school was concerned. But the functions of the theatre as playhouse make a case for the setting up of wider connections. We must cease to think of an audience as any haphazard collection of people that has paid for admission to a show. Truly under present conditions in big cities it is no more. We find one successful play stuck in a theatre for a year at a time, one section after another of the public is appealed to and exhausted, and the play is kept going for months maybe merely by the favour of the shifting hotel population. This last has increased greatly of late years, and has been particularly catered for (certain plays, one would say, find their chief support in it from the beginning), so that even the loosely established " connections " upon which theatres of better reputation used a little to rely have been dissipated. Any theatre, however, by a simple persistence in policy, may acquire a reputation which will encourage constant attendance, may secure an audience whose taste, while it may not amount to much, will but need in some simple fashion to find a voice for it to be a valid and valuable and a definitely consultable part of the theatre's constitution. A theatre manager talks now of the public taste. He deceives himself, for as far as the drama is concerned there is no such thing. He addresses himself to nothing so constant and integral as a public. He caters for the casual appetites of a mob. And more money is lost, more time and energy wasted, in efforts to calculate the incalculable than would suffice to endow a dozen theatres with at least the virtue of self-respect. Once a public is found and formed, though, it may develop a taste well worth respecting. The problem, then, will only be how to render it articulate; and, as far as our exemplary theatre's integrated public is concerned, how best (for one thing) to represent it upon the governing body.

An integrated audience and its representation
A big university might—and why not ?—run a theatre entirely for the benefit of its students: for those that would easily fill it as audience no less than for those going more intimately to school there.

174

In America, under such a scheme, undergraduate
bodies would almost certainly be given a voice in its
policy. In England, if such theatres were the
fruit of undergraduate enthusiasm, they would be
good ground for some experiment in this direction.
The working-men's theatres, so common in the
German-speaking countries, solve this problem, of
course, without any difficulty ; for they start, so to
speak, with an organized audience. The bodies,
by the bye, most likely to emulate them in England
are not the trade unions but the co-operative societies,
which have ample experience of the financing,
at least, of enterprises not so dissimilar in intention.
They might do worse than consider the question.

Still, sectional audiences, whether of manual
workers or shopkeepers, or doctors and lawyers,
or stockbrokers and bankers, are not in themselves
very desirable. A university audience would only
be better because it would at least represent a
section cross-cut through the whole community.
And there are objections to be urged against any
process which will produce in a theatre the atmosphere of the coterie. It would be a pity if a choice
could only lie between the intensity of a coterie
and the anarchy of the mob. Those theatres are
the most fortunate in their audience that have a
naturally mixed community of negotiable size to
draw upon. But how large a town must be to
provide a steady five or six thousand theatre-goers
a week is too crude a speculation. We must think
qualitatively in the matter ; we want a census of its
leisured class ; by leisured not meaning idle.
Taste in drama will be found to have a very direct
relation with industrial fatigue ; the worst audiences
being those with minds dulled by occupational
routine or debilitated by the lack of any.

When an audience can be adequately spoken for by those that represent the community in other public matters the problem is at its simplest. There is no reason that every sizeable town should not possess its theatre and control its theatre as it does any other of its public services. If the elected representative has not superfine taste in these matters it is probably as good as that of the majority of the electors ; if it isn't let them look to it, for perhaps he is betraying them in other imponderable matters as well. But with as great a reliance on expertize as they must have for their education system, for their local hospital (as close and as loose a bond as commonly binds this to elected authorities would be no bad measure of the relations of a theatre) we can easily see how the study and interpretation of drama might be brought under civic protection. And in the larger, less comprehensible communities, where sectionalism of some sort, of taste, class, or income, has more excuse to assert itself, it will be well to counteract its worse effects by assorting the governing body very variously indeed. This council (let us tentatively so call it) should certainly represent the audience of the playhouse, in whose interest also that of the students, past and present, of the school would be bound up. But it should stand, furthermore, for the theatre's dignity, and for the fulness of its public purpose.

The political influence of the theatre as a public institution Upon such principles, though with many variations in practice, councils of national, municipal, or university theatres might be formed. And it is worth while, in passing, to remember how extraordinarily wide is the play of the influence of any theatre that has the status of a public institution. The Théâtre Français is not only the possession of the Parisian, and a shrine that every provincial

Frenchman with a sense of his national culture must make pilgrimage to ; but is it too much to say that it stands for every visitor to Paris, that most visited of cities, as something far more vividly interpretative of France than the galleries, museums, shops, and hotels which are probably his only other haunts ? What deeper insight into the cultural tradition of France can the casual stranger hope for than he will find in this expressive place ? The Londoner takes his cathedral, his museum, and national picture galleries as a matter of course. Destroy any of them ; cover Ludgate Hill with shops, or Trafalgar Square with an hotel, and—for all that he may be but a passer-by of these shrines, not twice in his lifetime a visitor—he would as a good citizen feel impoverished and insulted. Has he not imagination enough to note the gap in his city's crown, where the national theatre should be ? Does it never occur to statesmen, in the intervals of their talk of the bonds of empire, that in a national theatre they could have a perpetual public meeting, so to speak, where the knot of a racial fellowship in apprehension and understanding might be tied with a better, because a less obtrusive, eloquence? * National theatres will come, no doubt, in England and the Dominions, too, and the political importance of such a one in London might well outshine the educational aspect which we have been at pains

* Moreover, we are out to fashion bonds for the English-speaking races that shall subject them to no political chafings. Why do all good Americans, when they die, go to Paris, and possibly even greater multitudes in this life ?   One answer, at least, is that there is very little to bring them to London instead.   As a result of its serious study in their schools and colleges more and more Americans of the younger generation are interested in the drama. But they travel to France and to Germany to refresh their ideas about it—never to England now.

to emphasize. No reason the outshining should harm it.

A council at the head of affairs; its constitution; its work

The problem of the right adjustment of an institution to a community's demands upon it is first of all the problem of how its governance should be constituted, of how, in the case of our theatre, then, its council should be made up. Only the principles involved need concern us, for this part of the institution more than any other is likely to depend upon the circumstances of its creation. There will be, however, certain dangers to guard against. In too many such councils is felt the weight, if not of the dead, of the dying, hand. For a museum or a gallery, where products of the past are to be tidily tucked away, this may not so much matter. But in the control of a theatre, which must renew its life day by day, to give even the power of responsible criticism too predominantly to minds that must more naturally judge the present by self-defensive memories than see it as preparation for a future which they themselves will not see might have a very deadening effect. Why should we not find in our council—along with government or municipal representatives and nominees of the vested interests of the older generation—the younger people voicing there their insurgency and discontent? To begin with, insurgency *within* such a body would be far more use to the theatre than attacks from without and the calling for revolution and secession would be ; not to mention that it would make for a healthier and a livelier time than usually falls to the lot of these august assemblies. The theatre would profit by being subjected at such close quarters to the impertinence of youth, by having to match its settled habits with the irresponsibilities of those whose interests were vested

178

mainly in their hopes for the future. Students' associations, bodies of teachers, church councils, chambers of commerce, manufacturers associations, local trade unions—any or all of them might be given nominations to the council. Certainly the students in the theatre as school should be well represented. But it would be a good opportunity for the devising of fancy franchises. Why should not a nomination be given to the upper forms of a neighbouring public school (the nominee himself perhaps being of full age)? Eton could probably be trusted under likely circumstances to return a Radical member. And electoral bodies, of course, could be formed without very much trouble from among the frequenters of the theatre as playhouse.

Into conditions of the council's tenure we need not go. Service for one year or three or seven or a lifetime ; the filling of vacancies now and then by co-option—these are important but mainly circumstantial matters. For numbers twelve is convenient, twenty full large. But the question of the council's powers is important and trenches on principle.

Such a body, we must assume, would find itself *The council* already part of a constitution. But within these limits *as the* it would be the legislative authority of the theatre. *conscience* It would be a court of appeal: the interpreter both *of the* of the constitution and of its own laws. It would *management* be the target against which the public would be invited to hurl their, no doubt, numerous complaints. And if it did not get complaints it would be its business to formulate a few ; for here would lie its greatest constant usefulness. The council should be the collective conscience of the theatre's chief official—the director, let us call him. The better a director the freer hand will he demand, but he will not wisely want that freedom which is isolation. In any artistic enterprise the difficulties engendered by criticism are genuine and great. Should it always be listened to ; should it ever be listened to ? Much of it is apt to be hopelessly uninstructed, much more of it—educate one's critics all one will—is unlikely to know when to make allowance for an artistic intention still imperfectly realized. The sponsor knows that if he does not resolutely pursue his own path he is lost, but it may be the wrong path for all that. Now the theatre is peculiarly susceptible to this sort of trouble in both its simple and its complex forms. To begin with, everybody thinks himself competent to criticize drama. He is a modest man indeed who will not venture to say whether a play or its performance is good or bad. And, indeed, it is true that every-body ought to be competent, in some degree, to criticize drama; there is nothing esoteric about the art. But one must remember that, as far as its acting goes, not only an actor's work is criticized, but inferentially his whole personality, his physical, almost his moral, being. We must not wonder that he, at least, is sensitive even to morbidity. Then, again, the co-operation in drama is so complex that it is seldom the incidence of criticism, however just it may be as a whole, will fall justly. To tell who, among the many contributors, is really responsible for failure, and what the degree of blame, needs a very acute eye indeed. The result, as we have else-where noted, is that, while criticism is ostensibly much counted on in the theatre, it is assessed, one fears, in very cynical terms. There are good notices and bad. Praise has a certain commercial value; blame may show in the balance-sheet.

Where public blame should fall But with immediate commercial considerations largely ruled out, as they would be in a theatre

where on the one side was a classic repertory with
its prescriptive claims and on the other every encouragement to be patient and not panic-stricken in
the pursuit of the untried thing, one would be inclined to urge a director rather to ignore casual
criticism altogether than to let his policy be in-
fluenced by it, swayed this way and that.   Every
soul in the theatre will be to some degree sensitive
to what is said about them—that is human nature.
Very salutary indeed that they should be, just so
long as the tenor of their work be not unreasoningly
deflected by it.   But the completer the co-operation
of actor, author, producer, designer, and the more
perfect, therefore, this organism of the theatre, the
more will praise and blame fall upon individuals
very haphazardly.   Let the head of the whole
affair, therefore, take all the blame to himself,
even though he leave the praise to be appropriated by
whomsoever it will comfort most.   Then he will be
glad enough, the director—if he is not to become,
on the rebound from subservience to the polite
mob, completely Bourbon—of a chance of that
frank question and answer, free from attack and
defence, which a finely working conscience can
supply.   And it is for this purpose that his council
should be chiefly fitted.   They would have power
over him, power to insist that their general policy
should be carried out, and if he would not, or if he
could not, bring them to like his interpretation or
amending of it, to make him resign.   But these are
mere penalty provisions.   This little parliament of
the theatre, working with good will, a wise director
being keen to consult it, its members having just
enough technical knowledge to quicken the dis-
cussions, would provide something like that collective mind which we have noted as the peculiar

virtue and strength of drama ; would be, in fact, in kindred sort, an epitome of our vision of the theatre at large.

The council would formulate criticism of its own, constructively one hopes. It would be the filter through which any formal public complaints must be passed. Its meetings should be, finally, occasions for the casting up of other balance sheets than those which the business management will bring before it. The council is the one body to which one can recommend the pursuit of self-satisfaction, since, taking no part in the work but being a part of the theatre, it must satisfy itself continually that the work is well done. And it might report yearly in due form to the general public its considered opinion of the theatre's progress, justify policy, explain good fortune and bad. It should, in fact, be for the public the Theatre Articulate, when there was need to say anything that good work could not say for itself. One would hope that its elections might inspire a little interest and a very definite confidence be reposed in it.

The theatre's director and his autocracy   The director of the theatre should be an autocrat, and that his autocracy may be effective it must be strictly limited. His council will tell him, for instance, to do what he likes. Without this freedom, illusory though it must sound, he could not hope to do anything at all. But the theatre, school and playhouse both, company, teachers, students, can never be disciplined into an automaton, carrying out orders without question, whatever the theoretical powers over them may be. And if any such institution could be so conducted it would lose just that spirit of individual and diverse effort which alone can keep it a healthy living body. Therefore all the director's ability to direct and to

182

manage (in the true sense of the word) will be needed, every ounce weight of it; and it must be free to flow in this one direction. He must be ready to justify to his council what he has done : if he had first to spend strength in persuading them to let him do it the division of effort would sink him. He will be glad enough, probably, to limit his freedom towards his subordinates, to lighten its burden both by regulation and by much delegation of power. A common rule for the students, common conditions of service for staff and company, will make his relations with them the easier. He must limit his powers, too, according to his own human capacity to work, and to work well—according, that is, to the bent of his talent. He is not very likely, for instance, to be an able financier. That qualification will at least, one supposes, not have a prominent place in the list when he is chosen. But there is no good reason, once the scope of the theatre's work is determined and the proportions of its budget adjusted, that its finance should not be a department almost, if not quite, autonomous, subject to the council's oversight alone. Encroachment upon a director's time by such matters would always be serious enough ; and it would be even more serious if, as is likely, he resisted the encroachment. Indeed, there are no matters in which a director, right for everything else, might, through sheer inability to change his spots, find himself more often in the wrong than money matters. He would be well quit of their burden.

Another limiting of power and lightening of *The choice* responsibility wants careful compassing. We must *of plays* deal at length with the problem of the choosing of plays. For purely practical reasons a director must, over this, if not delegate his powers, at least contrive to extend his faculties very considerably. He cannot hope to read a tithe, or even to consider upon a fair report a half, of the manuscript plays such a theatre is likely to receive. Yet this reading, and the encouragement or considerate discouragement of the author, is a most important part of the theatre's work, too important to be entrusted to private secretaries (who in any case would not be found capable of doing it), or to be left at the point of vague and polite letter-writing. Apart, for the moment, from the theatre's relations to the authors of established reputation, and from its concern with the play-writing work of its students, its touch with potential authorship, its fostering of a future supply of play material, must be a matter of great importance. It is not that one would try to " attach " playwrights to the theatre ; no return to even a remote likeness of the tamed hack, turning his stuff out to order, would be either possible (one hopes) or desirable. Even when a young dramatist has studied in the theatre as school the sooner he could shake free of its influence the better ; and if the teaching there is not largely a preparation for the shaking free it will be ill-considered. The best use any student can make of his knowledge is to forget—not the knowledge itself, but the fact that he knows it. And for nobody is it more important than for the dramatist to escape from this vicious tendency, common to all institutions and their inmates, to revolve perpetually in the circle of his own ideas.

The dangers of institutionalism   The danger to the dramatist is as great a danger to the theatre. There will be the classic plays, accepted material both for study and performance. These apart; if experience counts for anything, the institutional tendency is always to keep in with a school of writers, whose approximation to classic rank

184

would really seem to be their exceeding dulness; though we may more charitably see them as seeking safety—safety above all things !—in the empty prisons of form, beautiful houses once, but only for the souls that built them. This would be bad enough; but far worse is the trick by which, with an air half apology, half reckless abandonment, the institution brings itself up to date by the belated patronage of some revolutionary dramatist who, a generation ago, was thought to be going to do very desperate things indeed, but somehow has never done them, nor anything else worth mentioning. From such arrant foolishness some defence must be devised ; though truly it is not easy to find means whereby Satan shall be compelled to cast out Satan, to make rules by which the tyranny of rule can be broken. What one needs, of course, is simply an atmosphere, in which the human being can breathe freely and be human. Then men and women, who, strangely enough, cannot live without breathing, will be happy to come and work in it.

There clearly must be in any important theatre someone of authority and understanding whose chief business it will be to deal with plays and— more importantly—with playwrights. He must *The need for a play-reader of unusual importance* have authority, because a good man will not work without it; and only a good man, a man of individual ability, will be listened to by people whose independence of the theatre is their very virtue. And he must probably be given a playreading secretary, so that his mind may not be utterly dulled and his standard hopelessly lowered by the contemplation, day in and day out, of the miles of manuscript upon which there is no possible comment but " Thank you." Every few miles or so, for all that, there is always something worth the stopping to consider.

From the attempts of the younger generation, with their study of the technique of playwriting and, even better, their improved chances of some association with a theatre in being, the quite impossible play is disappearing. It is amazing, though, how literary men of distinction will still produce stretches of dialogue, divided into acts and scenes, which to them, apparently, look like a play and (if they ever read them aloud ; though that, one thinks, is doubtful) sound like a play, but have about as much relation to a play as a picture of a house has to the house itself. But out of the training in technical form for a literary generation or two will come, one hopes, what is far more valuable, its individualized development. This may, encouragingly enough, run into strange paths and to the use of untried material. Now it will be a not unimportant part of the business of the play-reader to help, if he can, to make these experiments fruitful. To-day the best intentioned theatre can do little but accept a play or reject it. The occasional middle course—suggestions of this alteration and that, or for a rewriting with a more practised collaborator—is looked on coldly by the author (if he can resist the material temptations attached to it), who only sees the individual growth of his idea cut mercilessly and soullessly to a commonplace pattern. And the manager does not often find the plan worth the trouble it involves. But while rejection is easy enough, acceptance of a play is, for any theatre, the beginning of responsibilities which few people and very few authors seem able to realize. Anything like a reckless policy of experiment is really not possible. For not only the author and the finance of the theatre is involved in failure. A play is, indeed, very much a house of art. The material, the de-

The difficulties of experimenting in play production

186

coration, may be fine. But unless you can be reasonably sure that its construction is sound, that it will not come rattling about their ears, you cannot in decency put a defenceless company of actors into it. It is true enough that very professionalized actors can often be unnecessarily hard upon plays, which are more simple in content or more tentative in method than the robuster stuff they have grown accustomed to. But the question of a play's effectiveness can never be begged. And if actors seek for this quality first of all, and are ready to ensue it rather to the neglect of others, it still does not follow that the test of professional performance is a wholly unfair one. For, after all, when it comes to the point of performance the actors have to make the play effective. And if the author has not supplied them with what they feel to be legitimate means they will turn to illegitimate ones. It may well be that in their anxiety they will, after all, have only obscured the play's true effects. Then the fault is, of course, theirs. They are interpreters, and have no right to force the dramatist's intentions into the mould of their absolute habits. On the other hand, if the dramatist cannot convincingly indicate to his responsible interpreters as they study his text how the promise of it (so to speak) will be fulfilled in performance he courts misfortune. And it comes to this, that in any theatre where the actors are at home but the dramatists are strangers there will be little disposition to run risks. It may be said that with eggs in so many baskets one breakage is no great matter. But it is also true that both the time and space for production of plays will be very precious in our theatre ; there will certainly be none to waste. We have tried to provide in the work of the school for a modicum of sheerly experimental production. But that alone will not take us very far, and it must rest with the play-reader of the theatre to see that no playwriter, bringing anything of dramatic value, is either let go quite empty away or, indeed, quite let go.

The play-reader's qualifications and powers

For the gist of such a task one can lay down few laws ; its very feasibility will depend upon the play-reader's personality. But such men (and women, though as yet, with their own worlds to conquer, more rarely) do exist : men whose personal ambitions have been absorbed in an unselfish regard for their art. Theirs are not very dynamic natures, perhaps, but they are receptive and sympathetic. They have dropped the burden of their egoism, have broken the many mirrors of their youthful minds. If ill-luck has left them disappointed that trait may yet be sweetened with humour. They look now to find their account in the passing of the torch to swifter runners.*

The play-reader would have behind him all the resources of the theatre, within which there is every sort of close collaboration making for the completed drama except this one. The playwright necessarily works elsewhere. For all the association of his student days, for all the active collaboration that he must welcome in the completion of his work, if he does not, in its initiation and development, keep both a solitary mind and a mind in contact rather with realities than shows—never with the show of shows at least—he will have nothing of

---

* Such men are to be found in most universities. But there the contact with a monotonous succession of immature minds may dull them till in time they react to nothing save the obscurities of their own ; and the soft nature grows softer or the hard harder. But to be dealing with fully, variously developed men is another matter.

188

value to bring, nothing that could not be better improvised within the theatre walls. It is literally true that a fresher freer drama could be generated by actors and actresses trained to elaborate variations upon accepted themes than results from the formal literary interference of the dramatist, who, by re-fixing the worn subjects and phrases in would-be novel forms, nailing them down once more in the outline of a play, does but impoverish and deaden the theatre's art.

Our problem, however, is how to give the play-wright backing, even when it must, by force of circumstances, fall short of a complete production of his play. We are concerned here mainly, of course, with the adolescent playwright, so to call him ; still adolescent in his art, whatever he may be in age or other education. It is not the cheap commodity of advice we see being handed out to him; not that alone, at least, though when that will suffice the play-reader can be free with it, and, one fears, a poor play-reader would rely on it over much. There would be far more worth in a few weeks' association with the theatre. A man's work might be brought, perhaps, to the preliminary stages of production, there being admittedly no chance of taking it further. But it might be handed for a few days to a seminar of the students, or discussed with the author and play-reader by a committee of such of the actors and actresses as would be likely players of it ; talks even with producers and designers would not be—should not be, in a sensitive author's mind—barren of result. Not only the contact with individuals would count, but the dramatist's entry, even for that little time, into the theatre's general scheme of collaboration. Attendance at rehearsals, at play-readings, at the discussion of productions : these are things that cannot be offered by the ordinary theatres of to-day, where, with all eyes to performance, nothing else counting except as cost, they are scamped and rushed—hectic, irritable affairs, best concealed. But when the study of the art is an end in itself, and perfected co-operation the recognized means to that end, a visit to a theatre may come to mean something other than the moral discomfort of intruding upon a few painful rehearsals or indifferently sitting out a show.

One would have hopes, too, that the atmosphere of this theatre (to venture upon that vague and hackneyed phrase) might be a very sane one. It is not less true of playwrights than of other people who plan things on paper—and really a written play is no more than our plan, our theory, of what we hope the completed thing will be—that divorce from the practical difficulties of bringing them to being is but too apt to turn would-be servants of the single cause into sectaries, righteous in their own eyes, since they see but themselves matched against chaos. In no art, certainly, are the pretensions of the theorist hollower, or the backings-up of phrases by phrases more vain. There is room in the theatre both for the reformer and the rebel, and for the conventicle as well as for the Church. But there is no health whatever in the editing of tracts by scholars (whose view of the stage is like the Swiss mountaineer's of the Mediterranean), in the drawing of two-dimensional designs for the three-dimensional theatre, nor—to outrage the illustration a little—in the writing of one-dimensional plays for many-dimensional acting. All this may be excusable enough when, as now, the disastrous conditions of the theatre exclude from its service

190

man after man whose scholarship, artistry, or inspiration asks some further encouragement and
recompense than cash in hand. But, when better
encouragement is to be had, it will be well to
remember that the art of the drama is as pragmatical
as the art of architecture, and most effectively to be
preached by practice.

While the play-reader himself should have every
latitude in granting the freedom of the theatre to the
potential playwright, whether, when there was a
direct question of the production of a play, his
recommendation and the director's acceptance or
rejection would cover the ground of this most important business, is to be doubted. If not, it being
hardly practicable to turn director and play-reader
into a committee of two with equalized powers,
the only feasible plan seems to be the addition of a
third authority.* We have rejected the notion of
any large committee of actors to exercise this power.
Schemes by which the students or the actors or the
council themselves or committees elected by the
audience might have power to dictate one production in so many are really hardly worth playing
with. The provision of such backdoors is a token
of weakness, and the use of them generally a demoralizing business. The choice of plays will be
a dominant part of the theatre's policy, and it must,
above all things, show consistency of purpose.
For this reason much could be said for letting the
director's be the sole voice in the matter. In a
theatre where his other work left him time to
grapple with it—could he be certain, too, of ideal
relations with his play-reader—this probably, for mere

*A third voice
needed in the
choosing of
plays*

* This plan is worked out, as are most of the others for the
staff of the theatre as playhouse, in " The Scheme and Estimates
for a National Theatre."

simplicity's sake, would come so to be. But, apart from the amount of detached attention involved, there is the perennial danger of hardening taste and narrowing mind, in no direction likely to be greater than in the choice of plays. The third authority, then, must be someone who can hope to keep himself as free as humanly may be from this particular risk. And, while the play-reader would try to bring the playwright into tentative collaboration with the theatre's work, the part of this third chooser of plays would be to keep out of touch with it altogether. He should never be tempted to consider plays from the point of view of the ease with which the theatre could produce them, never for their sheer effectiveness or their chances of immediate success. Ideally he should possess one of those sceptical, critical, troublous minds, unattachable to any movement, frankly at odds with acquiescence. He should be a discoverer of the talent that would not be drawn into the theatre's orbit. One sees him, perhaps, travelling on its behalf. He would be constantly out-voted in the committee of three. That would not matter. The flavour of his opinion would abide.

These limitations noted—the financial and the play-choosing, the second being less really a limitation of power than an extension of faculty—to enumerate the director's positive tasks would be but to imply limitations the more. Nor will an attempt to describe a desirable personality for the post be of much more avail. To say that the ideal director must be born and not made is but a way of saying that the man and his qualities—the qualities to fit the man, rather—can but emerge from the development of the institution itself ; for his abilities must be as near as may be an epi-

tomized reflection of its activities. And, in addition,
he must have the administrative qualities that
should pertain to direction anywhere. Well, there
are no such people. And the story of all government is the story of the failure to find them, the
wisdom of the search, and the necessity of putting
up with the next best thing.

The fallacy of trying to get every-thing right at once

But for the direction of the search a principle
is involved which it may be as well, as far as this
theatre is concerned, to examine.

If we do not look for the institution itself, with
its accumulating traditions, to give birth to the
director,* and by its own virtue to make up for his
inevitable deficiencies, then not only this plan, but
the very idea of such a theatre as this, had better be
scrapped. And there is much to be said from this
standpoint. The argument, familiar to every enemy
of an academy, that, if you confine an art within set
boundaries which are alien to its inner purposes,
you do, *ipso facto*, prevent its healthy development,
is doubtless a strong one. But the theatre, it must
be remembered, depends, as no other art does,
upon organization. Of necessity more co-operative
than any other, its workers profit most by the perma-
nencies of an institution. We may at least look
round at this moment and justifiably protest that it
has profited enough, and suffered too much, from
the vagaries of individual genius. Within the art's
generous boundaries there should be room, no
doubt, for two policies—institutional and free,
traditional and iconoclastic ; the one policy does
not prosper, indeed, at more than a brickbat's

* Whether, a century hence, the man appointed were actually a
product of the theatre, or an outsider, is a small matter if his professional qualities were those which it is the theatre's object to
cultivate.

range from the other. But the " free " theatres, dependent upon some individual of genius or some lucky combination of talent, had better remain, organically, comparatively simple affairs. Then there need be no regret at their natural perishing when the circumstances that sustained them change ; and, above all, there should be no attempt to keep them artificially alive. Lilies that fester smell far worse than the wholesome cabbage. But a continued new creation of elaborately organized institutions is not to be faced. These, if they are desirable at all, must be designed to endure, and an inevitable condition of their endurance will be for the theatre itself, and, above all, the *idea* of the theatre, to take precedence of any individual talent.

Now, in practice, this condition will rule out all sorts of attractively easy plans by which a theatre may be brought at high speed to artistic eminence. Find the director of outstanding ability, give him his head, fill his pocket, and the thing is done. Such is the common cry. That the thing might be begun in such a way is possible. Indeed, as things generally, like people, do *not* begin as they go on it might be the best way to begin. But from the very beginning such a director would have to plan his own obliteration ; and it would not be an easy matter, though he were a model of unselfishness, both to suppress himself and to advantage the theatre to the full by his personal prestige. He may make the best job possible of carrying his burden up the first steep ascent, but if he cannot hand it over when the level is reached, so that he stands from beneath it quite unnoticeably, his work will have been wasted. In his staff, his company, and students he must inoculate loyalty to the theatre, not to himself. And while it may be called the United States—or the British—or the Pittsburg —or Nottingham—Theatre, yet, if from beyond the memory of man (which dates back in such matters for five or ten years) the work there is too much associated with his name, the public (that always likes something to complain about) will take offence at his leaving. So the problem presented is very difficult ; in the flush of success, moreover, it is always ignored.*

One need not press the point further ; and it is obvious that to complicate the difficulty with financial considerations will greatly worsen it. The farming out of such an enterprise, the sharing of profits (for one thing, there should be no such thing as the making of profits)—the more admirable, from what is called a business point of view, such plans are, the more futile, shortsighted, destructive are they, as a rule, to the final purpose of the theatre.

All these things should be obvious. Compromise of some sort, when things come to the starting-point, there has always to be. One must do as one can, and take the openings that offer. But one should be quite certain that it is compromise and opportunism, and should know where the right road lies. There is an absolute morality in business methods, no doubt, but its pretended application to artistic enterprise is too often a shifting of responsibility, if not, indeed, a left-handed attempt at sabotage. That may seem a hard saying ; but one has seen too many expeditions in altruism bidden to sustain

---

* Where was Antoine's theatre without Antoine ? And, conversely, the Odéon swallowed him like a grave. Why could not the Lessing Theatre Company hold together after Brahm's death ? The Théâtre Français survives all defections. Is that only because of its national character and its subsidy ?

themselves upon terms that their sponsors would scoff at had they been concerned with commercial profit, not to be sore sometimes at the spectacle of the right hand of the man of business outstretched to receive congratulations upon his public spirit.

*The libra-
rian ; the
making of
prompt books;
the conser-
ving of
tradition* A functionary barely existent in the theatre of to-day, but of some importance to such a scheme as this, would be the librarian. His work would be two-fold. For the playhouse he should be concerned to conserve tradition. There he would be the permanent head of the staff of prompters (a further word about them soon), and responsible for the proper recording of each play's production; for the writing of a small history of its casting and development; for the preservation in some interpretable form of the designs for costumes and scenery ; and, above all, for the making of that particular record known as the prompt book. This last is a difficult business, mostly muddled nowadays, for no one concerned seems to know quite what is wanted. No producer but has been driven distracted, at the revival of a play, by a carelessly marked prompt book. After tangling himself and his company for a few days in its toils he finds it simpler to cut loose and begin again. But meticulously marked books, for all their fascination (perhaps only a producer feels it), are even more dangerous friends. For, as a rule, they show no distinction between the main features of the play's scheme—that skeleton upon which the rest is hung—and all the minor matters, positions, movements, which not only can be varied without injury, but very constantly should be if its acting is not to stiffen. To rehearse a play by such a guide is a poor business and takes the heart out of everyone concerned. The principles of prompt book

196

making will be implicit in our later discussion of the production of the play itself. But in practice it can, at least, be no mechanical matter. One might compare it to the full score of an opera, but that there the effects of the instruments are calculable, more or less. Now, even if we could tie our actors to notes in their voices and precise liftings of the eyebrows, we presumably would not—cinema and gramophone records would be of little positive value. The secret of the art of acting and its whole glory lies in this very impossibility of reducing it to set terms. The prompt book must rather record, then, the meaning of what was done. It should be an over-writing of the play. Not that one wants anything remotely like what is called the novelization of a drama. Better to retain and elaborate a strict technique of expression by which to detail entrance, exit, and movement in general; that will deter the recorder from indulging in fanciful phrasing of his own. On the other hand, the comparative importance of these movements and of the cadences of the dialogue and their purpose needs to be indicated; above all does the distinction between essential and permissive things. The dramatist himself, one presumes, will so annotate his work as to give its interpreters what guidance he thinks necessary for their imaginative approach to it. There is an art in doing this so as to feed without choking the actor's imagination. But the prompt book record should differ in kind, should be clear statement of what was done, implication merely of what should be. Acting is an ephemeral art, but it is an encouragement to continuity of effort that its achievements should be intelligibly enshrined and its traditions formed and preserved.

The library—the room full of books—would

be a necessary resource for both playhouse and school. If one considers all the subjects upon which workers in the theatre need to be currently informed the very number of books involved is a large one. Books on architecture, costume, manners and customs, topography, not to mention a quite surprising amount of writing upon the art of the theatre itself, will make up but a part of the list. And a certain amount of pure research work would doubtless be sponsored by the school, which must therefore be equipped for it. Where better could the visiting student find his books with less chance of suffocating his learning in the dust of them ?

The prompters themselves With regard to the corps of prompters—let us prefer the old-fashioned simplicity of this slight misnomer to the pretentiously exact "assistant stage-manager "—there is a little to be said. The job— once its drudgery were reduced to a minimum by the means of organization and good stage machinery— is such an educative one that it should, if possible, be left for the students and beginners to tackle. A sharp dose of the work, even at its crudest, inoculates a man well enough with the practical habit of the stage, but refine it as one may it has not many more possibilities of development than has the kindred job of fagging at a public school. It is a task that everyone should be keen enough to undertake, and no one should want to stick at. A man who did want to would be already devitalizing into one of those bits of dead wood which must be resolutely cut away from the theatre tree.

This prompter's job should be practised first in one of the play-study seminars, then in the experimental staging of a play by the students, finally in a full-fledged production or two. He is the secretary, the convener, the recorder, the
198

remembrancer. A passive agent for the greater part of the time, he is best able to soak in the general effect of the work done. When a student has been concentrating his attention first in one direction, then in another, in no better way will he recover a conspectus of the whole than by taking the prompter's seat. He must master there the technique of recording the production as it develops ; a complex and rather troublesome business this should be for him, as we have seen, but well worth the trouble to anyone who is later to be concerned in producing plays, and possibly in itself, by reason of the close attention and the powers of clear exposition that it needs, an educational study.

We come now to the staging of plays; and, in the first place, let us decide that shoddy has no place in the theatre. Just because some scenery may be meant to create an illusion, because the rooms that one sees are not real rooms, nor their furniture amenable to scrutiny, nor to more than a reasonable resistance to usage, it does not follow that such things are, in any derogatory sense, shams. *The workshop*

The worst of illusion in stage scenery has ever been that it lends itself to claptrap, to tricks ; and one of the best things to be said about formal decoration is that it sets a sterner standard of accomplishment. Craftsmanship, and not craft, will be called for ; the work must be beautiful and right in itself. Is it too fanciful to contend that in the theatre the various sorts of shoddiness are interdependent ? One need not hold that we can promote sound thinking in our playwrights by means of sound carpentry on the stage. But, conversely, it is undoubtedly true that fineness of feeling in the essentials of the dramatic art must, for the sake of its own preservation, extend itself to a care

199

for the fitness of the practical accessories, even the smallest. Interdependence in the theatre is complete. When it is not, something is functioning wrongly or not functioning at all. But for ill, as well as good, the rule holds; and slovenliness in the setting of a chair will react throughout the whole body of work, so subtly at first, perhaps, as to be worth no comment; and coarser tastes may for long be impervious to the effects. But finally impoverishment is sure.

We must think well, however, what we mean by fitness. The actor's performance of Charles Surface will hardly be improved by his sitting before the public upon a genuine Chippendale chair, though one might argue that some appreciation of the merits of Chippendale would not come amiss as a flavouring to his study of Joseph ; and Moses, no doubt, had a good working knowledge, to be evidenced in glance and gesture, of *objets d'art et de vertu*. But we may certainly contend that, starting from the nucleus of four boards and a passion, the passion may be just a little sublimated by the boards being well chosen and, perhaps, scrubbed ; till, arriving at the complex mechanism of the modern theatre, there is no part of it, not the furnishing of the stage, nor the dressing-rooms, not the artistic lives of the actors, nor the trade pride of the carpenters, but will reflect and be reflected in the spirit of the whole.

Really it stands to reason. For our aim is to make of the theatre a place where the senses are sharpened to immediate response, most immediately in the actors, contributively in all the workers ascendant or distributed, resultantly in the audience. It follows—does it not ?—that there will be response to coarse stimuli as to fine, and always an easier letting down into the slough of bad taste than a tuning up to good. Therefore one cannot afford to knock a nail in wrong.

It follows then that the decoration and furnishing of a play are as integral a part of the theatre's work as its study and acting, and are to be admitted to the same co-ordination. Hence the need, in any theatre aspiring to completeness, of a studio, or, more properly, a workshop. By preferring that term we both emphasize, again, the uselessness for these purposes of mere paper designing and the practical impossibility of carrying on very much abstract study. For this last, indeed, there should be not much need. The æsthetic principles involved are not rooted in dramatic art any more than is the craft of carpentry that will, among others, be practised in the same connection.

In the theatre as school a certain amount of teaching of the subject can be devised. There can be lectures at large on the history, the theory, and practice of scenic decoration and costume design. But a great deal more learning can be done by students admitted to watch and assist in the carrying out of the practical work. Not much good will come, however, from playing about with half-inch models. That is a showy business, but to use such things for show is to misuse them. They are properly workmen's devices—no more—and not very efficient ones at that. Scale drawings, though not so attractive, are far more useful.

The workshop, then, must be primarily a part of the theatre as playhouse, though it may pass as many student apprentices through a course of its work as it can do, profitably to them, and without deflecting its own purposes to any sort of dilettantism.

The amount of attention to be given to stage decoration

Now comes the question what proportion of time, attention, and energy should a theatre give to this side of its work ? Note that in the last analysis it will be energy and not merely money that will be absorbed. Lavish expenditure is, no doubt, a tempting devil ; but it is the business manager's task to put this behind us. The more seductive deep sea, however, is the notion that fine artistry and a free hand are in themselves all-sufficient and utterly desirable. But far better four boards, creaky and unscrubbed, as a stage for our passion than that it should be choked by a collection of bric-à-brac. And what else do scenery, furniture, costumes, however fine in themselves, accumulate into if they have not the right and intimate relation to the production as a whole ? And in nineteen cases out of twenty their relation should be subordinate also. For to surround a play with foreign bodies of scenery and costume which, alien in origin and in intention, only obscure its meaning while they pretend to illustrate it, is an artistic crime. And a greater one still is the attempt to bolster up poverty of acting (the heart's blood of all true interpretation) by even the most genuine accessory riches, however brilliant, however attractive they may be.

The right apportionment of energy, it will be said, will differ with each production. No doubt ; and we have admitted the twentieth play to which sheer beauty of staging may be the most important contribution. But we are searching for a formula which will serve generally, and if there were æsthetic, as there are scientific, laws some such definition as the following might possibly be valid. Allow for all the energy that can profitably be expended upon the simple interpretation of a play, then the surplus *and* the extra energy and enthusiasm engendered by the work of interpretation will allow for just so much external beautifying as will properly complete the whole. If one could follow such a rule strictly the result might be a simplicity of presentation almost unbearably severe. But while it cannot be worked out as a formula, it can stand as a safeguard against temptation. And it does certainly point the way to a rule of simplicity for the great play which needs nothing more, which will by its own virtues absorb the attention of an audience as it should have accounted for the full energies of the actors; and, on the other hand, to a latitude of fancy in embroidering the slighter fabrics, which do not by their own strength and completeness forbid such attentions.

Undue emphasis, one feels, has been laid of *The easy way* late years upon stage decoration. There was, in- *of visual* deed, a crying need both for the practical reformer *appeal* and the inspired prophet. Scene-painting had touched depths of dulness, ugliness, and ineptitude from which a few instances of honourable craftsmanship and creditable imagination could not save it, while the occasional intervention of an artist of academic reputation, superior and aloof, made only specious pretence at a rescue. But the trail of reform once blazed, there was a rush to it : the reason being, one fears, that this is such an easy way to the " new " theatre, while it looks even easier than it is. If sticks and canvas were the main content of drama, and limelight the liveliest thing about it, what a simple business it would be ! Who suddenly discovered that a bare stage, bounded by a wall with its whitewash gone grey, and lit by a shaft of sunlight from the dust-stained windows above, was in itself a most decorative thing ? It is upon these phenomena, commonplace enough to theatre folk, but always impressive, one would say, to the stranger straying in the day time into the empty, echoing, shrouded house, that the new gospel was based. It was indeed necessary to strip scenery of its sophistications and become again as little children in the matter. But we do not want to go on playing about for ever with these pseudo-simplicities as with toys, and playing (it really is!) upon the innocency of the public. There are signs, however, that the public begin to be as bored by them as for some time past the initiate have been.

But there is always the temptation of the easiest way. And nothing is easier in the theatre than to overshadow the mental-emotional complexity of the drama, with its sharp demand upon our full attention, by the primitive appeal to the eye or by the hypnosis of sound—melodious dronings lulling the intelligence to sleep. Which of us has not heard entranced playgoers, as they passed out from some tremendously decorated, softly boohooing séance to the clattering reality of the streets, exclaiming: "How beautiful! How *artistic!*" Though what it was all about they no more knew than did old Caspar the cause of the battle of Blenheim!

Theoretically, every play should be approached by its decorator as the actors approach it. He also is to interpret it to the full extent of his—and of its own—capacity for individual expression. But in practice one had better admit the two admirable safeguards against excess of zeal—convention and economy.

Artistic economy Quite apart from the economy which a business-manager, balancing one branch of the theatre's work against another, will very wisely impose on the

204

workshop, there is an artistic inhibition of over-
expenditure of energy or money upon the decoration of any play. For, after all, its production is an
ephemeral thing. And if, time and time again,
everything must begin from the beginning, a company be collected, rehearsed, dressed, instilled with
the feeling that this is a matter of life and death—
all for what ?—after a little the mature mind ceases
to respond to the fantasy of such demands. So it
should reasonably be with the scene-making. If
the efforts are to be such as would almost suffice
to build a city, the artist, if he has in him any touch
of that supremely artistic quality, a sense of fitness,
will rebel. And then, if he must stick to the job,
for careful design he will substitute brilliant
sketches, which make for effect but have no substance behind them. Now, this may be fine
artistry of its sort; but translated to craftsmanship,
to the three dimensions of the theatre, to a stage
peopled with humanity, it opens the door to
shoddy, and is generally the beginning of debase-
ment. There is then a fitness to be found in more
than the appearance of simplicity, and the measuring
of means by end will prove a positive artistic
strength.

And the development of conventional staging, *The salutary*
quite apart from its particular dramatic fitness, *influence of*
answers the same purpose. Just as a standardizing *conventional*
of the measurements for doors, windows, platforms, *staging*
steps, is a help to the carpenter, so is the conven-
tionalizing of a scene to the designer : his imagination is set the freer by the very limitations within
which it must work. These must vary very much
according to concrete circumstances, and their
proper extent will always be arguable. A Greek
play, for instance, torn from a Greek theatre, where

its convention of staging was built, so to speak,
in very marble, is already sorely at any producer's
mercy. However, if Greek tragedies are to be kept
alive in the English climate they must submit to
the conditions of a new playhouse. It would be
best, of course, to reproduce the theatre at Athens or
Syracuse on a suitable scale, covered and warmed ;
and, were a hundred thousand pounds of no consequence, London might well be possessed of such a
building. But the practical course is to adapt our
modern theatre to the necessities of the case. That
is not difficult. Minor disputes will arise—as to
how far, for instance, in providing those essentials
of the old theatre which are reflected in the stagecraft of the plays, the "accidentals" should, for the
sake of the so-called atmosphere they engender,
be reproduced, too.* Each theatre may settle this
in its own way and hold its own way to be the best.
The important thing is to re-establish the framework of a fitting convention. To have designers
and producers setting out upon one revival after
another with no equipment but blank minds and
a bare stage is the depth of folly. Greek plays
were written in obedience to a definite convention of acting and staging ; therefore the
acceptance of a convention as germane to it as
the gulf between Athens and out own time allows,
by producer and designer, by actors and, most
importantly, by the audience, is a necessary part of
their performance and enjoyment. Limitation this
is not ; convention is law to art, and only within it is
one's power of appreciation truly free. And the
designer will find that he has amply enough to do,
working within this accepted range, and quite
enough to ask of beholders without straying be-

* Personally I think they should not be.

yond it. Incidentally, it is roughly true that the more conventional the scene the greater value is given to the beauty and fine quality of its costume and furnishing. This is a question not of simplicity, but of convention and its acceptance ; the freeing from unnecessary astonishment of the spectator's mind and eyes.

To Mediæval and Elizabethan drama the same principles will apply, and over their application the same sort of disputes arise. The common quarrel over the staging of Shakespeare is a pretty one, and something more is involved in it than like or dislike of platform, stage, and illusionist scenery. The arguments for and against the adaptability of Greek Tragedy can be used with effect by either side. The strict Elizabethan should contend that an open-air theatre and the Greek language are the only allowable means of interpretation, while the advocates of the modern staging of Shakespeare should be content to see Euripides subjected to all the tests of realism—as sometimes they are. But it comes to this: what degree of translation will the plays bear—much is inevitable—and of what degree of translation of mind is the audience capable ? Drag Euripides by force across the centuries, strip him of everything which is not the common knowledge of a London street corner, and, however transcendent his genius, how much of him must we not lose ? The further that we ourselves can go back to meet him, recapturing—however hardly —a knowledge both of his intention and of what lay, besides, unconscious in his mind, the better our footing will be. Now, Shakespeare may be rhetorically not for an age, but for all time. It may be that his genius quite transcends the medium in which it worked—though surely at one moment to praise his

The need for agreement on convention between interpreters and audience

207

stagecraft and in the next to contend that in the problem of producing his plays it may safely be ignored is something more than paradoxical. It may be true that not the most Elizabethan playing will restore an Elizabethan psychology to the audience; though one would have thought that the world's experience of these last seven years would have taught us that—with appropriate stimulus applied—the nature of man has not changed so greatly with the ages. Nevertheless, since Shakespeare wrote as he did write and planned for the theatre he knew —not, in spite of all argument, as he doubtless would have done for the theatre of these times had he lived in these times—it stands to something which will pass for reason that, as he cannot now come to us, the nearer we can get to him the closer understanding we shall have of him. It is a question of degree, of give and take, and not, perhaps, so much of disquisitioning upon the psychology of audiences as of careful study of his stagecraft— study which can only be carried on in the actual staging of the plays themselves. Shakespeare is likely to be the corner-stone of any representative theatre in England as long as the impulse of the Elizabethan age—England's renaissance, her gathering of strength for the spring that has landed her upon what now perilous height !—endures. Therefore the problem is of more interest to us than its parallel of Greek Tragedy and the Mediæval play. It is more capable, too, of varying solutions. We are, at any rate, sufficiently near to our Shakespeare for the more and less of distance to count, and for the degree of proximity achieved to be disputable by canons of taste as well as reason. It is a problem which each representative theatre must work out to its own salvation. But it must be remembered that, in the establishment of a stage convention, not only the fancy of the decorator but the attitude of every contributor to the production is involved, and that this cannot be arbitrarily and constantly shifted from one pole to another. Producer, actors, and audience must not be asked to view "Hamlet" as a study in sixteenth-century manners one day and as a view of eleventh-century Denmark, filled by the rotundities of eighteenth-century classicism, the next. A convention is a treaty first between fellow-interpreters and then between them and their public.

Collaboration will be, in every instance, as obligatory upon the workshop as upon any other section of the theatre. This book both tacitly and *The workshop and collaboration* expressly rejects the ideal of the theatre which sees everything centred in the imagination and proceeding from the brain of one man. A good enough practical reason for doing so would be the scarcity of supply. If we are to wait for each theatre till the advent of an inspiring genius— no, we shall not wait a long time ; that is not what happens. We shall, as now, have many sham theatres in being and one or two real ones in the clouds. But the better reason lies in the sounder belief that the theatre in its very nature is a co-operative art, and that its chief glory is to be so. For if this sublimated single being must be duplicated into designer and producer, why should he not be triplicated into author as well ? Further, unless the actors are to be merely puppets, he should logically assume the burden of the acting besides. It is, indeed, noticeable that Gordon Craig—true genius and chief prophet in this kind, though, to our great misfortune, retired in these days to absolute supremacy in a theatre of the clouds—

has himself been sometimes driven to this conclusion and has sought refuge in an exalting of
the puppet play.   May one not write at the end of
such a proposition : Which is absurd ?   We all
strive for an absolute beauty, an absolute perfection
in our work, to the degree of our gift.   And if, in
solitude, we never reach it we may blame those
conflicting elements in ourselves, the penalty and
the promise of our very humanity.   The more, then,
should we approve the friendly art of the theatre,
which in its incompleteness is a truer reflection
of the life it portrays than in any unimpeachable
perfection of achievement it could be.

*The
workshop's
organization*

Collaboration admitted, the conditions need determining.   Should the workshop form as close a
corporation as the company of actors—and closer,
since its work would be more narrowly concen-
trated—or should it admit the alien designer, even
as the playwright must be admitted ?   One has
little doubt that it should.   But the workshop will
first tend quite naturally to evolve for itself some
such constitution as this.   Its head must be
established as administrator, teacher, and designer,
too.   He will be responsible for the working out
of the theatre's particular scenic conventions, for
continuity of policy, for craftsmanship.   This last
gathers great importance with simplicity of staging.
There is a method of producing plays by which
actors, scenes, and furniture are so smudged up in
soft lights that neither form nor colour can be
accounted for.   No doubt this is a method like
any other.   Perhaps it is the one best suited to
plays of muddled content.   And a little more
smudging with incidental music will complete
the characteristic effect.   Then there is a more to
be respected school of designers that relies upon

210

paint and the quality of the painting—no other. This method, though, just because of its striking possibilities, is but suited to a certain kind of play. But only the craftsman can make simplicity fine. For Greek plays, with their rejection of scenic illusion, and upon the platform stage of the Elizabethan drama every detail of workmanship tells, and the ideal of the school that has this condition of things to deal with is—to put it crudely—that you may turn all the lights full on if you want to, and not be ashamed to let the audience see everything just as it is. Not that the aim is to destroy illusion, but only to transfer it to the subliminal region of the actors' interpretation of the play. Not that the designer is after realism in the sense that he must have his gold caskets of real gold— a matter of mere commercial interest, the bankruptcy of all imagination whatever—but so that he may bring his material to the perfection which the circumstances fit it for. His appeal to the eye will be both intimate and candid, and in answering this a new bond may be knit between spectator and spectacle, and a new satisfaction enshrined in place of the out-worn pleasure of illusion.

What the measure of this craftsmanship must be *Craftsmanship* is a question. A good workshop will tend to do more and to do better than necessity demands, for good workmen will only be content to make things as well as they can make them. Experience will answer the question, and in each case differently. But certainly the answer will almost always involve the accumulation of a store of things that are fine in themselves and not to be destroyed or discarded. And apart from the things made, the conventional scenes themselves, and the rather comic medley of a theatre property-room—the banners, orders, caskets, thrones—there will be the things collected, the furniture, carpets, and hangings. No reason at all that it should be a meaningless, haphazard collection. There can be a policy, and a continuity of policy, in the matter.

The stranger designer It would be, then, into a workshop so constituted that the stranger designer would at times be invited. Not, be it clearly understood, any casual painter or architect, who thinks he would like to have a flutter in the theatre (the architect, of the two, would, by the way, have the better chance of making a steady flight). It no more follows that a painter can design scenery than that a novel writer can write plays. But with enough technique of his own to enable him to collaborate with the theatre craftsman he will be welcomed even as the playwright is; allowed, too, the pre-eminence of the playwright, for the sake of the imagination which other and broader interests should have kept fresh. The parallel is a close one. As the playwright may often be—and should always be if possible—his own producer, so the designer with full knowledge of the theatre crafts could be, from beginning to end, responsible for the carrying out of his designs. Needless to say, there will be no room at all for the man who can but do brilliantly on paper. One must distrust a designer—if for no other reason—when his drawings are attractive at first sight. This, a truism in architecture, still needs some emphasis where scenery and costumes are concerned, if we may judge not only from some theatrical art exhibitions, at which the ecstasies of the amateur may be excusable, but from the pious but futile professional attempts that are made now and then to translate into actuality wonderfully attitudinized pictures. But also, as with the play-

212

wright—for the " solidifying " of a production is a lengthy and troublesome and a highly technical process—there should be some mitigation for the men to whom work in the theatre would remain a very occasional business. To the mastery of that simple situation comes naturally the workshop's head. He can edit the work. If the designs are of costumes to fit into his conventional backgrounds to some extent he must do so. And this must be the final qualification for his post, one akin to that upon which the play-reader is to base his services to the theatre: the tact of hospitality.

It is surely the most foolish of mistakes to suppose that artists are not capable of co-operation. Much of their work, as of much other work, must be incubated in solitude, of course. But this image of an unreasoning egotist—vainglorious, preposterous—was, one might almost believe, a product of nineteenth-century fiction, an item in its calculated flattery of commercialism. Or, where the reality does exist, it may have sprung from these very conditions, so bitterly hostile to all art. Let it stand as a living witness against them.

The average artist among his fellows is very like the average man, and a workshop is his natural environment. Here is an arena into which he may cast his idea for profit by dispute, and gain a new— an objective—delight in its over-fashioning. Friction will not often be more than wholesomely warming ; here is no audience to embitter a quarrel. And while imagination may be solitary and absolute, craftsmanship is a commonwealth. A workshop might well be the happiest place in a theatre, for its material is kindly and acquiescent. Moreover, the worker can go home and leave it. He is free from the ever-haunting self-consciousness of the actor, who sheds but his clothes in his dressing-room.*

Machinery   Some time before the scene designer proclaimed himself the saviour of the drama the contriver of stage mechanism had come to the fore. He did not, it is true, take on the airs of a prophet, but in the sacred name of efficiency he cumbered up the stages of certain theatres and absorbed the energies of their managements, passionate to be up to date. But the result of much experiment with stages that lift and lower, run back or run off sideways, with lights reflected from a colossal " heaven " and electrical contrivances galore, seems to be the verdict that the best basis for any production is a bare stage.

Having said so much in condemnation of machinery, which, while pretending to help the producer, only hinders him, it is fair to qualify the statement. Much of it was crammed into unsuitably built theatres, some of it was put in only by halves : and, at any time, no machine is better than half a one. But such a contrivance, for instance, as the ordinary revolving stage is mainly a nuisance. It is cramping to a degree, drives the scene-designer into (literally) hole-and-corner ingenuities, which by their novelty are too conspicuous and in their repetition (the bag of tricks is soon exhausted) become wearisome. A drama may yet be written æsthetically fitted for the re-

* There incidentally is presented a dilemma. Shall the actor escape it by creating a graven image—a sub-conscious professional self? No; for that will not suffice him for serious work. This is every artist's problem, but, above all, it is the actor's—that artist in self—to develop such sanity in his work that he never needs to escape it. Or he might keep a sub-conscious self to live by: life being unimportant. Not a happy way out of the difficulty, this!

volving stage, but Shakespeare, eighteenth-century
comedy, and most modern plays are grievously misplaced on it.   If Shakespeare does not need the
staging for which his work was designed he certainly
demands a forthrightness and uniformity of action
which is not occasioned by a twisted, tricky background.   It is always the method of acting to be
employed—the producer's first consideration—
which should dictate the main form of the scene.
But it must not be forgotten that the scene will
—if that has been first considered—equally im-
print itself upon the action of the play, and so
largely influence the very readings of the actors'
parts.   The ordinary revolving stage, too abun-
dantly used (and machinery imposes itself), makes
neither for spaciousness nor dignity of production,
nor for simplicity nor repose.

The whole question, however, of stage machinery *The right*
is involved in the larger one of the theatre's plan *sort of*
and purpose.   The modern form of theatre build- *auditorium—*
ing marks but one stage of the drama's development. *and the*
For plays of the so-called realistic school of the *wrong*
nineteenth century little is needed but a picture-
frame proscenium and an auditorium made for some
intimacy of effect ; and there must be no gallery
which will elevate the actor's chin to an angle of
disadvantage in the eye of the stalls, or exhibit
little more than eyebrows and hair-parting to
the patient gods.   Even here, though, one may
protest, in passing, against the pattern of theatre *
which ranks the seats in long straight rows,

* Dictated in the beginning, I believe, by the Hobson's choice
of sites in New York, where theatres must be built to the most
economical pattern, extra space being measured off—almost
literally if extra frontage is involved—in four-inch hundred dollar
notes.

admirable for a view of the stage but—and this consideration has been characteristically neglected in a time when everything has been forgotten about the drama except that it is a paid entertainment—nullifying any friendly relation in the audience to each other. One of the results, accidental possibly, of the accustomed horseshoe formation was that the spectator never quite lost consciousness of his fellows. The effect could, no doubt, be overdone. In the smaller Court theatre at Munich, if you sit in a side box, the party opposite is full in your eye, while from the stage comes but a sidelong contribution to the entertainment. There are compensations if the opposite party is interesting and the performance dull. And in many opera houses, of course, the assumption is that people sit in the boxes as much to be seen as to see. But there is more to the question than the encouragement of such agreeable vanity. The relations of the spectators among themselves are a part of their united good relations to the play. One of the tests of a good performance is the feeling of friendliness it creates among the spectators. When the curtain falls on the first act, and a total stranger turns round to speak to you and you respond without restraint, you may know that the play has achieved one of its secondary— and presumably, therefore, has not failed of its primary—purposes. It may be art of the crudest sort that has this effect on people, but it cannot be *poor* art. And the physical disposition of the audience contributes not a little to the ease with which their emotions may have play. Imagine an auditorium in which people sat blinkered like horses. However excellent the performance, the whole affair would be as flat as if—however excel-

216

lent the dinner!—the diners sat at a long table
all facing one way. A double question is involved: the physical focussing of attention, and
the relative importance of one's own concentration
upon the play and of being in touch with one's
neighbours. Were it possible to sit round the
stage as one sits at a circus, that would be equally
wrong. The spectators would be dominantly in
touch with each other but distracted from the play.*
The question is of first importance in the designing
of an auditorium.

No playhouse, however, such as we have in mind *The differing*
can be built with an eye to one sort of drama only. *requirements*
It is difficult to foresee the future, but quite possible *of the*
to provide for the past in this matter, if one sets out *different*
straightway to do it. It is true that no one who *drama*
has produced a Greek play in a Greek theatre will,
for its own sake, ever want to bring it indoors again,
though the watcher, shivering in his fur coat under
the rigours of an English June may wish it there—
or further. But if in any modern theatre a Greek
play must be scenically incongruous, while a mediæval play in a picture-frame proscenium will be as
well placed as a picnic in a drawing-room, they
can at least both be housed so that no essential
quality of their stagecraft is warped. And though,
it might be argued, one could not distract a
whole building scheme for the sole sake of
Aeschylus and the author of " Everyman," there
would still be the problem of Elizabethan drama to
be solved—to any English-speaking audience a
very vital one. No need to argue in detail the

* Reinhardt's well-remembered production of " The Miracle "
was, to my thinking, largely spoilt by being played under these
conditions. And his circus playhouse in Berlin has comparable
drawbacks.

217

question between those who are for the Elizabethan stage—and that only—and those who contend that Shakespeare, not for an age but for all time, is for all sorts and conditions of staging, too. The main point of difference is involved merely in the presence or absence of a proscenium ; and upon it most others hang. The questions of swiftness of speech, of the treatment of the soliloquy, of uninterrupted action, of whether scenery should be realistic or decorative or whether there should be none at all, have been developed by the structural development of the theatre from the platform to the picture stage. This, with its relation to contemporary stagecraft, reacted characteristically upon the performance of older plays. Not till the breach is wide and the accommodation bridges are broken can it be seen in such a case what principles are involved. And now the issues must be fought out experimentally, point by point. But the thrusting of the plays within a proscenium, or the attempt to drag them half out again on to a platform stage which has been added as a structural afterthought in defiance of lines of sight and other such practical considerations, is quite too empirical to be enlightening.

A theatre can undoubtedly be so designed as to provide, not only the picture stage, but a platform with footlights abolished and suitable entrances for Elizabethan plays : it can provide, too, for the converting of a part of the stalls into an arena for a Greek chorus. The architectural problem is not an easy one—but it can be solved. An effectively disappearing proscenium should not be hard to contrive. The trouble here has always lain in a lack of space above and around the stage. The gridiron should be more than twice the height of

218

the auditorium ceiling, and the width between the fly-rails more than the auditorium's practical width. Limitations of site and of building cost stand in the way of this extensiveness. One suspects, too, that architects may have shrunk from the effect of a great square central tower in the midst of the structure; though one wonders why, as it looks well enough in a cathedral.

Machinery for the expeditious making of these constructive changes should be a part of the equipment of every playhouse with a comprehensive programme. For the rest one wants nothing self-assertive. And in command of this department should be a stage engineer,* solely concerned with the practical working out and the economical running of the schemes of the producers of plays. But the less they are tempted to dally with the marvels of machinery the better. Innocent, child-like beings, beguiled by a new toy, they always find themselves before very long dancing to its clackety tunes.

Note.—Personally (in a very limited experience, it is true) I have never seen a satisfactory working stage. The first requisite is space, not an extravagant amount of room to act in, but ample space around it. A normal proscenium opening of thirty feet or so is ample, contraction to twenty-

---

* The stage-manager whom he would replace has become to some degree an anachronism. He is still supposed to be interested in the play itself, to watch the actors, rehearse their understudies, and to be responsible for the artistic upkeep of the performances generally. But the coming into fashion of the producer has deprived him of any initiative in such matters, and nowadays he is chosen mainly for his power of controlling the stage staff, his technical knowledge of scenery, and his ability to keep accounts. The position would be better filled by a man who frankly disinterested himself in the dramatic side of the business altogether.

219

five is sometimes useful, extension to forty—that is, effective abolition of the proscenium altogether—should be considered a necessity for Greek and Elizabethan drama ; and the stage's working width should be at least a hundred feet. Working depth depends, of course, upon the line of sight from the theatre's top places ; most architects exaggerate its value. With the proscenium in use sixty feet should be ample. With the proscenium removed—that is to say, when there are no effects of illusion to be obtained—it should be more than enough. Simple decoration and acting do not ask, as a rule, for unoccupied distances.

Cellar room has its uses; for machinery for altering the stage level is, perhaps, the most practical of all in this kind, and in the construction of scenes it trebles the value of a turntable. This, indeed, is of little general use alone, and of no good use at all unless it can be placed so far back that its diameter can considerably exceed the normal width of the proscenium; and then—obviously—no complete scene can be set upon it. Lighting is too complicated a matter to discuss here ; it is the Achilles' heel of most stage equipment. Incidentally, though, every theatre could—and should—be so designed that plays can be performed in daylight.

CHAPTER V : THE PRODUCTION OF A PLAY

W E come to the kernel of the whole matter. *How plays*
And the first thing to note is that condi- *are now*
tions of play production in any such *thrown on the*
theatre as we are envisaging bear no relation at *stage*
all to the methods that are thrust upon the managers
and producers in money-making theatres to-day.
For the simple sake of the contrast, however, it
may be well first to envisage these. The money-
making (and losing) manager finds himself, at best,
with a building he can call his own and a few
constant collaborators. The rest—play, company,
scenery, dresses—are brought together to be welded
to a whole for the occasion only ; the entity will
be dissolved and its material scattered when the
occasion is over. For good or ill, then, the manager
must work upon very constricted lines. He has,
it is true, in theory the widest possible choice of a
cast for the play. Anybody in the world that's
available may be had—at a price. But in practice—
competition plucking the first fruits of talent—the
freedom to choose among a swelling crowd of
people with whose work you cannot be very intimate and to whose methods of work you are inevitably more or less of a stranger, is a doubtful
blessing. It means much to the producer to be
familiar with the ways of an actor he is to direct ;
it will often save him needless anxiety, friction, false
starts, wasted time ; it will mean even more to the
actor himself, who is apt to be as nervous as a
new found cat at rehearsal—if he is not it is no
good sign. So, for all their freedom of choice,
managers tend to select people they have worked
with before. The London stage in particular is
accused, from time to time, of being a close corporation. It is. And it is only broken up by
the advent of new managers who bring some know-

ledge of new actors with them. The system has, indeed, many of the limitations of the old stock days and none of their advantages.

The scratch company

But the company collected will still be, at best, a scratch company. For, though the manager may know them, though they may in the round of their work have met each other more or less often, they certainly do not come together now with any corporate sense ; they are, at best, artistic acquaintances. Observe, then, that the foundation of a good performance, which is just this corporate sense, has to be laid at the very same time that the superstructure—the work upon the play itself—is being built. A manifest impossibility. The acting of the average play to-day is all superstructure—and mostly façade ! If it gives one no sense of stability of intention, of there being in the whole thing any abiding worth of idea (for though the play's execution cannot abide, this may), it is mainly because the performance is not built upon this deeper sub-conscious understanding among its actors.*

The hurried rehearsals

Moreover, since the company have been brought together for this one production only no time must be lost. Rehearsals must be hurried on day by day. To pause for reflection or to correct a mistake is a costly business. If the production is a very simple one, if no demands are being made on the actors but to repeat, with a few variations, the physical and emotional posturings to which they

---

* If artistic worth were calculable in percentages one might estimate a 50 per cent. increase by the crudest, most haphazard cultivation of this corporate power; and this would in its turn add another 50 per cent. to the worth of the individual actor. But that is cheapjack estimation. Due cultivation makes a difference which amounts almost to an organic change.

222

and their audience are accustomed, some success may emerge. But the best that can be expected from such a preparation is a general hard competence of execution when the way is plain, and, at any complexly difficult moment, either a helpless clinging together for safety or a plunge into bustling bravado. For the rest, the individual actors and actresses will take care to rouse what delight they can by the exercise of their personal charm ; exercising it, though, as often as not directly upon the audience rather than primarily upon the play. They have their excuse. To surrender this personal power to whatever unity of effect can be gained in three weeks' work or so among a strange company might be to lose it altogether, and to get nothing in exchange—so thinks the theatre-wise actor; therefore, while rehearsals go forward he holds it carefully in reserve. There will be some genuine co-operation in the duologues, no doubt. It is necessary, and not very difficult, to work up a sort of mutual responsiveness in these; for the rest, each for himself and the critics take the hindmost! But this is not to vivify a play. It is at the best but a setting up of its bare bones, and we can be thankful if they are straightly articulated. External elegance may be exhibited, and while our eyes and ears are sufficiently entranced our minds may seize detachedly upon the bare meanings of the author's text. But no wonder we rise in æsthetic rebellion against the theatre. For of that fine interplay of visualized character, of (shifting the metaphor) the living tapestry of pictured thought and emotion into which the stuff of a play can be woven in its acting, what have we seen ? Hardly a beginning. Nor by any such means could we hope for it. Yet so used are we to the shackles of the

223

present system that in all the advocacy of the reform of the theatre—from the training of actors to the capturing of audiences—one finds no apparent realization that (the proper production of plays being, indeed, the mainspring of the whole matter) this is not a way by which any homogeneous work of art can be produced at all. We need to think the whole matter out again from the beginning.

The limita-tions of the human medium

One word of warning, however. The medium we work in is human, so there can never be a perfect production, nor is there such a thing as an ideal cast; nor should we even try by circumstantial safeguards to make our play's performance fool proof. In any theatre there will arise, when certain plays are under consideration, the practical question: can we command an inspiring or even an adequate Lear or Œdipus, Peer Gynt, Cyrano or Undershaft? If we for the time being cannot it may be more sensible to hang up those plays. But, again, as what we look for is interpretation, not realization, so with most plays a faithful and lively interpretation of the whole will always add more in value than we shall lose from individual inability to do full justice physically and emotionally to one or two parts. The unity of our interpretation will be the best measure of our approach—not to perfection, about which empty word and teasing thought we should not even bother ourselves—but to self-contained vitality.

The beginnings of a play's preparation by the company differ so little in theory from its purely educational use by students, as this has been outlined in "The Theatre as School," that we may avoid recapitulation here. In practice, no doubt, the company will get to the gist of their work far more expeditiously. One only hopes they will not be too expeditious; that the wheels, so to speak,

224

of their well-oiled and well-balanced artistic faculties will grip the road. They will make, too, a rather different use of these earlier stages when plays are in hand that call for certain technical brilliancies of accomplishment.

Take, for instance, "A Midsummer Night's Dream." This is less a play, in the sense that we call "Rosmersholm" a play, than a musical symphony. The characterization will not repay very prolonged analysis. It can best be vivified and elaborated by the contrasting to eye and ear of individual with individual and group with group. Then the passing and repassing from the lyric to the dramatic mood has to be carefully judged and provided for. To hold an audience to the end entranced with the play's beauty one depends much upon the right changing of tune and time, and the shifting of key from scene to scene and from speech to speech. From the time, for instance, when Puck's and Oberon's bungling with the love juice begins to take effect the action quickens and becomes more and more confused, the changes of tune and time come more frequently, more and more suddenly. But the greater the effect of speed that you want the less haste you must make over it, the more the effect of confusion the clearer cut must your changes be. And all the time it must all be delightful to listen to, musical, with each change in a definite and purposeful relation to what went before, to what will come after.

Setting to work upon "A Midsummer Night's Dream"

Now, once you get to rehearsing the action physically and your actors are occupied with their movements and business—moreover, once off the stage for a moment or two, out of touch, as actually out of sight and hearing, with what they have left going on there—it is impossible for them to

How physical action brings study to a standstill

build up their parts in such a scheme with a continuously abiding sense of the value of the whole, even if this has been arbitrarily formulated by the producer, annotated for the actor line by line and impressed upon him note by note. Besides, one wants no such arbitrary method ; a producer even now resorts to it only in desperation. To suggest, to criticize, to co-ordinate—that should be the limit of his function. The symphonic effect must be one made by the blending of the actors' natural voices and by the contrasts that spring from the conflicting emotions which their mutual study of the parts spontaneously engenders. Even over things that seem to need the exactitude of orchestration the scheme of the play's performance must still, as far as possible, grow healthily and naturally into being, or the diversity of the various actors will not become unity without loss of their individual force. And we must never forget that to put a play into action on the stage is to pour it into its mould ; once there it tends very quickly to set. If the performance of such plays as these is not to become mere repetition of ritual they must be kept fluid and experimental in their preparation till appearance and purpose both, fineness and sincerity united, can be relied upon for the tempering.

But in nearly all plays (except, of course, those of pure mime) the physical action is extraordinarily unimportant, the mental and the emotional action all in all. Delay, then, in entering the physical phase should not trouble the experienced actor. He has no business to be agitating his mind at rehearsals (much less at a performance) over physical movements, unless they are such matters of gymnastic as fighting, dancing, or the rough and tumble of farce. His training should so have equipped

226

him that all such things come without thought ;
come one way or another, with one way as right as
the other. His thought he needs to match with
the play's thought, and it is not so often he'll have
any to spare.*

But passing the period of argument and criticism, *The*
which are common to actor and student both, we *mysterious*
come to the point where their paths part company *process by*
—the student sustaining his criticism, the actor *which the*
pledged now to the mysterious process by which he *identifies*
identifies himself with the character he is to play.† *himself with*
A lot of rather irritating nonsense is talked about *his part*
this. Amateurs and very young actors tell you
solemnly at rehearsals that all will be well (all being
at the time usually very ill) once they get into the
skin of their parts. The hardened old actor sup-
presses (or does not suppress) his contempt, because
he knows very well that this must happen if it
will happen, that effort does not avail, that even by
prayer and fasting it may not come; on the other
hand, that rehearsal time is too valuable to be spent
standing mentally idle in expectation of the miracle.
Still, it is a miracle that yields, if not to contriving,
partly, at least, to explanation.

The phrase " to create a part " is embedded in
kindred nonsense, but in it there is sense, too.
That the actor can add something all his own to
the dramatic material he is given no one would deny.
And if one must be disputing his claim to be called
creative and original, let the dramatist at least remember that he, too, does but capture, to inform
with something of his own life and pass forth again

* For all that, though, I have known an experienced actor
worry himself almost to death about how he should get out of a
stage room when, after all, the only way was through the door.

† But see also p. 245 *et seq.*

renewed, a brain-full of the ideas and passions which are the common possession of—which so possess—mankind. We are, indeed, interpreters all. Creation is not man's prerogative.

This admitted, the relation between the dramatist's way of work and the actor's will be worth investigating. An essential quality of any work of art is its homogeneity. For a staged play, then, to make good its claim to be one it would seem to follow that the actors must continue what the dramatist has begun by methods as nearly related to his in understanding and intention as the circumstances allow. And it is probably true that the staged play is a satisfying work of art to the very degree that this homogeneity exists. We have insisted time and again upon the secondary importance of the physical side of the play's interpretation, for all that in the end it seems to dominate the entire business, to the exclusion even, in innocent eyes, of the dramatist's own share. It would be an exaggeration to say that it stands for no more than does the pen, ink, and paper by which the play was recorded, but quite just to compare it to the technical knowledge of play-making that the dramatist has come to exercise almost unconsciously. And it is likely that the near relation of method, which we want to establish, does lie in this mysterious preliminary process by which the actor " gets into the skin of his part " : for, indeed, all else that he does in performing it can be related to mere technique of expression. It is this mystery, then, that we must investigate and attempt to explain.

The dramatist's method, which the actor must follow   To begin with, how does the dramatist work ? He may get his play on paper quickly or slowly, but the stuff in it is the gradual, perhaps the casual, accretion of thoughts and feelings, formed long

228

before and now framed in words, or arranged into action, for the first time. How much of this process is conscious, and how much unconscious or sub-conscious, he probably could not tell you. If we say that the experiences are unconsciously or sub-consciously selected and consciously shaped we may not be far wrong. Wherein does the actor's method fellow this ? Certainly no such process is to be found in the stuffing of his memory with words, and the whipping up and out of whatever emotions his repetition of them happens to suggest during the half-drill, half-scramble of the three or four weeks' rehearsing, while he fits himself as best he can—his corners into all the other arbitrary corners—of that strange shifting Chinese puzzle which is called to-day an efficient and businesslike production. As a matter of fact no actor worth his salt relies upon this sort of preparation ; he has other resources within himself. If he worked, as does the dramatist, in solitude, if he too were a fountain-head, his methods would be of only theoretical interest, our care but for the result. But his job is derivative and co-operative both. Therefore we must know the rules, if rules there are.*

* That this creative collaboration among actors and between them and the dramatist can be brought to a high pitch we can have evidence by comparing performances of a play that differ, not in brilliance of execution, but absolutely in the meaning extracted from the play and in the observable addition of dramatic values. I have seen a performance of Tchekov's " Cherry Orchard " in Moscow, and to read the play afterwards was like reading the libretto of an opera—missing the music. Great credit to the actors ; no discredit to Tchekov. For—and this is what the *undramatic* writer so fails to understand, though in Tchekov he may find a salient example—with the dramatist the words on paper are but the seeds of the play. How be sure, as he writes, as he plants them, that each seed will be fertile ? Well, that is the secret

Tension and conflict

We must consider certain constituents of the problem. With but a three hours' traffic in which to manœuvre all the material of a play, the longest part can but appear on the stage for a comparatively few informing and effective passages. To find the inferential knowledge of it that he needs the actor must search, so to speak, behind the scenes, before the rise of the curtain and even after its fall. This is a commonplace ; and all actors who can be said to study their parts at all, not merely to learn them, do, instinctively if not deliberately, work in this way. But unless they do so in concert with their fellows they really more often harm the rest of the play than help the whole. For an isolated performance, of however great interest,—if the rest of the acting is sagging, vague, helpless, unattached, or perversely at cross purposes—must distort the play's purpose. No matter if the one seems to be right and all the others wrong. Nothing is right unless the thing as a whole is right. A play is founded upon conflict ; the dramatist,

of his craft. How to cultivate and raise the crop ? That is the secret of the actor's art. There is demanded, no doubt, something *more* than acting, if by acting one only means the accomplishment, the graces, or the sound and fury of the stage. For these externals of the business may spring from nothing purposeful, be independent of any dramatic meaning, and then, for all their charm and excitement, they come to nothing in the end. It is only when they are the showing of a body of living thought and of living feeling, are in themselves an interpretation of life itself, when, in fact, they acquire *further* purpose, that they rank as histrionic art. That there are rules for so incorporating them in this creative process of collaboration we may learn from the Art Theatre in Moscow, where they have to some extent elaborated them, though without pretence at finality, only for the convenience of mutual understanding. Much that follows, indeed, was suggested to me by my memory of a talk with Stanislawsky. And I have, by the way, seen a performance of "The Cherry Orchard" elsewhere.

230

to get the thing going at all, must bring his characters into collision, among themselves or with fate or circumstances. He must keep them all in an equally effective fighting trim; if he betrays one of them, denies him his best chance in argument or action, for all that it may open an easy way out of a difficulty, end a scene quickly, bring a curtain down with effect, the fabric will be weakened, the play's action may be dislocated altogether. It seems obvious, therefore, that the play's interpretation must be founded upon corporate study by the actors, which should begin as an argumentative counterpart of this struggle and develop through the assumption of personality into the desired unity with the play itself. We have outlined the argumentative process elsewhere. Let us now consider how the unity is to be achieved.

It is to be hoped that the very subsidiary matter— *Never* which now bulks so largely—of learning the words *commit words* of the play would be swamped in the process of *to memory* argument. Words should never be learnt, for the result—as with action, if the play is brought to that prematurely—is that they harden in the mind as actualities when they should merely come to it as symbols. All solitary study whatever is (once again) to be deprecated. For to study the play, apart from studying your fellow-actors in the play, is to prefer dry bones to flesh and blood. There is much to be said for the method of the seventeenth-century music-teacher, who locked up the instrument upon his departure for fear that his pupil might practise. Actors might well leave their books behind them on the table. It is in the untroubled intervals between meetings that ideas may make good growth and opposing points of view tend to re-conciliation. That sort of solitary study by which, so to speak, with your mind quiescent, the matter in hand seems to study *you* is profitable enough. It is even, for most memories, the easiest way of assimilating the dialogue. A sensitive mind rebels against nothing so much as getting words by rote.

The mystery of iden- tification again

And one hopes that even the most expert actors would not come to argue their way very slickly through this preliminary period. No play should move in an efficient straight line between first re- hearsal and performance. This time of survey and discovery is the time, too, when the first tendons are being formed which will come to unite the actor's personality with the crescent figure of the character itself. Here is the mystery; the gestation of this new being that is not the actor's consistent self though partaking of it ; that is not the character worn as a disguise; individual, but with no absolute existence at all, a relative being only, and now related alike to the actor as to the play. It will be slow in coming to birth : the more unconscious the process the better, for it does not work alike with everyone, never at the same pace, never to the same measure. Wherefore the producer may discover that, to rally his team and to save them from a premature awareness of themselves and each other, it may be well once or twice to move from the table to the stage and engage in the business of a scene or two. This exercise should not last too long, nor should the scenes that are tried follow too much in sequence ; for, above all things, the physical action of the play must not be defined while the thought and feeling that should prompt it are still unsure. But the shock of the change will be re- freshing. It will check the too easy growth of an agreement, the creation of a unity of purpose based only upon words, whether they be the play's

232

or the actors' arguments round and about the play.
Quite literally the company should be allowed to
feel their feet in the play, to stamp up and down
and restore the circulation which too much talk
may have slackened.

Having got thus far by the aid of two minor *Productions*
negatives, let us lay down a major one. The pro- *must be born*
duction itself must never be shaped before its natural *and not*
form has declared itself. By shaping we are to *made*
understand, of course, not only the physical action
of the scenes, but their mental and emotional action
as well—everything, indeed, that could be regulated,
were our play an orchestral symphony, by time
signatures, metronome markings, sforzandi, rallen-
tandi, and the rest, even by the beat of the conductor. It is tempting to compare conductor and
producer, but one must do so mainly to remark
that their powers, if not their functions, are very
different. To wield a baton at rehearsals only,
and even then to have neither terms nor instruments
of precision for explanation or response—the
limitation is severe. It is better to remember that
compared to music—and to a far greater degree
in comparison with painting, sculpture, and poetry
—acting is hardly capable of verbal definition. For
by admitting the weakness, by abjuring fixation and
finality, one can the better profit by the compen-
sating strength, the ever fresh vitality of the purely
human medium; and so the art will gain, not lose.
Some fixity, however, there must be, for the practical
reason, if for no other, that co-operation would be
impossible without it. But there is the æsthetic
reason too, and the theatre's problem is concisely
this: how to attain enough definition of form and
unity of intent for the staged play to rank as a
homogeneous work of art and yet preserve that

233

freedom of action which the virtue of the human medium demands.

Nothing is easier than to plan out a production in elaborate mechanical perfection, to chalk the stage with patterns for the actors to run upon, to have the dialogue sung through with a certain precision of pitch, tone, and pace, to bring the whole business to the likeness of a ballet. But nothing will be less like a play as a play should be. Here, too, it is the letter that killeth and only the spirit that giveth life. Even when such a poetical symphony as " A Midsummer Night's Dream " demands for its interpretation a rhythm of speech matched by rhythm of movement—individual, concerted, contrasted—which can only be brought by skilful hard practice to the point where it will defy forgetfulness, all this must still be taken the step further to the point where its cumbering recollection is defied, too. Rehearsals, be it noted, have always this main object of enabling an actor to forget both himself and them in the performance.

But preparation having been brought by one means and another to the stage when the play— now a grown, or half-grown, but still unshaped combination of the work of dramatist, producer, actors—has acquired life enough to be about to go forward by its own momentum, our *positive* rules (if they are discoverable) must begin to apply.

The two categories of a play's action: the conscious action

We must now divide the action (using the word comprehensively) into two categories. To the first will belong everything that can be considered a part of the main structure of the play (again using the word comprehensively to express the play, not as the dramatist left it, but as it has been so far brought to fuller being). And everything so included must be capable of clear definition: its

234

execution must not vary, it must rank for constancy
with the dialogue itself. It is obvious, for instance,
that the characters must come on and leave the
stage at particular moments in particular ways ;
we may take it for granted, too, not only that at
certain fixed times in fixed places certain things
must be done, but done always with the same emphasis and intention. This is common form. And
thus far (the inconstancy of its human medium always allowed for) the drama moves in line with the
more static arts. Into this first category, then, will
fall all ceremonial—the whole movement, for instance,
of such a play as the " Agamemnon." It will also
hold the broad relation in tone and time between act
and act, between scene and scene, and the emotional,
no less than the physical, structure of the action of
each scene, its muscular system, so to speak, as apart
from its integument, blood and nerves. We should
be right to rule into this category any features of
the play's interpretation which we hold must be
common to every production of it. We might well
include, too, all features which, peculiar to this one,
called for and were capable of any definition which
could be genuinely agreed upon by the interpreters
concerned; the greater the number of them the greater
the need of agreement, but the less easy its achievement. But these abstract terms become both too
vague and too positive. We must cite examples,
remembering, however, that no one will ever dup-
licate another and that as to each opinions may
legitimately differ ; such are the drawbacks to
æsthetic law-giving. And, as we must quote a
known play, we can but exemplify a second-hand
approach to it. To take, then, the occasion of the
screen's falling in " The School for Scandal " as a
simple case in point. The intention of the author

is obvious and the tradition of its expression recoverable if broken ; and it may not be practically worth while in this instance to do other than register both in the traditional form. But at each reproduction of the play there must be something like a fresh approach to the situation, and as that may—theoretically, at least, and tradition apart—dictate a remoulding of even the main lines of the interpretation, let us assume for the moment that we are wholly free. The treatment of such a situation must obviously be a matter of clear definition and, let us say, of honourable agreement among the people concerned. One uses this last epithet because it allows for the greatest possible freedom within the bounds of the understanding. You do not want, even for the sake of the most brilliantly concerted effect, suddenly to change your Charles Surface from a man into an automaton, nor must you dictate to your Sir Peter how he should feel and find his way, breath by breath, to this emotional trysting-place. If you do you will sacrifice to the second's mechanical perfection the life and the liveliness of whole minutes leading to it and away from it. Certainly there must be mutual concern here for far more than the words spoken and the places occupied in the scene. But we only need to establish an identity of *intention* among the actors, so that they may make of the saliency of the moment a knot, so to speak, into which they may tie, simply and surely, those strands of the play's purpose that they severally hold. A most expert feat, no doubt, if it is to be as perfect in its execution as its purpose, and one which can by no means be left to happy accident. But it will be most fruitfully achieved if there is no closer agreement upon means than is absolutely needed to compass the ends. And the closer the agreement upon the end—that is to say, the more skilled in sympathy the group of actors are—the less will the precise means be found to matter. In the production of plays, as in many other things, the art lies largely in discovering what not to do ; and quite certainly the less you are ever seen doing the better.

One could multiply examples and doubtless find better ones. But the constricting fault of most modern play production is to treat every possible moment with the utmost severity of regulation, and it is more to our main purpose to insist on the needlessness of nine-tenths of it. And we can do so inferentially by going on to consider our second category.

If the first, for the sake of a single adjective, is to include all the conscious action of the play the second may be said to hold all the unconscious or —deferring to the psychologist's lingo—the subconscious action. Into it, then, we are to bring everything in the play's acting—movement, expression, emotion, thought—which may, without disturbance of the production's structure or to the distraction of fellow actors, be carried forward in any one of fifty different ways. We say fifty, as we might say a dozen or a hundred, simply for comparison with the single way of the first category. And there may be in theory as good an æsthetic reason for exactly enumerating the fifty as there is for prescribing the one. There will appear, indeed, in our plan an indirect method of prescription of the fifty ; for the sub-conscious self has still to be regulated. But practically what we are after is a consciousness of complete freedom. And though the freedom can never be quite complete, neither can any action in the first category be made perfectly accurate, for in each case the work is done in the incalculable

Unconscious or subconscious action

human medium which defies (and perhaps despises) exactitude. We aim, then, through this freedom at an appearance of spontaneity. This may seem to some people a very little thing ; if it does they have not a very discriminating taste for acting. That spontaneity itself is unattainable a ha'porth of knowledge of the art will inform us. The task of ensuring its appearance has exercised other writers than Diderot, and this and the many underlying problems are in one way or another stumbling-blocks to every actor worth the name.

The Scylla and Charybdis of automatism and self-consciousness
The hardening effect of the " long run " upon acting will be admitted. We may owe to that system in England a care and a finish—if a trade finish !—in production that was unknown before. But the art of acting has incidentally well-nigh been destroyed by it ; for it has reduced art to automatism. No wonder people talk of the cinema as a substitute for the theatre when they are content in their ignorance to see and applaud an actor's thousandth photographic reproduction in his own person of what was once (perhaps) a piece of acting. It should be plain to anyone that no human being can *act* " Hamlet " eight times a week, if acting is to involve anything more than physical gymnastic. He must, to escape intolerable wear and tear, keep the finer parts of his human mechanism out of commission for at least two performances in every three. And the actor of Rosencrantz is brought to a self-defensive automatism for the very opposite reason. If he did not make himself into a machine, the little round of the part travelled over and over would reduce him to a state of histrionic imbecility. What a piece of work is a man that we should bring him, even as Rosencrantz, to the state of a squirrel in a cage !

238

But the tendency to automatism, though lessened, is by no means abolished by the simple expedient of putting on a play three times a week instead of eight and letting the actors play other parts on the remaining nights. Other influences make for it : disciplinary rehearsals ; or the actor's own effort to build up, by one trial after another, the best possible performance, and having, as he thinks, attained it, then to register each item and try to preserve a constant combination of them all. This is a tempting method; for who does not want—on the stage or off —to be always at his best ? But it is a vain desire, both off the stage and on. By all means should a man at performance, as at rehearsal, be alert to eliminate clumsy touches of expression. But the quite conscious replacing of them with touches more effective (once the preliminary periods of preparation are over and if he and his part have grown to a single artistic entity) will result in his considering these details rather than the entity which was the objective of his first study, and altogether obliterating under these effects his apprehension of the cause, which is that artistic entity's life. If he anchors himself to this bit of business, to that intonation, even to a particular trick of thought or emotion which he finds he can command, his performance will become in time a mosaic of excellent fragments : disturb one, a dozen others are loosened, and then, with the oncoming of fatigue, the whole may begin to break up, for there is no vital principle to unite them. He may satisfy himself at some moment with a particular reading of a passage and then, by a stroke of his mind, be able to transfer his conviction of it to a sub-conscious self which will faithfully record and can later re-express the idea : his conscious mind thus being freed again for the larger

239

view of part and play. But even so, when, in time, a mass of such detail has accumulated and is brought into action as a concrete whole by the sub-conscious mind, no inner conviction will be prompting it: it will be invariable and lifeless.

Pure conven-   The problem is no easy one. There is the
tionalism   natural effort after economy to be counted with. At one time and another an actor of Hamlet must try and live through the emotions of Hamlet. But if he were so spendthrift of his energies as to try to re-experience them all at one performance it would be long enough before he could rise to another. Some conventionalism of feeling is as necessary as is, for the sake of economy of thought, the reduction to rule of the play's main movement.

And we can conceive, no doubt, purely conventional acting of a very satisfying and beautiful kind, appropriate enough in its place. The ritual of the Mass is a performance of this sort, and most imaginative people prefer it to the ranting, personal appeal of a revivalist meeting. Greek tragedy, with its religious element, sustains conventional treatment well—our modern difficulty being mainly to establish an agreement between actors and audience upon the alphabet of its convention. But in the theatre of the last three hundred and fifty years the element of individual interpretation has come to occupy a dominating place, has developed in complexity and intensity quite beyond the compass of conventional expression. That is clear. And though we may lose thereby in dignity and force it is to be hoped we gain something in vitality
The limits of and subtlety. It is possible, too, that the advance
the personal of interest in dramatic art, with its mirrored effects,
appeal is due to civilized resentment of a too direct emotional appeal—to fear of it, if you will. There
240

is reason in such an objection, sound reason. We resent the ranting preacher and the frothy demagogue because they are too intimately connected with the message they bring. If we dislike the men and their method our would-be welcome of the matter is hindered, though as often we may disapprove the matter and yet half-wittingly be caught by its terms. God and our country, our honour, morality—it is a stiff wrench even to seem to be turning our back upon these nobilities; yet he is a poor demagogue that can't wave some such flag—dressing his part, too, for still better effect, in uniform or canonicals, the frock coat of the statesman or the tweed cap of Labour.* But give us the *oratio obliqua* of art and we are at our ease. Its appreciation puts us to some trouble, no doubt. Anyone can sit still and be preached at, but to get the sense out of a play, a picture, or a symphony we must learn to do our share. But then, upon this third factor of the play thus intruded we can exercise our criticism without prejudice: or we can give sympathy and still withhold judgment. We can enter, friends and adversaries together, into a world of make-believe. This is an exact and no derogatory description of it. It is in that world, where we are free for the moment from self-consciousness, self-seeking doubt, and fear, that our true beliefs are made.

And so it becomes plainer, perhaps, why in the theatre, where the personal appeal is naturally so strong, we need by some means to detach the actor from himself. Effort to charm us by chorus girl's smile, comedian's wink, or by a tragedian self-

* There was a certain Labour leader about 1906 who, after dining out, carefully changed back into more plebeian broadcloth before reappearing in the House of Commons. But the other day one turned up in a dinner-jacket. He was a privy councillor, no doubt.

centred in the limelight is the demagogy of drama, and rightly to be resented. And it is to be the more condemned; for, at least, the politician drags in no playwright as an unwitting accomplice.*

To ask for sheer impersonation will not serve ; playing at disguises is only a good child's game.† We need interpreters, but it must truly be the characters of the play which they interpret. Working in full consciousness they cannot do it; self will be asserted. Identification of the actual with the imaginary, of the actor with his part, asking for a murderer to play a murderer and for a saint to appear as a saint, is as impossible as the fiction of personation is puerile. And so we are brought to the need for a creation in the actor of something like an integral sub-conscious self.‡

---

* Not that one condemns chorus girl or comedian for their goings-on, as long as they make no pretence to be practising the art of the theatre.

† Besides, it is not really a practical game in the theatre. Mr. W. T. Stead displayed the logic of it when he demanded, in joke no doubt, that an actor should play but one part throughout his career, lest illusion be spoilt. *See* also p. 164.

‡ It might be claimed that there is in all of us, as product of our civilization, a third and entirely unconscious self that operates as automatically in expressing itself in simple movements and gesture as it does in breathing and digesting food. But this is not artistic expression. It is true that this self, the product of civilization, should be perfectly—that is, healthily—regulated if the artistic expression that will later be founded upon its activity is to be beautiful and complete. But this task we relegate to general education; and if our school of the theatre specially provides for such training it should do so with little more particularity than any institution of the sort might provide a gymnasium in which the students could keep themselves fit. Animals are un-self-conscious, and in their natural beauty, having nothing further to express by it, put to shame poor human beings engaged in artistic enterprise. For this reason they should never be brought upon the stage in a play. The two values contradict each other.

In this creation a double process is involved: first *The mystery* the mental search and the provocative argument into *yet again* and around the character and the play that we have described ; then the sensitizing of the actor's receptive faculties, mental and emotional, too.* It should be a concurrent process ; and the argument will promote the mental receptivity—it will, at least, if the parties to it direct their attention more to the play, the third factor, than to each other. The emotional part of the sensitizing process is not so demonstrable. It is difficult enough even to define sympathy, and, in human relations, it is certainly a fatal error to try and cultivate it by prescription. But even in the world of make-believe one can affirm no more than this : let the actor surrender himself wholly to the idea of his part as it forms itself to his apprehension under the spell of this generous study, and there will, by his Muse's grace, be added unto him, as fruit of the personal surrender, this mysterious second personality, which will be not himself and yet will be a part of himself. He will be wedded to his idea. We make poetry of such a relation between two human beings : we see or experience the shadow of it sometimes. In its fulness it must doubtless remain an ideal. Nor is its realization quite to be desired ; for no two lives can run wholly together, nor must one yield passively to the other's way. Life demands separate and uncompleted service. If in some other world union could bring perfection that would be worth preparing for. But here and now in the world of art the impossible is possible. Surrender to an idea robs no man of

* One is tempted to add physical. Wave your hand suddenly within an inch of an actor's face and watch for the automatically released mobility of expression.

his birthright : these wedded beings born of the actor's art live for their one purpose only, and will perish unsustained by it. While they live, though, their very limitations give them power, and perfection, too, to a degree. In any fine playing of a part— of Imogen, shall we say ?—there is a power not the player's own, and a beauty which certainly does not accompany her off the stage. Nor can the complete effect be accounted for by adding together the words of Shakespeare, the woman's looks and voice, the theatre's lights and scenery. Pick the whole thing to pieces, and you'll no more find out the secret than you'll find a soul in the body's anatomy. If it does not lie in the surrendered self, and the possession for the time of the obedient body by the changeling idea, then where? Diderot explains the matter carefully and cleverly. One must answer that he never can have acted a part in his life and *The actor* *let himself go* in it. That phrase is pregnant. Now, *"lets himself* every actor has experienced, more or less, the sensa-*go"* tion of being under his part's control. Mind, there can be delusion as to this, with direful consequences. Letting yourself go, when no rounded and complete idea does control you, is like losing your temper, and may result, likewise, either in feckless screaming or a helpless inarticulation. Being soundly angry with anger's cause behind you is another matter, as everybody knows. One may test and value the masterly sensation both in life and art by the extraordinary coolness and clarity of mind that should accompany it.

Once you have learnt the secret; then, as you act a part so studied, while you may still choose what to do, you can feel assured that whatever you may do will be characteristically right. Impulse, moreover, to do this or that will not wait upon effort or for a particular call. Through the sensitive channel which the interpreter has now become will flow unchecked the thoughts and emotions generated in the part's studying. These will have been shaped (we recapitulate) ; those of them upon which the play's structure as a work of art depends, definitely and consciously—and they must not be vague or varying, and at each fixed point the interpreter must consciously control and direct them. He must, moreover, never let this side of the part's playing escape his quite conscious control, or it will degenerate into automatism; and automatism will not do. But to the rest he need only sub-consciously attend. To demeanour, tones, gestures, and the like he need now oppose no mental bar.* And as they shape themselves spontaneously they will be fresher and more vital ; they will come and go with an ease which interposed calculation could only deaden and destroy. If the underlying idea is just and consistent, if the interpreter is physically trained and mentally and emotionally sensitized—if his faculties, that is to say, are sufficiently at one with his conception—then all that he does or can do will now have appropriate value and stand in right proportion to the whole. And this will be so even though the appearance of what he does may never be twice alike. Indeed, it never will be, because the process is in a very near sense natural and not mechanical at all. And it never should be if we are to take full advantage of the human medium. Far better, though, that this principle of change, thus kept constantly in flow, should not, half the time, be discernible in definite changes at all. To try to save

* If one may borrow a simile from electrical engineering : he need not pass their current through the converter of his conscious mind.

a play's acting from hardening by arbitrary changes which only disturb its right rhythm and melody is to gain for it a very indifferent freedom. No one wants a scene done differently every night. An actor's response to a situation and a line, his own or another's, may well seem to be identical six times out of ten. One only wants to be sure that it is a genuine response.

There is a possible extreme of self-surrender to be noted and avoided. Against extra passivity the actor must be on his guard, or he will find himself, within this second category, the victim of automatism again. He must remember with what amazing swiftness, within such artificial limits as a play's performance, habit is established. And unless the quiescence of the conscious mind helps the receptive, sub-conscious, emotionally expressive self to be only the more keenly alive—and, even when in complete physical quiescence, to be actively alive *— the method fails.

* I find an instance of how this may be in the memory of the Art Theatre at Moscow and a performance there of Tchekov's " The Cherry Orchard." It will be remembered how, in the third act, Madame Ranevsky comes out of the ballroom to hear of the sale, asks but a couple of brief questions, and then stays listening till the curtain falls, never speaking another word. It was not till I re-read the play after seeing it that I was reminded that she could not have spoken a word. The impression left on me by Madame Tchekov's silent performance was that she had played a chief part in a long and strenuous scene. As she had. But how was the effect produced ? One could answer : by doing nothing. That in a sense would be true, if one means that there was not— as far as I could detect—any elaboration of business which, however discreetly contrived, must have taken attention and detracted value from the figure of Lopakhin, who, flushed with his triumph, struggling with a sort of shyness, vocally dominates the scene. For such a figure at that moment, and throughout the play, is Madame Ranevsky that had the actress deliberately done *anything*

246

Faced with a school of histrionic sleep-walking we should return with joy to such a confident brilliancy of execution as the competent player deals out to us upon a piano. That is not to be despised, upon occasion, even when translated into the feebler conditions of the theatre. But we are now seeking for the peculiar quality which the constituents of this

at all she must not only have captured all eyes herself, but have blinded us to everyone else on the stage. The stage directions say that she weeps bitterly, and any actress might regard this as an invitation to " score " by that simplest of all methods of scoring. As far as I remember, Madame Tchekov sat down at the table as the curtain fell, and that was all. But whatever she did was enough. It left her, as she should be, the central figure of the scene. But more would have been more than enough, and would inevitably have obliterated the others. Now we can be quite sure that such an effect was not gained by doing nothing. That would allow the construction of the play and the mechanical arrangement of the scene, with all their virtue, far more than their due. And if this is doubted, substitute in such a case any one actress equally suitable in appearance and manner for any other, and see if the result is the same. It might be more to the point to argue that Madame Tchekov reaped at that moment by entire passivity what she had sown in action during the rest of the play, and that having set her face as one sets a clock she could have safely left her Lopakhin to play the scene while she thought of what she would have for supper; and that if she would do no such thing it had only to be from respect for the rest of her performance, or self-respect generally, or regard for her audience. Why bring in this last consideration? How can an audience distinguish the state of mind, or the degree of emotion, present behind a carefully expressioned face and an appropriately attitudinized figure? An answer is implied in the fact that to no discerning audience, or upon any important occasion, would the most callous performer of a part risk impoverishing the scene by distracting herself from it. Is this mere superstition, to be yielded to when fear is upon you, or is there any value in this sub-conscious activity? If so, by what process is its power conveyed? Are we to suppose that emotional rays of some sort emanate from the still, silent figure? I do not pretend to say. But personal magnetism is a very palpable thing, and why it should not be controlled, characterized, and directed, I do not know.

art of acting can be made to yield us; and that must, it would seem, reside in some particular virtue of the human medium itself, since that is the drama's distinctive possession. We see its vices easily and often enough, an egotism that must dislocate any *Acting the* artistic form.* Its virtue, then, should probably *art of* be sought in the opposite direction. And this may *sympathy* well be found in the very human faculty of sympathy —experience transmuted to instinct—in its integration and epitomising, under the guise of art, of that great human achievement, by which to the calculable sum of fellowship there is added a mysterious gift. We call it the spirit of a race, the moral of a regiment, the character of a family or an assembly. For as with music;—when melody and harmony have been accounted for and praised, through these we have been spoken to, we find, of supernal things—so it is, too, with great drama finely shown us. What is that, seemingly, but the repetition of words and the movements of men and women for an hour or two upon a lit and painted stage? And yet, by furthering with their best thoughts the thoughts of the poet, and more, far more, by yielding themselves utterly, body and spirit, as instruments to the harmony of the play's purpose, a company of actors does bring to birth a thing of powerful beauty that was not in the play before, that is not in themselves, but has now some of the absolute virtue of fine music, some of the quality

* Let me, however, record my personal experience that only bad actors are artistic egotists (though there are other sorts to be found in the theatre, as elsewhere), or, at least, that their badness is generally in direct ratio to their egotism. But then it is badness in relation to the play, not to their own performances—which, alas, are all that the undiscerning public (and therefore success-hardened actors) seem to care about.

248

that can make small things great.   There is honour
in this art.

As yet, in our modern theatre, the art of acting *The*
has been but outlined.   We guess at the fine ritual *childhood of*
of Greek drama, at the splendid crude pageantry *the art*
of the mediæval stage, we can recall to life something of the passionate enjoyment of swift words
which must have fired the Elizabethan actors.   The
drama of that fifty years was like a tongue of the
Renaissance flame licking into splendour our English common life.   The eighteenth century gives
us the comedy of manners; truly not much more.
But good manners were of artistic value upon the
stage when they were valued in the world, and they
might be appreciated now for other reasons.   The
eighteenth and nineteenth centuries have seen also
the dominance of the " star " actor with his pocket-
ful of popular effects.   One does not mean to
smother in such a category the fame of a Garrick,
a Kean, a Salvini, a Duse, whose genius must have
shone bright in any surroundings ; one could bring
other names besides to the completion of an honourable list.   And even the pretenders to great title,
who do more harm to their absolutist cause than
good to themselves, are more sinned against by the
system than they are, to begin with, wilful sinners
against their art.   A " star " is not necessarily a
being whose one aim is to outshine.   His plaint,
on the contrary, is more often that he cannot find
adequate reinforcement for his beams.   He patheti-
cally asks why.   It is an innocent question, but for
all that such a pertinent one that in the validity of
the answer lies the theatre's whole destiny.

Let us think of a performance to which the
audience should come, ignorant of the play, its
author, producer, to be given no programme, nor told

249

the name of any actor there. If this were an ideal, its fulfilment, as with most ideals, might be a little too arid to be quite desirable. But the supposition does point to a concentration upon the acted play and upon nothing else whatever. It presumes that in favour of this it is as important to de-personalize actors, producer, and dramatist as it is for the audience themselves to sit attentive and anonymous. Who has not been at a play with great persons prominent in a box, and half the spectators wondering how they were taking it? It is a difference of degree—not of kind—if, while the first act drags, we are saying to ourselves "Wait till Miss Smith comes on," or, when the curtain falls on the third, " How well Mr. Brown did that ! " And though the star's supporter may think that in his playing of Rosencrantz he gives himself wholeheartedly to Hamlet the play, and the player of Hamlet the Prince believe of himself the same, at the best they both reckon without the idolatry which is innate in the whole affair from the moment the one " sees himself " as Hamlet and the other is engaged to "support" him, down to the arrival of the audience intent upon the attractions of their favourite actor, and only deepening damnation by saying reverently under their breath, "And in Shakespeare, you know!" It is for this idolatry that we must somehow substitute a faith in the living drama itself. Still, let us not be too superior. We have most of us joined at some time in the " roar of applause " to which the popular actor has so modestly bowed his head, and have enjoyed the roaring as much as he has— possibly more, for with accustomed success there comes, even at the moment, weariness and a bitter aftertaste. And if this sort of thing may be said only to fit the childhood of an art it is the more welcome, therefore, to the child-mind in ourselves, nourished on those games of make-believe in which we ourselves were glorious protagonists. The joy of the theatre to many of us is that it stimulates the fading memory of them. But it may be, too, that perennial regret for the days of the great actor marks more than the personal ageing of the particular grumbler ; it may show some general maturing of mind through a cycle of theatrical culture of whose curve we are not yet aware, under whose influence, also, the race of great actors, in the sense of our use of the epithet, is perishing. And it does certainly seem that in these days—in answer, it may be, to our present need of an interpretative art—there is being precipitated from the jolly crudities we have so far enjoyed a new idea of the theatre which—little more than an idea as yet— is making other and harder demands upon actors and audience both, but has a far richer promise to fulfil.

This demand, as it has fallen on the playwright, *The demands* he has honoured fairly so far, even if we must *of its* qualify the response as at times rather rigid and per- *adolescence* verse ; the inevitable consequence, this, of his estrangement from a living theatre. He has been lucky and unlucky both in this detachment : the crippled, half-dead theatre has been only luckless in this as in other deprivations. And upon the actor, powerless to save his own artistic soul—not having, indeed, in isolation any soul to save—the accumulated demands of a renaissance are now heavy. His obedience must be asked to a stern and searching training of body, mind, and imagination. Next, he must turn his back upon all the attractive tricks which save him so much trouble and can earn him such applause. And, finally, he must

251

be ready to surrender himself and to merge his carefully cultivated artistic identity in a company of his fellows, believing that when in each product of their mutual work it again emerges, if he will often not have gained as much as he gave, yet he will not have given in vain.

This may be much; but it is, after all, no more than the world asks of most of her workers. Is the actor to take his place among them, or does he want to stay playing with the other spoiled children?

He, in his turn, may ask of us, his audience, what taste we'll show for the results of all this. Well, it is the privilege of truth to make itself believed, and of true art to command respect, but of neither, doubtless, to hold us by their first tentative strivings. To these we must extend patience and an interest more in the end than in the immediate means. Few of us have the eye of faith, though, or the knowledge that goes out to meet, or even the sympathy that will sustain the single-minded adventurer. And many strivings in the theatre fail because allegiance to an uninspired and uninstructed audience means the making of the best of that world of approval even at the expense of the more dimly seen salvation of an empiric art. Therefore it is that this third factor in the theatre's future is all-important. An audience there must be. Not the finest playing of the best play in the world can fully exist without it. Its presence is the logical extension of the co-operation between actors and playwright, and between the actors themselves, upon which the whole art rests. Not many steps further can the theatre even go than its audience will wholeheartedly follow. Nor should it wish to, for in this wider partnership is the art's final strength. In the collective consciousness so formed by playwrights, actors, and

252

audience we can gain from the acted drama an understanding of human relationships deeper and subtler than words and their reasoning can give. Sensitized by art, overtones are added to our nature's scale. And what more wonderful instrument has man to play upon than is this living self? What greater capacity for an orchestration of humanity, with all its thoughts and passions, will he find than lies in a company of men and women highly attuned?

THIS book's concern is to establish a point of view of the theatre that is unfamiliar perhaps, if not new. Much successful achievement, therefore, under the present system falls outside its scope, and many efforts at reform must be seen at an obscuring angle. Not that one wishes to decry either success itself that has no further cares, or the gallant struggles of the victims of the present commercial circumstances to reconcile contradictory causes and effects. Belief persists in them that if only the thistle seed is good enough some sort of grapes will result. Why should not art and twenty per cent. go hand in hand ? All we should ask for is a good play well acted. What can the system matter ? And it is true enough that when it comes to putting ideas into practice there will always be unsuspected difficulties, one's own incapacities not least among them. Then is no time to be discussing the right way. One does the best one can. So it may be worth our while now, perhaps, to end by surveying some of the minor problems that will beset compromise ; to demolish, if we can, a few of the fallacies that haunt the indeterminate space between the two worlds which one will be pledged to make the best of. For this is the worst of such a situation ; once committed you must protest your satisfaction with it or go forward, or go back ; it is the worst of a half-way house that, as no road is ever straight, you are bound to be a bit in the wrong direction when you rest there. And the best of a point of view is that it overlooks difficulties. But one does not occupy it unsympathetically for all that.

Compromise and catchwords In the theatre, though, the path of compromise is hard. " Certainly," says the patron of art to the ardent young reformer, " give me good plays well

254

acted. I ask no more," and he puts down some money. He might as well go to a nurseryman and ask for a fully developed garden by Thursday week. The nurseryman could, no doubt, produce the effect of one which would last, say, till Friday fortnight. A close parallel. The money is spent— some theatre landlord probably gets most of it— the patron of art then bethinks himself that the drama is an extravagant pastime and an unsatisfactory business. But it isn't a pastime, and any business would be unsatisfactory run on such lines. And even if you only want to have good plays well acted, that isn't a business enterprise either.

And the theatre suffers from catchwords. The word " repertory " has become almost a curse. In America the term " Little Theatre " has acquired so many significances as now to have none. One may best qualify a little theatre by saying that if it is a success you wish it were bigger, and if it is a failure you wish that it weren't there at all. A repertory theatre, according to the enthusiasts, may be anything from the Comédie Française to a band of beginners who produce plays haphazard in a back drawing-room and are animated by what they call the repertory idea. What, in heaven's name, is that ? You might as well have an idea that you run a motor-car by pouring petrol in somewhere—into the radiator, perhaps. If the term " repertory " is to keep any specific meaning at all it should only be used for an organization by which plays are kept as ready for the stage—to make comparison between a simple and a complex business— as books are kept to your hand in a library. If a clearer definition is needed—and if one is to argue the advantage of a system one cannot be too clear—it will be found that, as a matter of practice, the

" repertory idea " must consent to be bound by conditions very near akin to the following. In the theatre expressing it no single play must be given for more than two or three performances running, or for more than three or four in a week, and at least three or four different plays must be performed in a week; so that as a consequence no one play can be performed more than about a hundred times in a season. But it may be played in every one of a hundred seasons, as, no doubt, certain plays in the repertory of the Théâtre Français have been. And a theatre is not worked in this way because of some vague ideal behind it, but because the demand if thus fulfils involves this particular sort of organization, and can be satisfied by no other—as is demonstrable and as we had better proceed to demonstrate.

A " stock " theatre, with a permanent company producing fresh plays week by week, or month by month, is not a repertory theatre. A permanent company is in itself a very desirable thing ; but to produce a play at one time, let it lapse, and revive it at another is no more to keep it alive than it would be if the process were applied to a human body. Nor, again, is a season of a few months or less, in which half a dozen plays—for all that they are played variously week by week—have been rehearsed at a stretch by a company especially engaged for them, more than by courtesy a repertory season. It is at best a temporary lath-and-plaster façade for a repertory theatre. Walk up the steps, push open the door, and there is nothing behind. There are, moreover—it may be stated pretty dogmatically— only two logical and economical ways of organizing the drama as a continuing and professional activity: by a full-fledged repertory system, if artistic economy is what you are after ; for long runs, if you want to make all the money you can in the shortest possible time (you may equally lose it). All com- promise between the two systems means waste of money or of energy, extravagance, and treble the work for half the result—not even for half, indeed, but rather for a different kind of result altogether.

Now it should be freely owned that there is much *The defence* to be said for the long-run system from the public's *of the long-* point of view, something from the playwright's, and *run system* a great deal from the business manager's : its dominance, indeed, is the charter of his own.

In a big, busy-living city it is a convenience for the playgoer to know that a play is at his service upon any evening he may be moved to go to it. For this all he seems to sacrifice is the loss of those plays that exhaust their demand in a single month of his absence or over-occupation, but as they are mostly classed as failures he hardly regrets them. As to the plays that have little chance even of a thirty-day popularity, managers, as a rule, do not produce them at all. But he does not stop to think what he misses in this direction. A play to him is (quite reasonably) not altogether a play until it is. to be seen in a theatre. So the average playgoer in a big, theatre-filled capital city will never actively complain of the long-run system. At the worst he wearies of the plays he does find, for so many of them seem to run, not for a hundred nights, but (under changing titles) for ever, and he slackens in his playgoing.

The city whose theatres are served by the touring system barters, so to speak, a disadvantage in this par- ticular form of the long run, for some of the advantages and some disadvantages of the old stock theatre ways. The playgoer in Manchester, Liverpool, Glasgow,

Boston, Philadelphia, and Pittsburg does certainly seem to get his drama fresh and fresh. But in practice he rather receives it stale and stale. Plays either reach him when their popularity in London and New York has been exhausted and their principal players are sick of them, or as slavish imitations of the original production. And in these days of high wages and costly transport many do not reach him at all.

But the long-run system, under whatever guise, suits the business-manager.* It suits him best if he owns or runs the theatre building and lets someone else in to produce the plays. By letting the temporary partner out as quickly as he let him in— and quicker !—he can cut his losses on the failures, while he takes profit on success equivalent not only to the commercial merits of the play, but to the preferential value of his building, for that has enabled him to strike a good bargain with the producer beforehand. In any case his finance is simple ; and that is a great thing. He invests in a production, sucks it dry, and scraps (or all but) the material, turns off the hands employed, starts his next venture on a new and appropriate basis of expense, and keeps his overhead charges at a minimum.

The system seems to suit the dramatist, but he is unwise to believe so. Certainly if his play is a success he makes money quickly. And he has all the available acting talent of London or New York to choose from : he has the monopoly both of the theatre's resources and of the attention of the cast, while he coaxes or drills them, or watches them being drilled, to a clockwork precision of ensemble and a meticulous obedience to the last comma of his text.

* I use the term here in its general, not its particular, sense.

But a slight objection to the whole glorious business (and the dramatist should have been the first to note this) is that it tends utterly to destroy the art of acting. This cannot prosper under such conditions of employment. It may profit a little by failure, but what it cannot endure is the numbing monotony of success. So acting's place is taken by the artifice of stage effect, a mechanism guaranteed fool-proof, which makes, therefore, for the encouragement of fools both among the actors and in the audience. It may really be asserted that most young playgoers of to-day do not know what acting is. They yield themselves happily to the emotional illusions of the play itself, but the stage attitudes they are accustomed to, that bear the stigmata of the art of its interpretation, have about the relation to acting that an oleograph has to a Rembrandt.

Verdict : the long run guilty of the destruction of the art of acting

And this alone should suffice to condemn the long run system, whatever may be its convenience to public or financier, for one cannot too often insist that the art of acting is the theatre's very flesh and blood. Besides this, however, it keeps from the stage, year in and year out, about seventy-five per cent. of the best drama written ; leaves it to grow dusty on bookshelves, while as a discouragement to the new writing of plays fit to survive what could be more effective ? The qualities that look for slow gathering appreciation and make for survival are naturally no more in demand in a profit-seeking theatre than they are in the business of publishing best-selling novels and popular magazines. The publisher however, helped by cheaper manufacturing conditions and easy distribution, may, and usually does, put out an assortment of books good, bad, and indifferent. But the long run manager, if he be a consistently good man of

259

business never nervously or hypocritically hedging in the direction of " art," should rather try to specialize in the production of the unfit.

The " short run " little better

But to replace the long run by the short run, by the experimental matinée or the hastily concocted " repertory " season, is no remedy; and not even the use or misuse of that blessed word " repertory " will make it one. We may protest in the interests of the actor's art against his repetition of a single part eight times a week for six months or more,* but it does not follow that either in his art's interest or his own he will welcome the slave-driving and the uncertainties, artistic and financial, which mostly characterize the alternatives offered him. The long-run system with its careful preparation does at least ensure him against making an unpremeditated fool of himself. Personal success may be longer in coming, but it is obviously easier to sustain when it is partly measured, not by how many plays he will appear in, but how few. The financial conditions he finds either very good or very bad, but that uncertainty has its own queer attraction. Besides, this is the tune that is called, and apparently he must dance to it. London success brings him leisure also, which he can employ in playing golf, or collecting pictures, or even in a second occupation. Lastly, as many of this stage generation have never learnt to act at all, but only to give exhibitions of stage artifice, they really do not suspect what an absorbing business it can be. It should be added, though, that the younger people do struggle against this crippling of their opportunities. And for this

* A recent theatrical entertainment has survived for something like six years. But, indeed, there seems to be no reason why, when a theatre serves a city of six million people and its rising generations, not to mention its visitors, a play should not run for ever.

260

we have to thank both the stirring of their spirits by such institutions as the Academy of Dramatic Art and the example, for all their failures, of the compromising reformers.

But let us now analyze the artistic conduct of a few of these reforming efforts, and discover why, with all their good will, based as they are upon a contradiction, they cannot serve as solutions of a difficulty. As essays in discontent they are admirable, and as evidence of a readiness to do anything rather than keep on grumbling even more admirable. But they had better not lay claim to essential virtues. *Why many gallant efforts at reform have failed*

To begin with, there can be no continuously fruitful combination between the efforts to sustain a play-producing establishment as a sound competitive business enterprise and the desire to make a theatre a home for dramatic art. Financial results may be as good—or as bad—in the one case as the other, and even the artistic results may look, on the surface and for a time, alike. But, aims differing, counsel will always be divided; and, indeed, the outlook, intentions, and the methods employed towards these separate ends should differ absolutely and totally.

The efforts to reform the theatre during the last fifteen or twenty years in English-speaking countries can roughly be split into two classes : those that have had enough capital and those that haven't ; ten per cent., perhaps, have been of the first class and ninety of the second. And one besetting danger has been that the capitalist, measuring the probabilities of success by the amount of money provided, and yet in his heart rather doubtful of the whole affair, has been apt to demand immediate results, financial or artistic, preferably both. This demand has, of course, led to an inordinate expenditure of capital energy, difficult to sustain. The promoters were making, it may be, for full-fledged repertory, but you cannot, so to speak, stick feathers into such an enterprise. For a theatre worthy of its purpose is a complex living organism—a thing of growth. It will grow, moreover, in seemingly unpredestined ways and at uncertain pace; so many influences does it owe life to. The strain of trying, god-like, to create at a stroke a full-grown thing, the impossibility of avoiding serious mistakes when neither time nor energy can be allowed for their correction, must lead to an exhausted smash. One is then told that the theatre wouldn't " pay," or that it wouldn't "work." Of course it wouldn't. Good heavens, a fisherman spends more patience to get one trout; and, what is more, it is the fishing he enjoys !

The cautious capitalist   Then there have been the enterprises of the cautious capitalist, who watches his expenditure with care and plays for the safety of each step he takes. These have endured better, but naturally at the cost of a limitation of enterprise, and, as a general consequence, of a low standard of work. For some degree of comprehensiveness is a necessary virtue in a theatre, and you cannot, moreover, retain talent in your service unless you give it good opportunity. Into this category would fall most of the "short-run" theatres, which by misplaced courtesy are dubbed " repertory."

There is something, of course, to be said for the short run, though nothing that is unequivocally in its favour. It enables a theatre to produce a number of plays ; and, if the audience could be perfectly mobilized—if, that is to say, any theatre could rely upon the constant and immediate sup-

port of a definite number of people for every production—the system would be so provokingly simple
and so financially sound that its artistic defects and
limitations would be too easily forgiven. But the
system's rigidity is its undoing. On the artistic
side this is patent from the beginning. On the
business side, why ever expect to achieve such a
mechanically perfect thing? And if the business
ministered to the art as it should do, instead of art
being asked to fit itself to business requirements,
the attempt would never be made. But business
has the whip hand; and the scheme seems so thrifty,
and if you have only so much money and do so
want to do something relatively worth doing the
temptation is great. We, however, must concern
ourselves with the absolute objections to it.

Should such a theatre have a permanent com- *Practical*
pany? The answer being inevitably Yes, several *difficulties*
difficulties at once arise.* If the size of it is to be *for*
suited only to plays of short casts then your choice *"practical"*
managements
of productions will be seriously limited. But if you
enlarge the company you must keep members of
it idle perhaps for weeks at a stretch; and, apart
from all other objections, good actors will not stay
with you to be kept idle. You may adopt the
" practical " compromise of calculating the size of
your company by the length of an average cast
and trusting to special engagements to fill the gaps
that a larger cast would show. But in the first

* This " inevitably " may be disputed. Well, one could plan,
no doubt, to furnish a theatre with rapid relays of productions,
each one cast *ad hoc*. But the effort, the friction, the waste of
time, energy, and money would be so stupendous that it is hard
to see how such a scheme could endure. It would, exhaustedly,
adapt itself before long to long runs or short runs, or to the touring
system, or to any other that showed some consideration for human
fatigue.

263

place you will be lucky, indeed, to find good actors waiting on a rank like cabs, ready for long rehearsals and a short run (in any case a most thriftless way of engaging them); and in the second a revival of the particular play would be very difficult, for you could not expect to make the same special engagements over again, and a second posse of strange actors would mean rehearsing *de novo*.   In practice the solution of this problem is evaded by the avoidance of plays that involve this difficulty.   But a policy which dictates the avoidance of good plays is a pretty poor policy.

Then arises the question : how short are the short runs to be, and are they all to be equally short ? Much hinges on the answer.   The length of a run must be settled beforehand.   At least if that is not a rule made to be only very occasionally broken, if the plan is simply to be one of taking off the failures and letting the successes run on, what management will be so consistently strong-minded as ever to limit the tide of success once it is flowing ?   And a course of short runs would come to mean that the theatre was involuntarily specializing in failure.

The outsider may say that a management with a well mobilized audience should, after a while, be able to guess pretty well the amount of attraction each play could be trusted to exercise.   On the contrary, the more experienced a manager the readier he will be to own that he can't.   And it comes in practice to his trying to strike a safe average run which will not expose his failures to too many empty houses, nor cheat his successes of too many full ones.   Further, as he must be tenderer towards his failures than towards the robuster success which, cut back in its prime, can be trusted to shoot up as strongly in a timely revival, he will rather set out to precognize a run that's too short than one that's too long. And so it happens that in this sort of theatre the preference has been mainly for a fortnight's, even for a week's, spell of performances.*

Here we touch an ineradicable weakness. If you are to change your bill so often, your productions must be scrambled and your actors shamefully overworked. The old stock company's way out of this difficulty was to hand to the actor, a while before the season began, a list of the parts he would play. With most he'd be familiar, for old plays made up about eighty per cent. of the programmes in those days. And the usual attention given to a new one can be gathered from the letters and memoirs of many an infuriated author. To-day, with matinées to consider, a fortnight yields not more than ten rehearsal days, ludicrously insufficient (with the laugh on the wrong side of the producer's mouth) for any play, old or new, if the time is to be used for anything like collective study. In stock company days it was the necessity of doing the job in about half the time that brought into being the curious technique of acting (misnamed

---

* At the Court Theatre, 1904–1907, it is true that while short runs—that is, runs of a length settled beforehand—were the rule they were varied in length, and there was never, I think, a weekly change of bill. But it is the one short-run experiment I know of in the West End of London, where there is a larger potential intake of audience, both mobilized and casual, than anywhere else (except, of course, in New York). And it must be remembered that the evening bills were almost exclusively drawn from the plays of Bernard Shaw, whose settled popularity was exceptional. Even with this, though—and an experimental matinée test to help one as well—good guessing was not easy. The Birmingham Repertory Theatre, I believe, with its mobilized audience steadily increasing, finds it possible to increase also the settled number of performances of a play. But the more these are increased the heavier does the penalty of miscalculation become.

tradition) more suited to dancing the lancers (which, indeed, it much resembled) than to the interpretation of a play.

The way out of the difficulty

There is, it is true, one method by which plays—new or old—can be produced under these conditions. The principal performer will be the prompter. The actor's study of his part will be the getting of a rough idea of the character and deciding what are to be its salient characteristics. The company will walk through the play once or twice, marking in their books where they come on and go off and their whereabouts on the stage at stated times. And that will be all. At the performance they will stand peeping at a door till the prompter from his central box beckons them on. The prompter will read the words *sotto voce*, they will repeat them loudly after him ; he can signal them if need be to their places, pantomime their business ; and, relieved of all such responsibilities of memory they can fling themselves into expressing the spirit of their parts. If plays must be produced under such conditions this is, perhaps, the best plan. It may be in any case the best. It may be that we make altogether too much fuss and take too much trouble over the job. Can we get all that is worth getting out of dramatic art by leaving it at the level of a living Punch and Judy? Possibly we can, in which case this book need not have been written.

It must be remembered, too, by people who wonder why we cannot restore the old stock companies to their prosperity that modern plays cannot so easily be stereotyped in casting or staging as could the old.* A return to the first phase of the

* Though the old plays were stereotyped in their acting it does not follow, however, that they should have been. And a queer consequence followed. The stock companies, composed of necessity

266

" star " system, by which certain eminent performers would go visiting with such parts in their
heads as Undershaft in " Major Barbara," Anthony
in " Strife," John Gabriel Borkman, and Abraham
Lincoln, while the resident company crammed the
rest of the play into theirs, and themselves as best
they could into the parts that remained ; the whole
then being subjected to a recognized ritual of production—this is possible, no doubt, but hardly
desirable. Better see the plays under such conditions, one might say, than not see them at all.
But modern plays are not generally remarkable for
the bravura passages which were the strength of the
old. They accord ill with the unyielding egoism
of a star player who treats his part as a personal
possession, while the rest move tentatively round
him, protesting or apologetic, disguising as best
they may their strangerhood. One disinherits a
modern play of its privileges of commonwealth at a
performance's peril.

And in what selection of modern parts a "juvenile,"
or a " heavy lead," or a " first old man " would
set out to equip himself in the hope of an engagement is almost beyond discovery.

The short-run theatre is in fact a short-sighted, if *Old methods*
heroically meant, attempt to provide for the new *and new*
drama by the old methods which the new drama *drama*

of actors following " lines " of parts—juveniles, heavies, first old
men and women, ingenues, soubrettes (there was even a curious
creature called a "singing chambermaid")—were, almost equally
of necessity, so catered for by playwrights anxious for production.
Hence arose a drama with characters drawn, not from life, but
from the resources of this Noah's Ark. Carefree, Charles, his
friend, Alderman Glutwell, Mrs. Glutwell, Angelina, their daughter,
Sophia, her cousin, Maria, her maid, Toby Taproom, an apprentice. It was a convention, like any other, grown to a tradition.
Robertson broke it. I think we cannot seriously mourn its loss.

267

itself rendered obsolete; an attempt, therefore, logically foredoomed to failure. And if the logic of the situation cannot convince us, it is open to anyone's observation that each step the drama takes towards a finer artistic freedom makes the task of the new stock company—for all its goodwill and for all its disguising as repertory—more hopelessly difficult.

Does this seem a needlessly virulent attack upon workers in a good cause? A called-for blow on their side, rather; for they cannot bite the hand that feeds them, and it is, of course, the financial feeding that is most often at fault. Of all the stupidities that pervade the theatre financial stupidities are the worst and really the least excusable. In London and New York more money is thrown away in a year in theatrical speculation and extravagance than would suffice to endow half a dozen genuine theatres. That is a truism. A truth, though, that still needs enforcing is that most of this money goes in things quite inessential to plays and their acting : profit rentals, advertisement, " library "* commissions, inordinate taxes, licence fees, water rates. Even as an industry it is neither well treated nor self-respecting.†

The good business man and the theatre But an industry it is, with its practice and ever-growing precedent; and a paying industry, or

* In English theatrical parlance a " library " is an outside booking-office. What a target for scorn in the phrase !

† As an instance of its ill-treatment one may quote the conduct of the London Water Board, who, to make up a deficit in their budget, imposed on the theatres rates which they did not even pretend were equitable, on the ground that the theatres could afford to pay. The fairness of the present Entertainment Tax may be disputable. But lack of industrial self-respect is evident in the balance-sheets of nine out of every ten theatrical enterprises. Quotation would take us too far.

268

people would not meddle with it. Bring a scheme, then, for the establishment of a genuine theatre before any average body of business men, and by instinct they consider it in the light of the dominating industrial conditions, for all that these may be demonstrably both the fruit and the root of insensate extravagance. And they cover their ignorance by such commercial platitudes as " The theatre must be economically managed." Excellent. But outline to them the genuine economy of a genuine theatre and they stare. " That needs a great deal of capital. The return will be slow, but will it be certain ? Why not a simpler scheme, a more modest beginning ? " Their minds are by this time havering uneasily from the theatre as a gay speculation to some glorified reminiscence of their own back-drawing-room experience. If it were a factory * they meant to build they would realize easily enough that money must be spent on equipment, on experience even, not to be returnable in a year or so. And the theatre, a higher organism than the factory, needs more liberal consideration, not less. If the enterprise is to be public-spirited then the good business man will opine that while, of course, it must not be expected to pay in any commercial sense (cent. per cent., or total loss, he will mean by that) it should, to justify its existence, be made to " pay its way." But that does not take us very much further, for it is its way that is in question. There are, of course, many very uncommercial ways of paying. It would be inconvenient, perhaps, to make a theatre as free to the public as is a picture gallery or a museum. Theatres are not places (even if galleries are) into which people should be

* But even in factories nowadays we are told that it pays to consider the human factor. Why ever suppose that it wouldn't ?

269

encouraged to wander idly. But suppose performances at twopence, fourpence, and sixpence a head, which, though crowded to the doors, would still stand very thinly on the credit side of a balance-sheet—would this justify the existence of a public-spirited enterprise? Or, again, if we put the value of dramatic art before public entertainment, is it better to perform a good play to a half-filled house than a worse play to an overflowing one, and, if so, why not a better play still to a house quite empty? Are plays always—or ever—to be judged by their immediate appeal? And if the theatre is a public-spirited enterprise what claim has a minority audience to consideration?

These questions may be academic and may seem foolish. But it is only by answering them and their kin, and by analyzing his own answers, that the good business man will be brought to a reasoning, if not reasonable, attitude towards an attempt at the founding of a genuine theatre. And if its promoter does not at this stage push controversy hard he must not grumble later if, when his first streak of luck fails him (and most of these schemes have, at least, a short attack of success—a sort of measles), he fails. Though there will follow from this a worse result, at which we may all most legitimately grumble. For from every such failure the whole cause of the theatre suffers. And a promoter may rightly argue, as he fights for conditions or against the misunderstanding of his aims, that far more is involved than his personal success or the prosperity of a single enterprise.

The one thing needful to begin with is that everyone concerned should agree upon what it is they are up to. No one will propose to give art a free hand and a Fortunatus' purse to dip into.

Whether they ought to may be a question, though it is a good case to argue that artistic self-sufficiency would, in the long run, do little but harm. And no one, presumably, will suggest that such a theatre's success should be judged merely by its money-making powers. Crowded houses are exhilarating, but the cause of the crowding must be any management's concern. What is wanted is a determinant.

This can be found, it would seem, in the audience *The* —that essential part even of the artistic completion *integrated* of a play. But by no means in the haphazard *audience* collection of people that we now describe by the term. If the audience is a completing part of the play's performance obviously its quality and its constitution matter. As well, almost, cast a play haphazard as suppose that anyone dropping in can, by virtue of paying half a crown or half a sovereign, carry through his passive part of the performance with credit. There is an art of listening. Five minutes' test will distinguish a good audience from a bad one ; and numbers have nothing to do with it. Now instinctively we write our plays and plan our productions with an eye to a perfect audience. Or, let us say that we should; for it's obvious that to do a thing less finely than you can do it for fear of misunderstanding is a fault in art. Therefore, not the least of the tasks of any theatre is to develop out of the haphazard, cash-yielding crowd a body of opinion that will be sensitive, appreciative, and critical. And when such an audience has been formed it can be regarded as an integral, if a not too rigidly calculable, part of the theatre's constitution. Certainly a manager must lead his public's opinion, and not look to be able to follow it. He had better, indeed, force the pace at times ; go

boldly ahead with but a few to follow him, leaving
the laggards to catch up as they can, even at the
risk of having to stop and wait, or at the peril of
taking a wrong path. It would be possible, of
course, so to organize an audience that they could
make positive choice of plays and the like ; but
inadvisable. The business of a government is to
govern, and no manager should let himself be
robbed of his initiative : it is the touchstone for all
his other qualities. Besides, this audience, the
constituency of his appeal, need not be thought of
under a single aspect. It will show divisions of
taste more or less constant, definitely attributable
sometimes to the various sections of the community
for which it is the theatre's duty to cater, such as
schools, bodies of teachers, and students, or societies
interested in drama from one point of view and
another. But even as a whole—and, perhaps, better
as a whole—such an integrated public can act as a
determinant. One supposes, be it noted, a theatre
doing such a quantity and variety of work that a
confirmed playgoer may find fairly full satisfaction
in his attendance there. The theatre, in fact, by
its policy must look to form its audience's taste, but
after that need not be ashamed to regard it as a
guide.

And as a determinant such a public should
surely content the good business man engaged in
an enterprise of public spirit. He will not have
genius rampant and irresponsible, with nothing less
mighty than the universe to appeal to. He will not
expect the easiest entertainment of the greatest
number to be his theatre's aim. But upon the basis
of an integrated audience he can budget.

The need for
a budget   The budgeting will always be a tiresome business, and for some time must be a very chanceful

272

one as well. It is a great drawback to the English-speaking theatre that, while its art has been to some small degree fostered, hardly any practical knowledge of its proper economy exists—economy here meaning housekeeping, and not more of a tyranny than a good housekeeper needs to exercise. It has always been so much easier to apply the recognized commercial standards and—these again being so hopelessly vitiated by association with the speculative theatre that they offended one's every purpose—to salt them with altruism; to say, for instance, to the well-meaning manager : " Go ahead, and you may lose on your classical swings just what you can make on your popular roundabouts."

But this is an even more vicious method. Why should a self-respecting roundabout do more than support itself ? Oh, but if it doesn't the swings are to be starved ; and they will grow more than ever exiguously and forbiddingly classical. Then, as a remedy, are we to make the roundabouts more popular still ? Such a lazy-minded policy leads one deservedly into muddle and loss, and one returns to the brutal directness of commercialism with relief.

Nor can one save trouble by laying down golden rules. They are to be rattled off by the dozen; all excellent, and not one that cannot be dangerously misinterpreted. It is simple, and true enough to be worth saying, that a theatre, if it is to do public service, should be given the freedom of the city, released from rent, rates, taxes, the cost of light and police and the necessity of advertising. These things the public should be ready, directly or indirectly, to lose if they are to profit by the theatre. It is worth noting that the smaller the scope of a theatre's work and the shorter the time the estimates cover, the greater will be every cost in proportion.

And it follows that every limitation of necessary equipment is an extravagance, not an economy; and every expenditure upon temporary needs equally an extravagance. If there is money to burn at first, and you accumulate a large store of scenery and clothes; a little later, their effective appeal to your public having been made, you are left with the obligation to go on using them ; and this will tell probably at the very moment when that back-wash of enthusiasm comes, from which all such enterprises suffer, and when you'll be needing, above all things, to set free inventiveness and fresh ideas. One lays up this sort of treasure only to wish that moth and rust would corrupt it sooner.

But there is one rule which, if not pure gold, has at least been tried in many fires. Always from the beginning pay the market-rate for everything and everybody, and if by good luck you get anything cheaper, write down the difference in pencil on the debit side of your accounts. For the deadly back-wash of that first wave of enthusiasm sweeps in among workers as well. If it were only the individual that had to keep himself up to the mark ! But the collective courage of a theatre is a very un-controllable thing, and if, at an unexpected and difficult moment, it may be sapped by a loss of energy, which for some reason is no longer to be given for nothing, but for which there is no proper provision of pay, from that moment, perhaps, dis-integration will begin, unobserved. And most likely it will not be observed until too late to check it. *Vice versa*, sell nothing under the market-rate ; or, if you do, see that the buyer suitably acknow-ledges the bonus, and that *somebody* pays the full price and knows what they are paying for. No complimentary seats should be allowed unless the cost of each compliment is written plainly somewhere. No privileges to patrons and guarantors and the like. If they want special seats for first performances with their monograms worked on the back, let them be paid for, in oneway or another, at the right rate; and a little extra for the monogram would not come amiss. More enterprises have been ruined for the petty convenience of their avowed supporters than all the hard words of their true critics could stimulate to success.

But confront a manager with his theatre and its *The pyramid* problems in the concrete; and now he will be wise to *of policy* build the pyramid of his policy from the bottom up, ideals at the top, the base of expedients tested and tried. He must know first what he wants to do ; he should be allowed time and some money for sheer experiment ; but, above all, he should ask patience from his supporters and authorities while he assembles his resources stone by stone. He will be wise if he makes neither attempt nor promise to bring the theatre to normal running conditions in less than three years. He should see that every experience is made illustrative. Let the theatre be set its various tasks. He can size up the gross cost of each with some accuracy and, at a guess, the likely return. Prize plays and their like should have special funds set apart for them. A play which is being studied that term in the city's schools must certainly be performed in the theatre. Very well, put the gross cost on one side. Whether the children see it free or at sixpence a head, and how the account is balanced (balanced it must be), is a matter of convenience. But the incidence must be made clear to everyone concerned.

The theatre's main task is, of course, to stand as drama's representative with its audience. Now, a

275

*A Shake-
spearean
parenthesis*

library—to which we have compared our repertory of
plays—does not buy one book here and there by a
recognized author : it has their works on its shelves.
The theatre moves more slowly and under obvious
disabilities, but the parallel should hold. The
whole canon of Shakespeare, for instance, should be
brought by degrees into the repertory, certainly of
any purely English theatre. And if parts of it
cannot hold a place there on their merits we may
debit some of that loss, at least, to the literary
fetichism by which a frank understanding of the
playwright has been obscured. But the gain from
the rest when it accrues will probably bid fair to
surprise those good people who accept the national
poet as they accept other national monuments—
St. Paul's, the Abbey, the Column in Trafalgar
Square, shrines to be passed unnoticed on three
hundred and sixty-four days in the year, to be
livened by bunting and liturgy upon patriotic
occasions. Nelson, the man of deeds, and his
peers in the great city crypt or under the transepts
at Westminster pass into the shadows of history,
but Shakespeare, the man of mere words, does not.
Statueless, unrecorded, what they were and did and
the meaning of it would be lost in our barren ingrati-
tude. But it is utterly right that we should know
next to nothing of Shakespeare himself, and the mild
curse of wasted time is upon him who tries to re-
articulate those bones. And it is entirely appropriate
that a silly posed statue, surrounded by music-
halls, should be the only attempt of the sort to
memorialize his fame. On the day that the nation
he has honoured thinks to satisfy its conscience by
decreeing some magnificent mass of marble to his
name we may fear, indeed, that his gift to them is
finally buried beneath it. We still hardly guess at
276

the gift's value. How can we till we accept it? Promoters of Shakespeare theatres dutifully exploit their possibilities. Certainly it is our duty to provide a home for the plays. Most certainly that alone will be his fitting memorial. But wait till these good memorialists have turned their backs upon the opening ceremony with a sigh of relief and a human resolve—after all the squabbles and intrigues which wearily accompany the collective doing of such good deeds—never to go near the place again. That will be Shakespeare's chance, his moment, which will last as long as the England lasts which his light illumined. It will not be for all time. His meridian may have passed already. Perhaps we have delayed too long; history does not bear out our cheery optimism of its being never too late to do anything. Already a tithe of his phrases, the little things that made him laugh, many turns of his thought, are strange to us. But that is no great matter. His spirit flashed upon the sky reflections of an age which was big with the future of our race. Is it still in the fulfilling? How long before the travaillers feel within themselves the joys and burdens that the prophet's soul foreknows? Poets, it is certain, come to their own at no accountable time. But, seeing that the history of these three hundred years shows the common people that Shakespeare sprang from and despised more than a little, moving doubtfully and painfully—slipshod, stupid, helpless, heroic, passionate always for something better than they know, and better than they are—towards the heritage of their being that his genius seized and showed, is it not very likely that these English may find now, at this expansive moment of their career, as never before they could have found, in the pageant of

277

his work a picture, vivid and informing, of their master-meaning to the world ?

Theorizing is vain : one can but bring the matter to the proof and, even so, not beyond argument. But let us be clear that upon the last three generations at least the power of Shakespeare the playwright has never been proved. Needless to say that reading his plays in school is not the way to do it, nor even is taking the children to see, as a treat now and then, a little selection of them acted. Only when they are there to be picked out as a man picks up popular tunes—hearing the lot, whistling those that appeal to him time and again, letting slip those that don't—shall we know what real hold they have. A tradition of their acting, generally accepted in its essentials,* must first be recreated. For if it

* Not in the detail of costume or scenery, but in the broad method of playing and staging, yes. Our so-called Shakespearean traditions of to-day, it must be remembered, date, the most venerable of them, from no earlier than the eighteenth century, an age of some great actors, of much well-polished playing, but, if we may judge by its treatment of the texts, of a complete misunderstanding of the Elizabethan drama. It was generally held, then, that all tragic acting should be statuesque—witness the sensation caused by the revolutionary irruptions of Garrick and (later) of Kean. The imperfect artificial lighting which superseded the daylight of the early seventeenth-century stage may have had something to do with the growth of this "classic" tradition. For the actor—the leading actor especially—valuing the effect of his facial expression, naturally tried to keep himself anchored "in the focus" as it was called, where his audience could best see him. The influence of the French theatre counted for something, too. But from whatever cause the eighteenth-century players of Shakespeare did slow down the verse and over-ballast the action, and bring to the whole business a general heaviness of method from which we have not yet broken free. We still suffer beneath the meaningless oppression of the bass Claudius and contralto Gertrude, brass-bound effigies, a ton-weight on our chests. Mrs. Siddons, for all her genius and with much authority, so distorted Lady Macbeth from the subtle

278

is our inbred selves that are to answer to their call
familiarity with the sight and the sound of them
must be unquestioned, almost unconscious. Acceptance of tradition will leave room, moreover, for
an ampler critical pleasure in the plays' interpretation. Shakespeare a national heritage! The patri-
mony seems divided to-day between schoolmasters,
writers who find that his phrases flow easily—
too easily—down their pens, and orators upon
ornamental occasions. To the rest of us—among
whom we may number some thirty-five millions of
uncultured rich and poor—he is a name, a memory
of lessons, an occasional treat to the play, or a peg
for a good resolution—" I really will read 'As You
Like It' to the children!" But in all peoples, and
not least in the English, there is unmined wealth
of passion and humour and love of beauty. It may
lie so near the surface as to be peeping towards
expression, and a scratching will show it. And
perhaps this very jolly playwright—divest him of
the trappings in which a grudging idolatry has
choked him, give him simply what he asks of us,
the freedom of the theatre—it may be that even
across the space of three centuries he can do more
than a little to help set our spirit free. The dumb,
the deaf, the blind—no census numbers them,
or notes the unhappiness and danger that must lie
in any nation so inarticulate and so crippled.

feminine enchantress of Shakespeare's fancy (not less an enchantress
but more because it was her husband she held in her toils) into the
clarion-noted matron that weakling shadows of her great presence
haunt us still. Though the true tradition be lost, this is obviously
a false one, and the problem is how to recreate a valid succession
from the internal evidence of the plays themselves, with the help,
perhaps, of such glimpses of the psychology of both Elizabethan
actors and audience as we can gain. Here is, as we know, matter
for much dispute, but for very good fun.

The theatre's duty towards the drama No rhetorical urging will be needed, perhaps, to enforce upon any public-spirited theatre the all-obvious duty of representing Shakespeare to its audience. But more is implied. The theatre's attitude towards its great dramatist should be its attitude towards all drama. It should have truck with none that cannot hope to be admitted—however distantly—into this view. The business of any true theatre is, indeed (the simile serves yet once again), to build up a library of living drama. Now the limitations forced upon it with the cost and complexity of its machinery, not felt in the library of books, must make it more chary rather than less of being cumbered with experimental stuff. This is no condemnation to unrelenting solemnity. If a manager cannot make bold to say " That tragedy will be forgotten to-morrow, this farce will live for a century," he is not fit for his post. But it does demand some scheme of selection which, however else it may be evolved, can certainly not be dictated by the opportunism of a vague wish to please anybody and everybody. Even the selected audience whose judgment may be respected will only form itself in response to a programme. There is no such thing as public taste. The democratic world of culture is, but for some few strongholds of purpose and hope, lost in the anarchy of pleasure-seeking. Haphazard armies of fashion march hither and thither under irresponsible and unknown leaders. What should the theatre do here ? It can only exist as a stronghold; self-respecting, even self-sufficient, single-minded. Seek out, hat in hand, bowing and scraping on its behalf, that personified monster the Public, and what does one get ? Halfpence; and, more deservedly, kicks. Coax the monster if you think you can into a reason-

able and articulate mood, and ask—not what he
wants, for the answer is "Find out," and many have
been the lives wasted at that task—but ask "How
should this theatre of yours stand for the drama?"
and with the utmost reasonableness he will reply
"Why ask *me*?" But, politely ignoring him, use
the theatre (it will be noted how the phrase, though
twisted a little, flows all too easily down the pen)
according to the drama's own honour and dignity,
and he, unmastered a little, will soon find his use
in it, if pleasure and use are to be found.

A director can find tasks enough. There is the
Shakespeare canon, there is eighteenth-century
comedy, there is now not one school, but many,
of English-spoken drama. There are the French
and Spanish, Italian, German, Scandinavian schools,
all worth their place. One could plan out with ease
a three years' programme—leaving spaces for plays
still to be written—which should have a consistent
purpose. It would not be an especially educational
programme, in the sense that plays would be done
chronologically, or according to any other inappropriately logical method. Nor yet should it be arranged as an elaborate exhibition of drama; not as
anything so soulless. Its purpose should be the
articulation of a body of plays and their acting so
ordered and balanced as to make of this theatre a
living thing. The peculiar property of the dramatic
art is that, by virtue of its human constituents, their
show among themselves, and our close touch with
them, it can stand as a symbol of that larger life of
sympathy given and granted, that extension of
personal power, the membership one with another,
which is civilization's only sure achievement up
to now. First has come realization of oneself;
then follows—a far and for long, indeed, a feeble

cry—realization of one's neighbour: this art's contribution to the second effort, being her childlike hints that neighbour and self are very much alike, especially neighbour.

The theatre's duty towards itself

Therefore, as both epitome and mirror of our social life, a theatre's first task is to realize a self, compacted, as a man's mind is, of heritage and circumstance. Then, without fail, a spirit will inform it. And so, with full title, it may take its stand as a living unit of that social world of man's creation—which is, as we begin to know, the grouping of groups and powers as much as of individuals, the complex following on the simple—its full task being just to make friends. The problem of this enlargement of the laws of individual association to a comprehension of groups and powers is admittedly a pressing one in these times. Why are mobs blackguardly? Why do men deteriorate in crowds? Must an assemblage be less moral than the individuals that compose it? Surely the art that offers to elucidate a little these confusions cannot be a negligible one.

A few sample plays

And the practical road to this ideal goal should as surely please the good business man if he wishes to travel in that direction at all. For he may first know where he is going, and at any point he can stop. If the theatre is a living entity, not a machine, there need be no iron rules for the construction of its programme. Give a sample of Euripides—Murray, a cycle of Ibsen, Gilbert's two early farces, Love for Love, The Critic, Le Malade Imaginaire, and—say—a couple more from Molière, a selection of Shaw, of Galsworthy, of Pinero, a Hankin comedy, Masefield's The Faithful and The Campden Wonder, one or two of the starkest of Barrie's plays, a de Musset, a Hauptmann, a Terence translated by Bridges, a Mystery play,

282

something by Herne, two or three by the younger
American school, a Browning, something by Davies
or Milne, by Brieux, Echagaray, Scribe, Sardou,
Giacosa, Benevente or Sierra, Tchekov (if you dare),
Holberg, d'Annunzio, and pick another half-dozen
English names from the good round dozen you can
find, not to mention Shakespeare—for one leaves
out the mention of bread in a diet. If the giving
is done with care, and there's careful watching of
the gift's taking or rejection, you will be able to
tell within a little as you go along just how firmly
and how usefully your friendships are forming.
You will not be a snob presumably, of either the
direct or inverted variety ; you will not bow the
knee to literary rank or money-making popularity.
You will do no play unless you like it ; and you will
never, never call a play a failure unless you feel that
it was badly done. If no one comes to see it—
if, when you've waited patiently enough, still no
one comes—you may say simply to the thousand
people that a theatre must call No One, " I am sorry
we cannot present you this excellent play again,
unless you choose to pay five times the present
price of your seats." No reason they shouldn't;
unless, perhaps, for their sake and this play's,
other members of your audience—if you have only
one building, so many actors, and as there are only
so many days in the week—are being deprived of
other good plays that they may wish to see. Just
as between self-respect and regard for one's friends,
so must these claims be matched with duty to the
drama's self. For if that stays unfulfilled, your
friends, come they or no to particular plays—this
may seem their horrid unreasonableness, but they
have better instinct than reason—will not in the end
give a dump for you or your theatre. If it is that
you cannot afford to fulfil your duty there is no

283

harm in saying so. But your friends must be frankly told, and the good business man be left quite clear where he and his money are failing you.

Drama and democracy The problem of social life is the problem of the balance of obligations ; and for the theatre, an epitome of social life itself, and at its truest a radiating centre of almost personal imaginative life, this is the key problem. The obligations to an audience are undoubted. One would like to see every theatre that takes its task comprehensively a popular theatre, crowded with all sorts and conditions of people : for its public should be comprehensive, too. The drama has always tended to be a democratic art ; and an audience class conscious to the point of self-consciousness is inevitably a bad audience. At its best it is apt to be a feeble audience in its passive politeness, or in its noisy ebullience, according to the custom of its particular class. Old theatrical hands will tell us to take it as a sure sign of success when, at the end of a second or third act, strangers all over the theatre turn and talk to each other like old acquaintances. The touch of art has succeeded in making that little assembled world kin.

In the looser bonds of our larger social world no one seriously stands for universal equality unless he may make reservations to his taste. Before God, before the law, in the eye of the bus-conductor—will the doctrine that all men are equal satisfactorily expatiate much further ? But we have founded much on the phrase, and it is worth while to make truth of it when one can. And some practical truth we may find, perhaps—if we prefer observation to theory—not in sweeping condemnation of all class distinctions, but by discovering where, in a so-called state of equality, class distinctions do actually lie. It is quite possible, for instance, to set up an equality

284

between the most diverse seeming people in the understanding and appreciation of a work of art. Is this such an unimportant matter as it perhaps appears? It is a passing fellowship, so we need not trouble it by measurement and analysis, or even disturb our generous conviction of the genuineness of each particular occasion. But of the cumulative effect of such agreements upon the dispositions of the partakers there can be no doubt, and it may even be the greater for not being easily calculable. A man will not actually say, perhaps, " I am nearer kin to that unknown who likes the same music and books and plays than I am to my cousin who cares for none of them." But neither will he even trouble to think that blood is a bond which will hold him, if its call comes, when material interests— the effective class interests—loosen quickly enough. Culture is a bond, knit by the common response to the thousand small voices with which the world of created thought daily calls to us. And therefore the contribution that this art of the theatre in particular can make to the comity of society is a very real one, insisting, as in its nature it does, there and then upon the common response, the mutual understanding. If it is true that the happiness generated in an audience of all sorts and conditions of people, who are at one only for this hour or two in their liking of a play, but who are made one, we may almost say, for that time by the play's virtue, is fuller and richer than any that will spring in an assembly whose bonds are but a commonly inbred prejudice towards life and the world, then here is indeed a service done to democracy. Must we find solvents for the arbitrary and ineffectual divisions of our changing society? Do we not then the more need signs lifted up, that will draw men together in the many fellowships of a life enriched by many interests, lest a material age, jealous of distinction, coin us all into a current drabness and dullness—tokens by the million of humanity's depreciation?

The danger of the clique

And for its own sake, quite certainly, the theatre must keep free from the prejudices of any artistic class. Whence it gets, to that only can it give; this is art's paradox. We go to the theatre, people say, to be amused, to be taken out of ourselves. No doubt; but into what? There is no world but this to write plays about. We can but inhabit it a little more fully in our imagination. We are too modest, though. It is not out of ourselves the dramatist must needs take us, but rather a little further in. There are no possessions of romance and beauty which are not our own, and the secret of appreciating art is first to believe this, and then, perhaps, to have a little patience. For one thing, if we are to enjoy to the full our imaginative inheritance, we need to be not quite so stupidly tired at the end of a dull day's work. There is, indeed, one social distinction which the good theatre must rely upon: it can only appeal to a leisured

The need for a leisured class

class—a class, that is to say, neither of people busily being idle nor of work-weary folk reluctantly set free. Ours has been called a quantitative civilization; it is true that we are apt to think in quantities both of work done and of holiday time. There is sound sense, no doubt, in a man's claim amidst the regimenting not of industry only, but (for apparently we cannot think upon two planes at once) of life, to have no more said to him than "Here are four clear hours to do as you like with." But leisure, if we may dogmatize, implies not so much an opportunity as a condition and a quality of mind. The ideally leisured man is one relaxing from keen, exhausting maybe, but, before all, well-balanced use of his faculties. To the measure of

286

its misuse in work his nature, in the receptivity of repose, will be found blunted or deformed. It is not apparently either quantity or kind of work that affects the matter, except as they first affect the man. Minds may harden more disastrously than hands, and a lawyer's imagination atrophy for the very reason that an unskilled labourer's is stunted. But the mass of the world's work to-day, it may be said, is too highly specialised to call for the exercise of well-balanced faculties. So much the worse then for the world's work and for its workers. That, at least, is the retort which art, with its sole obligation to man's complete humanity, must make. And if we set the theatre to interpret life, how can it hope to serve men who neither love life itself nor care to live it ? How can art in the end be any better than the reality of which it is the shadow ? It is its shadow, but then it is its illumination, too. The paradox helps us a little, is a reminder that we move always upon lines of seeming contradiction—oddly interlacing spirals, as they are, of effect and cause.

We may turn from a play because the life it paints for us is too familiar and too despised. Can the alchemy of art transmute it to some value for us ? To none greater, in the end, no doubt, than our own metal's worth allows. But in that mysterious process—through the lively symbolism of a play's acting, the actors' surrender to the dramatist's idea, the triple sympathy then set up—we do gain a vicarious experience that may almost stand for personal illumination. And art's teaching, heaven knows, is not more fallible than life's.

We get at last, no doubt, and not at very long last either, the government, the church, the theatre we deserve. But always at some point in the spiral's turn, by our goodwill—that only—theatre or church or government may manage to do a little of the

287

deserving for us. Effect, in fact, does sometimes seem to come before its cause. It may be ultimately logically true that art must await its full appreciation till every man works in his kind and to some degree, even as the artist does. If art interprets life, indeed, this must be true ; or art or life is in the wrong. For this perfection, though, of give and take, while art may wait, the artist cannot. He, with his own life and work in contradiction, still must go ahead and do his broken best.

The ideal theatre, playhouse and school, fount of a city's expression, sounding-board of its emotion and its thought, is neither to be built with hands nor planned on paper. It will be so intimate a part of the people's life—they or their teachers will have studied in the school ; the playhouse will be as much their own as is their church or their club— that no one will mark the boundaries of its influence. Press, pulpit, politics—there are powers these lack that the theatre can well wield; there are things they fail in now because, perhaps, the theatre does not take its share in the doing. Neither topically, nor in terms of direct reason nor of pure faith, but by the subtler way of art the drama works, to evolve from the sentient mass a finer mind, responding to the fine fellow-mind of the poet, expressed in terms of a common experience through the medium of human beings, whose art has that deeper significance that we find in the faces and voices of friends with whom we have come through the gates of understanding. This is the ideal, and towards it the paths are many.